KT-521-439

The Blender Book

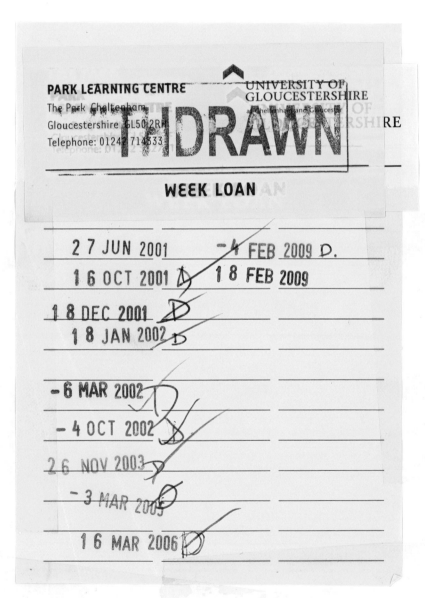

THE
BLENDER
BOOK

Carsten Wartmann

Translated by Nick Hoff and James Gray

An imprint of No Starch Press

San Francisco

Co-Publishers: William Pollock and Phil Hughes   Composition: Magnolia Studio
Project Editor: Karol Jurado   Copyeditor: Hilary Powers
Assistant Editor: Nick Hoff   Proofreader: Karla Maree
Editorial Production Assistant: Jennifer Arter   Indexer: Nancy Humphreys
Cover and Interior Design: Octopod Studios

The Blender Book is an English version of *Das Blender-Buch*, the German original edition, published in Germany by dpunkt.verlag (Heidelberg), copyright © 2000 by dpunkt.verlag GmbH. English translation prepared by Nick Hoff and James Gray.

Distributed to the book trade in the United States by Publishers Group West, 1700 Fourth Street, Berkeley, California 94710, phone: 800-788-3123 or 510-528-1444, fax: 510-528-3444.

Distributed to the book trade in Canada by Jacqueline Gross & Associates, Inc., 195 Allstate Parkway, Markham, Ontario L3R 4T8 Canada, phone: 905-477-0722, fax: 905-477-8619.

For information on translations or book distributors outside the United States and Canada, please contact No Starch Press directly:

No Starch Press
555 De Haro Street, Suite 250, San Francisco, CA 94107
phone: 415-863-9900; fax: 415-863-9950; info@nostarch.com; www.nostarch.com

Library of Congress Cataloging-in-Publication Data

```
Wartmann, Carsten.
[Blender Buch.  English]
The Blender book : free 3D graphics software for the Web and video / Carsten Wartmann ; translated by
Nick Hoff and James Gray.
     p. cm.
Includes index.
ISBN 1-886411-44-1 (pbk.)
1. Computer graphics. 2. Computer animation. 3. Three-dimensional display systems. 4. Blender (Computer
file) I. Title.
T385 .W3765 2000
006.6'93--dc21
                                                                              00-038012
```

BRIEF CONTENTS

CONTENTS IN DETAIL

1
INTRODUCTION

2
BASICS OF 3D GRAPHICS

3

QUICK START

4

BLENDER BASICS

5

MODELING TUTORIALS

6

MATERIAL TUTORIALS

7

LIGHT, SHADOWS, AND WORLD TUTORIALS

8

KEYFRAME, PATH, LATTICE, AND
VERTEX KEY ANIMATION TUTORIALS

9

INVERSE KINEMATICS TUTORIALS

10

GETTING SMALL: PARTICLE ANIMATION TUTORIALS

11

THE FINAL CUT: POSTPRODUCTION

12

PYTHON TUTORIALS

13

THE BIG REWARD: RENDERING

14

LASER TUTORIAL

15

ANIMATING A TORPEDO THROUGH A SCHOOL OF FISH

A

KEYBOARD COMMANDS

B

TIPS, TRICKS, AND USEFUL PROGRAMS

C

COMMAND LINE ARGUMENTS

D

OVERVIEW OF BLENDER MODULES

E

INSTALLING BLENDER

F
GLOSSARY
285

G
WHAT'S ON THE CD?

Index
293

FOREWORD TO THE GERMAN EDITION

It is now almost two years since Blender was released on the Internet. Only in my wildest dreams could I have envisioned what would happen in this time!

Blender is now used by thousands of professionals, students, and all kinds of people interested in 3D. The Blender community is very active on the Internet: We have many Blender sites and even more tutorials online.

Besides the Internet activity, Blender has received attention from book publishers around the world, with the publication of first a Japanese book, then an English book, and now a German book, which you read at the moment. Having read Carsten's book, I can say that I think it is definitely an excellent introduction to Blender for new users.

I'm very proud to present to you this guide to Blender, and wish you much fun in reading the book and working with Blender!

Ton Roosendaal, Blender developer
Eindhoven, December 20, 1999

PREFACE TO THE GERMAN EDITION

In the beginning of 1998, I learned on the Internet of a free 3D program; first available for SGI computers, it was soon to be ported to Linux. The software publisher's Web site, the Dutch company Neo Geo, looked very promising, and for several weeks I waited eagerly for the Linux version. In April of 1998 it finally came, and I loaded the file with "Linux" in its name onto my computer.

My first thought was that the 800 KB archive couldn't be the whole thing. But there it was, a complete 3D animation program, in under 1 MB! Getting started was a bit complicated, as Blender's operation can be quite peculiar. Still, in contrast, other 3D programs began to seem cumbersome and unwieldy to me.

As a result of Blender's rapid development and its developers'—first and foremost Ton Roosendaal—close connection with the Blender community, Blender became my favorite 3D program. And, after writing a couple of articles about Blender for German technical magazines, I decided to write a book about the program.

My thanks go of course to Not a Number, Blender's publisher, and especially to Ton Roosendaal and Daniel Dunbar, who have personally supported and motivated me. Thanks too to my friends Ingo Adamski, Oliver Ringtunatus, and Uwe Spenhoff, who tested the tutorials (often several times); Martin Strubel for his technical input; and Heiko Oberdiek for his help with LaTeX. Finally, thanks to my editor René Schönfeldt for a good and productive collaboration.

Carsten Wartmann
Berlin, December 22, 1999

1

INTRODUCTION

The amazing computer graphics of modern movies and electronic media are a real challenge—wouldn't it be wild to get those effects for yourself? Now you can! Whether you want droids like the ones in the latest *Star Wars* movie, an animation or 3D graphic for the Web, or your own animated short, Blender can do it all—and it's completely free! You don't need to spend thousands of dollars to get a professional animation and 3D graphics suite; just download Blender from the Web and let the fun begin.

First developed by the Dutch animation company NeoGeo as an in-house animation program, Blender grew and developed with each project NeoGeo took on. Then, almost as soon as the first free version of Blender was released on the Internet (in May 1998), NeoGeo went out of business. That's when Ton Roosendaal, Blender's "father" and main programmer, stepped in and founded a company he called Not a Number to further develop Blender.

Thus Blender became a product. Yet certainly an unusual one for the business world: The free version of Blender was not a restricted demo version but fully functional, and its license allowed unhindered use for commercial productions. So how did Not a Number make any money? In addition to selling the *Blender Manual*, Not a Number sold a software key that enabled many additional functions and turned the free version of Blender into "Complete Blender."

As Blender continued to grow, "Complete Blender" features kept migrating over to the free version. Most recently, Not a Number stopped charging for Complete Blender and expanded Blender 2.0 with functions that let you create entire interactive 3D worlds and make them come alive—a feature particularly important for creating computer games. But, best of all, Blender 2.0 is still completely free!

1.1   Who Is This Book For?

This book is not meant to be a Blender manual—the complete Blender reference is the *Blender Manual,* which is available directly from Not a Number. *The Blender Book* is intended for those who are looking for a fast, practical, and compact introduction to the world of 3D graphics and animation, without having to use expensive or functionally restricted programs. Because of its flexibility, Blender is suited for almost all kinds of computer graphics and has something for everyone:

- People with a general interest in computers can easily get started in the world of 3D graphics and animation for free.

- Students can learn the basics of 3D graphics with a program they can use on their home PCs.

- Teachers can equip their school computers without breaking their budgets.

- Amateur video makers can create animations and titles for their videos.

- Web designers can develop 3D objects for Web pages, VRML, and logos.

- Multimedia designers can use graphics and animations for their CD and DVD projects.

- Scientists can visualize their research results.

- Engineers and technicians can use animation to demonstrate how technical models and instruments work.

- Architects can visualize their plans and give virtual tours.

1.2   What Can Blender Do?

In its relatively short commercial life, Blender has been used successfully by all sorts of people because it offers features otherwise found only in expensive programs or not found in any programs at all. And Not a Number is also very responsive to Blender users' needs—many of Blender's new functions have been added in response to the large amount of user feedback on Blender's news server.

The following sections list Blender's most important features. If you're a beginner, you may not recognize many of the concepts, but if you've worked with 3D programs before you should recognize most of them. Wherever you are now, after reading this book you will be familiar with all of these concepts and be able to use them creatively.

General features

- Modeling with polygon frames, curves (Bezier, NURBS), NURBS surfaces, 3D texts, and metaballs

- Animation with keyframes, paths (objects and curves), morphing, vertex keys, IK systems, skeletons, and lattices

- Particle system for creating fire, smoke, explosions, fur, or even schools of fish

- Plug-in interface for postproduction, texture plug-ins, and a free development kit for programming your own plug-ins

- Programming language (Python) and text editor for expanding functionality

- Sequence editor for the postproduction of animations

- Rotoscoping, or the creation of objects and animations with the help of images or films

- File manager for managing all the system's files, including preview images

- Compact file format (`*.blend`) and full compatibility between different computers and Blender versions

- Inventor/VRML1, DXF, Videoscape imports

- Inventor/VRML1, DXF, Videoscape exports

- Support for Targa, JPEG, Iris, HamX, SGIMovie (SGI only), AmigaIFF, Anim5, and AVI (compressed and uncompressed JPEG) image and animation formats

Interface features

- Flexible windows and work space layout

- 3D window offering wireframe, solid, OpenGL, and rendered views

- Scalable button windows that can be adjusted to the monitor resolution

- Mouse-controlled translation, rotation, and scaling

- Layers, multiple work spaces, and multiple scenes per file

Lighting features

- Environmental (ambient) light, local lights, spotlights, hemispheres, sun

- Textured and volumetric lighting

- Fast shadow rendering with shadow buffers; soft shadows

- Selective lighting using a layer system

Rendering features

- Very fast scanline rendering

- Oversampling against aliasing (rough edges)

- Resolution up to 4096x4096 pixels

- Rendering in fields for video output

- Motion blur for animation

- Pre-gamma correction to adjust for output to different media

- Automatic environment maps for simulating mirroring and refraction

- Panorama rendering for creating navigable panoramas for games and multimedia CDs

- Radiosity rendering for lighting simulation

  All these features in one 2-megabyte program!

1.2.1 Blender Is Easy on Memory

During the writing of this book, I occasionally opened as many as three Blender sessions at the same time without a memory problem. Because Blender uses so little memory, it is an ideal 3D graphics program for slower machines. Commercial 3D programs, in contrast, take much more space and without offering much more functionality than Blender. They generally take up much more space even when installed with only a minimum of features (without materials or objects) and roughly the same functions—and you pay for the privilege!

1.2.2 Backward and Forward Compatible File Format

Thanks to Blender's ingenious file format, scenes save and load quickly. And, unlike those used by most similar programs, Blender files are both backward and forward compatible, meaning that older versions of Blender can open files created with the newest Blender versions with no problem. This feature is part of the system's basic design concept and the current intent is that there will never be a version of Blender that can't read old files. Moreover, someone working with an older Blender version will also always be able to read files created on a newer version and won't be forced to install the new version.

   All of a scene's pertinent information is saved in one file, including its textures and your personal settings. Yet in spite of this, an ingenious file management system allows each object in a scene to be loaded or linked into other scenes, facilitating collaboration among several animators.

1.2.3 Multi-Platform Flexibility

Another exceptional Blender feature is that it can be run on five hardware platforms and under six operating systems, making it one of the few commercial multi-platform programs in any software category. Thus it is possible for companies and institutions, even if they use very different computer hardware, to use most or all of their hardware when they construct render farms.

Of course Blender has its weaknesses, as do similar programs costing several hundred dollars. And if you're a specialist, you should take your personal requirements into account—other programs may better suit your needs (for example, if you need really realistic mirroring or light refraction in transparent objects). But if you need fast, high-quality renderings of long animations, Blender can certainly keep up with substantially more expensive programs.

1.3 The Intention of This Book

This book does not aim to replace the *Blender Manual*—and cannot do so. The *Blender Manual* is distributed directly by Not a Number and the proceeds from its sale are an essential reason for Blender's commercial success.

This book presents examples that encourage the reader to experiment and use Blender—not to simply scratch the surface, but to gain a deeper understanding of 3D graphics. The incredible number of functions in Blender makes it an almost impossible task to explain them all through examples. In contrast, the *Manual* gives short explanations of all the buttons and parameters, but without examples of their use—it's more of a reference book. At this writing, the *Manual* covers Blender through version 1.5 and Blender's operation has not changed since then.

1.4 Blenderspeak

Because Blender's development has often followed—or even preceded—the most current 3D graphics research, new technical terms that have not yet been universally accepted often appear in Blender screens and documentation. These concepts, dubbed "Newspeak" by Not a Number, are also used by this book (with the exception of the term *PupMenu,* for which I use *pop-up menu*). I hope this contributes to a universal Blender language and hinders the nationalization that divides users of many other programs on the Internet.

1.5 Conventions Used in This Book

In the *Blender Handbook* and in publications from Not a Number, keys are indicated by AKEY, BKEY, and so on. In this book, I'll simply write "press A" to indicate that you should press the "A" key on the keyboard. Keys that need to be pressed together are connected with a hyphen (for example, ALT-A means to press "ALT" and the "A" key at the same time). Text taken from a Blender window is printed as it appears in Blender—usually capitalized. Menus are written in a sans serif font as Add • Mesh • Cube, where the bullets indicate the next level in the menu structure. Buttons and sliders on the Blender interface are indicated by the same sans serif font used for menu options.

Although Blender is designed for use with two hands (one on the mouse and the other on the keyboard for keyboard shortcuts), it also has numerous onscreen icons you can click in lieu of the keyboard shortcuts. In a book like this, putting the icons directly in the text interferes with readability, so I'll be quoting function names in the text and putting the corresponding icon and name in the margin. For example, the icon for the Material buttons group, Blender's material editor, is displayed at left.

The color plates of figures in the middle of the book contain figures that are best illustrated in full color. I will reference these color plates as Color Plate X, with X being the plate number.

The CD-ROM complements the tutorials and their instructions (path names on the CD are indicated in this font: `directory/subdirectory/filename`). It includes files for each step in the tutorials in numbered order, so if you get stuck on a particular tutorial, look for the scene that corresponds to the step you're having trouble with. For example, if you're having problems with the middle of the roller coaster tutorial in Chapter 5, load `roller_coaster03.blend` to see if it corresponds to the step you're on. You can also use these files as inspiration and starting points for your own experiments or if you don't have enough time to complete the tutorial yourself. In addition, the CD also has textures, images, sequences, animations, figures from the book, and Python for Windows. See Appendix G for a more detailed list of what's on the CD.

In short, Blender is a completely professional animation program with an unbeatable price: It's available for free over the Internet and is not restricted to private use. And it changes very quickly since it is developed in close cooperation with its users; reported errors are often corrected within days. So be sure to visit the Blender Web site (http://www.blender.nl) frequently to read about new developments or bugs that have been fixed.

Enjoy!

2

BASICS OF 3D GRAPHICS

This chapter presents a basic, nonmathematical explanation of 3D graphics. Once you understand how 3D graphics are created and manipulated, you will better understand Blender's behind-the-scenes workings, as well as the limitations of individual techniques. A good understanding of 3D graphics will also make it easier for you to get up to speed quickly with other 3D graphics programs, and enable you to create better animations. (If you're impatient and can't wait to get started with Blender's 3D graphics tools, skip to the Quick Start in Chapter 3, where we create a very simple Blender animation, step by step.)

NOTE *To delve deeper into the subject of 3D graphics, read the articles published with Siggraph (http://www.siggraph.org), the most renowned computer graphics trade show. Also, at http://www.education.siggraph.org/materials/HyperGraph/hypergraph.htm you'll find a thorough collection of introductory articles on computer graphics, which are kept up to date with current developments. For the mathematics-related fundamentals of computer animation, I recommend the online site from Rick Parent (http://www.cis.ohio-state.edu/~parent/book/outline.html).*

2.1 Color

Color is caused by differing qualities of the light reflected or emitted by an object. When we see a color, we are really seeing light waves reflected or emitted by the object we are looking at. Color includes such measurable characteristics as hue, lightness, and saturation for both objects and light sources.

Colors are described as *primary* (basic colors that cannot be produced by mixing other colors), *secondary* (simple mixtures of two of the primary colors), and *tertiary* (mixtures of secondary colors). The hues that fall into each of these categories will differ, depending on the *color model*—the system of defining color—in use.

2.1.1 The Physics of Color

Radiant white light, from the sun or a light bulb, for example, is actually composed of various colors of light ranging from violet through red. When all colors are represented equally, we see the light as white. When colors are represented unequally, we see light that is other than white.

Two other factors, intensity and saturation, contribute to the way our eyes perceive color. The *intensity* of the light determines its brightness, while the *color saturation* determines its purity, that is, how much of the named color is present, as opposed to how much it is diluted by white. Saturation levels are typically represented as percentages; for example, 100% red would be vivid red whereas 10% would be light pink. Mild saturation produces pastel tones and impure colors.

2.1.2 Color Models

Colors are typically defined according to a *color model* (also called colorspace), which specifies the way primary colors (*not* wavelengths) should be combined to produce a secondary color. The upshot is that colors may vary when output to various devices, depending on the device's color model. For example, when making a film or printing an image, the switch to a different color model may result in corrupted coloration if you don't perform intensive *color calibration.* Color calibration is the process of tuning your input and output devices to ensure that colors are reproduced accurately according to an objective reference point.

Three color models are commonly used to produce colors on a monitor or in print—they are RGB, HSV, and CMYK. (Blender supports only RGB and HSV.)

RGB color model

The RGB (red, green, blue) color model produces colors using combinations of the three primary colors—red, green, and blue. RGB is an *additive* color model (see Color Plate 1), meaning that the primary colors are combined in various strengths to produce a desired color. RGB starts out with black (the absence of all colors) and adds red, green, and blue light to make white. Yellow is produced by mixing red and green; cyan by mixing green and blue; and magenta by a combination of red and blue. Computer monitors and television sets use RGB—electron beams produce red, green, and blue signals, which combine to create the range of colors you see on the screen.

NOTE *You'll find both a scene (*tutorials/chapter02/RGBSpots.blend*) and an image (*figures/CP01.jpg*) of the RGB color model on the CD. In both, the model is represented by a color triangle composed of three spotlights representing this additive color model.*

Mixed colors (other than white) are produced by adding the individual RGB component colors in various levels of saturation, with their levels ranging from 0.0 to 1.0 (0 means use none of that color; 1 means use that color at full saturation).

Colors are defined by entering the intensities of each component in a matrix. Each component has its own matrix and the matrices are additive. For example, to produce a completely saturated red, enter (1,0,0): 100% Red, 0% Green, and 0% Blue. When all three color components are combined in 100% saturation (1,1,1), the result is white (as shown here):

green (0,1,0) + blue (0,0,1) = cyan (0,1,1)

cyan (0,1,1) + red (1,0,0) = white (1,1,1)

Colors that are opposite each other in the RGB color model (see Color Plate 1) are called *complementary colors*. When mixed, complementary colors always produce white. Example complementary colors are cyan and red, green and blue, and magenta and green.

HSV color model

The HSV color model (hue, saturation, value) is more intuitive to understand and use than the RGB model. Briefly, when using the HSV color model, *hue* is the color being described, such as yellow, purple, or green; *saturation* is the purity of the color; and *value* is the relative lightness or darkness (intensity) of the color (see Figure 2-1).

When using the HSV color model, you choose a color tone with the hue setting, the desired color purity with the saturation setting, and the intensity with the value setting. The saturation setting of white and the intensity setting of black are mathematically added or subtracted. The saturation is the distance from the V-axis (see Figure 2-1) and describes the vividness of the color. The value along the V-axis describes the brightness (value).

CMYK color model

CMYK refers to a color system made up of cyan, magenta, yellow, and black. Cyan, magenta, and yellow are the three primary colors in this color space, and red, green, and blue are the three secondaries. Blender does not support the CMYK color model, but CMYK plays an important role in computer graphics in general, especially in desktop publishing. Printouts or other images on paper use CMYK, which is a subtractive color model in which the color pigments absorb or

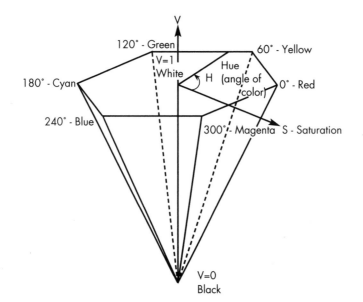

Figure 2-1: The HSV color model

filter the white light, and the reflected light determines the color of the image.

Color Plate 2 shows the CMYK colorspace. Unfortunately, when cyan, magenta, and yellow inks are mixed equally on paper, the result is usually a dark brown. Therefore, black ink is overprinted in darker areas to give a better appearance. (Black is the K in CMYK.) This compromise, the use of black to compensate for the real-world behavior of colors, makes things very complicated.

The following simple formula translates the RGB model to the CMY model:

$$C = 1 - R$$
$$M = 1 - G$$
$$Y = 1 - B$$

The formula only gives you a starting point, however. In practice, an intensive calibration of the devices is needed because the typical color pigments don't work precisely the way the formula predicts. The *Blender Manual* contains several images, also available on the Blender Web sites, that allow you to calibrate your monitor for CMYK output.

2.1.3 The Emotional Effect of Color

Color has a definite effect on our feelings—one that should not be underestimated. Still, there are no rules that govern the effect that color has on us, and certainly the rules discovered by science are not set in stone. In addition, the effect of color on each of us varies by person, and is heavily influenced by culture, presentation, and context. Therefore, when using color in your work, follow the rule that "less is more" and use color judiciously. Otherwise, you are likely to end up producing very chaotic creations.

Here are some ways that people interpret the psychological effects of color — see if they resonate with you.

Black	Serious, difficult, death
Dark blue	Stable, calming, trustworthy, mature
Gold	Conservative, stable, valuable
Gray	Integrity, neutrality, cold
Green	Growth, positive, earthy, go!
Light blue	Youthful, masculine, cold
Pink	Youthful, feminine, warm
Red	Danger, negative, excitement, heat, stop!
White	Pure, clean

Consider too that colors don't necessarily have the same meaning in every cultural group: Some think of white for weddings and black for funerals, others marry in black and bury in white.

2.1.4 The Psychological Effect of Color

When selecting colors, keep in mind the following, based on the way we see:

- Avoid combining saturated primary colors such as intense blues and reds, because different wavelengths of light cause the eye to attempt to focus differently. For example, a red point on a blue background seems closer than the background and appears to float on top of it. The eye keeps trying to correct its focus and quickly tires.

- Avoid using pure blue in text, thin lines, and small figures. Small blue elements are difficult to see because the center of the retina has no receptors for blue. On the other hand blue makes the perfect desktop color, because it makes a monitor's flicker disappear.

- Avoid color borders that differ from each other only in their level of blue. Blue does not contribute strongly to brightness cues, which are crucial for recognizing contours, thus blue-differentiated borders appear noisy.

- When edge colors differ only in color tone but not in brightness, viewers have a difficult time recognizing edges. The eye and brain have an easier time recognizing contours when differences in brightness exist.

- Older people need higher brightness levels to differentiate between colors.

- Complementary colors are easy to differentiate.

- About 10 percent of people are color-blind for some or all parts of the spectrum. Red-green color-blindness is most common, but some people can see those colors but not blue and yellow, and some cannot see color at all. Color-blind people cannot decipher graphics based on contrasting pure colors, because for them, such colors represent the same gray value.

2.2 Coordinate Systems

Switching from color to shape, you can picture any object as being made up of points in space. To give the exact location of each of the object's points in space, you use a *coordinate system*. This system consists of specific positions based on a predefined reference point, with coordinates typically given as *pairs* (two dimensions) or *triplets* (three dimensions) in parentheses. For example, one can describe the point, P1, in Figure 2-2 as follows:

P1(3.5,4.0,5.0)

These values show the point's distance from the origin, or zero point, in the directions x (3.5), y (4.0), and z (5.0), respectively. To reach the point, you move 3.5 units along the x-axis, then 4 units on the y-axis and, finally, 5 units up the z-axis.

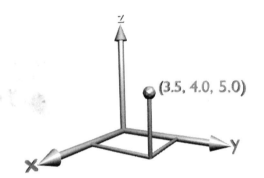

Figure 2-2: A point in Blender's coordinate system

2.3 Defining a Surface

Now that you know how to locate a point in space on a 3D scene, let's discuss how to define a surface.

2.3.1 Surface Coordinate Systems

On the left side of Figure 2-3 you'll see four points, labeled P1 through P4.

P1(0,0), P2(0,1), P3(1,1), P4(1,0)

These number pairs represent each point's x and y coordinates, which are stored and processed by all 3D animation programs. (The z coordinate is left out: Since the points lie in the same plane, its value for all points is zero.) The coordinate system indicates the direction of the axis.

2.3.2 Wireframes

You can create lines between these points (here displayed as cylinders), resulting in edges (E). Once you've connected all points with lines, you'll have a square (shown in Figure 2-3), with these coordinates:

E1(P1,P2), E2(P2,P3), E3(P3,P4), E4(P4,P1)

This coordinate information produces a *wireframe graphic*, an object portrayed by its edges only. 3D graphics programs employ wireframe models because wireframes are quick to display and offer a good overview of the scene. One disadvantage, however, is that the wireframe mode doesn't show depth too well, making it difficult to determine which lines lie in the front or back of the scene.

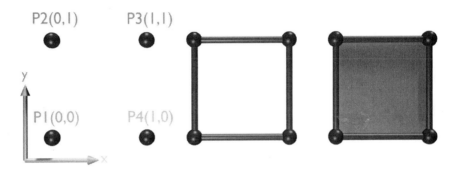

Figure 2-3: Moving from a point to a surface

2.3.3 Creating a Surface

A true spatial representation is possible only after spreading a surface between the points. The simplest surface is a triangle, whose surface lies between three points. The triangle is the building block for nearly all 3D applications. Every surface is either composed of triangles or (as in circular surfaces) approximated by them.

Now look at Figure 2-4, where we've added four additional points to the square from Figure 2-3. (We've also altered the perspective to avoid hiding the new points behind the front ones.) The resulting figure appears three-dimensional.

If you look intensely at the wireframe cube shown in the middle of Figure 2-4, its spatial orientation may suddenly change, with the back edges appearing to spring forward. On the other hand, the cube at the far right of the figure is recognizable as a three-dimensional model, an impression gained largely by lighting effects. (We will discuss lighting in the next section.)

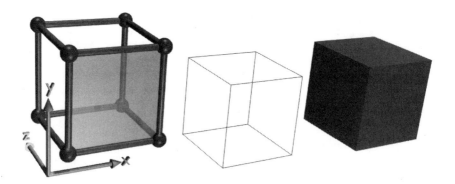

Figure 2-4: Presentation of a cube

2.3.4 Additional Ways to Portray Objects

There are other ways to portray objects besides using polygon surfaces. For example, you can describe objects using mathematical formulas, which allow you to pull objects away from each other, add them together, and so on. These mathematically determined objects also have the advantage that their resolution is not restricted. For example, a mathematical curve remains rounded regardless of how closely you view the object with a virtual camera. These alternative methods often peacefully coexist in many 3D programs, and complement each other nicely.

You can recognize polygonal objects by their multi-surface structure and the visible surface edges. Choosing the appropriate type of modeling for a particular object is an art form that every animator should master.

2.4 Rendering Light

Lighting an object, which adds shadow and depth, is essential to creating a realistic impression of the object. Figure 2-5 shows four spheres, each made with a different type of *light rendering* (calculating how light sources affect a scene or object). Sphere A appears as a flat disk with uniform color. Sphere B was subjected to a process that renders the strength of the light that falls onto each surface, which results in a stronger spatial impression. In C, the reflection point is also rendered, appearing matte on a reflective surface. Sphere D has been smoothed and has both a reflection point and a shadow.

The first three spheres appear to hover oddly over the ground, although they all occupy the same position *on* the ground as sphere D, which seems to sit there solidly. The trick is that a shadow is rendered for sphere D. Our sight apparatus uses the distance between the shadow and the object to determine the object's position relative to the ground. In addition, since individual surfaces are not recognizable, sphere D is smoother than spheres B and C. (You can achieve this smooth look by applying an interpolation technique, which allows you to insert smooth areas into particular surfaces.)

Figure 2-5: Different types of light rendering

Many programs exploit lighting models like those in spheres B and C, as well as the wireframe method, to display 3D scenes, mainly because a computer with a special graphics card can compute these scenes quickly, almost in real time. (This is also the reason why 3D games use these lighting models.) On the other hand, calculating shadows, as in lighting model D, is much slower, making the technique unsuitable for use in interactive graphics applications.

2.5 Transformations

Transformations involve the manipulation of objects in virtual space, including *translation* (positioning), *rotation* (turning), and *scaling* (changing size). In the real world, every transformation of a real, physical object requires a certain amount of energy. In the virtual world of computer graphics scenes, however, no energy is needed to make a corresponding transformation. On the computer, transformations are performed using mathematical calculations, typically matrix calculations. Fortunately, most programs insulate us from the internals of these transformations and allow us to perform them interactively, right on the screen.

2.5.1 Translation

To move a point from its origin at (0,0,0), to a new point (3,0,0) to the right, add 3 units to the x-coordinate of the point. To move more complex objects consisting of several points, make a corresponding addition to each point.

2.5.2 Rotation

Rotation happens according to complicated computational rules that a computer can process without much effort at all. All rotations have a center of rotation, which is either a coordinate axis of the object itself or a global coordinate system, around which the rotation occurs. Rotation around a particular point consists of repetitive rotations around several axes.

2.5.3 Scaling

Although translation and rotation are the most commonly used transformations, scaling is also useful. You can scale 3D objects simply by multiplying a point's coordinates by a scaling factor. When using a positive factor, the object becomes larger—the points move farther from the object's origin. Conversely, a negative factor moves the points closer to the origin.

NOTE *Explaining the mathematics behind 3D graphics is beyond the scope of this book. Nevertheless it is often helpful and fascinating to know the mathematics, even when a deeper understanding is not necessary to complete a particular task. You'll find supplementary information online at http://www.education.siggraph.org/materials/HyperGraph/hypergraph.htm, and the classic* Computer Graphics *by James Foley and others in book form is also highly recommended.*

2.6 Converting from 3D to 2D

At this writing there are no (affordable) devices that can effectively display an animation three-dimensionally as a free-standing image. Even 3D glasses use two-dimensional images that, for example on LCD monitors, transmit separate information to the left and right eyes. Devices that can output 3D objects actually constructed by the computer include a computer-driven milling tool and a stereo lithography system. (In the latter, a UV-laser cures synthetic resin and creates a truly three-dimensional object.) All other purposes require conversion to the two-dimensionality of the output medium—and there are different ways to trick the eye into seeing 3D.

2.6.1 Parallel Projection

Parallel projection, a method of projection that uses parallel lines and therefore does not produce perspective (foreshortening), is one such method of making 2D look like 3D. In the simplest case of parallel projection, the coordinates for depth are left out and both remaining coordinates are displayed on the screen, creating an *orthogonal parallel projection* (Figure 2-6). Orthogonal projection is a parallel projection—that is, it is projected with parallel lines so that lines that are parallel in the object remain parallel in the projection—with the direction of projection the same as the surface normal.

Depending on which coordinates you leave out when creating your projection, you get either a top, side, or front view. This technique is often used in technical drafting to create a three-sided view, which allows a craftsman to measure an object directly from a drawing—made possible because the object is displayed without distortion, ensuring proportional integrity.

3D programs offer the three-sided view too, which make the dimensions and position of a point or object easy to determine. Useful as it is for construc-

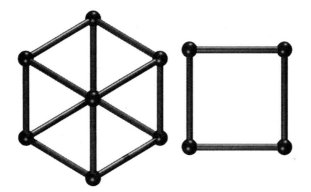

Figure 2-6: Orthogonal parallel projection

tion, however, the three-dimensional impression of this type of projection is uninspiring and bewildering to look at. As a result, the program must display a fourth view using another projection technique. This situation gives rise to the conventional layout in most graphics programs, which is divided into four main windows.

2.6.2 Cabinet and Isometric Parallel Projection

Two other commonly used techniques are *cabinet projection* and *isometric parallel projection*. You may recall the cabinet projection from your school days, whereby lines showing depth are shortened by one-half and drawn at a 45° angle. Many computer games exploit the isometric parallel projection with a slanted, bird's-eye view.

In isometric projections the height, width, and depth are displayed at 82 percent of their true length (see Figure 2-7) and the object is first rotated about the y-axis by -45 degrees, and then about the x-axis by 35 degrees. Because the normal surfaces of the object are no longer parallel or perpendicular to the picture plane, the image edges will appear foreshortened on each axis by 18 percent. The foreshortened view is called an isometric projection (Figure 2-7).

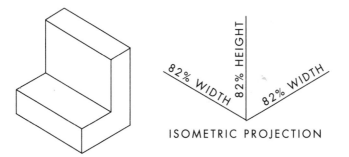

Figure 2-7: Isometric projection

2.6.3 Projections with Perspective

We perceive objects that lie farther away as smaller than they really are. This apparent size reduction makes up a large part of the appearance of space. Artists use this vanishing point trick (whereby all lines that lead to the rear of the image, if extended, would converge on one point) to produce perspective. Certainly you've seen this phenomenon in pictures where train tracks converge at the horizon.

This type of central perspective (see Figure 2-8) is the most commonly used way to display a 3D graphic in a two-dimensional medium. When working with a central perspective, one can apply methods such as a virtual camera in front of the scene or virtual vanishing point behind the picture level to calculate the perspective.

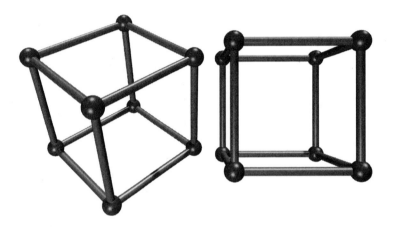

Figure 2-8: Central projection

2.7 Animation

Animation is the movement of an object in three-dimensional space. Movement is calculated to produce each picture by moving the object a small amount.

This technique is used in traditional animated cartoons and to produce certain special effects. For example, to make an animated comic film in which 24 frames per second are shown, you would have to perform each movement step 24 times for one second of footage!

2.7.1 Keyframe Animation

Keyframing (also *in-betweening* or "*tweening*") is another technique commonly used by animated cartoons. When keyframing, the lead cartoonist creates the main scenes while other cartoonists create the drawings that lie in between. As computer animators, we are lucky to have an extremely efficient and tireless co-worker—our computer—to do the in-between frames—the *inbetweens*—for us.

Figure 2-9 shows a keyframe animation. Two keyframes were defined—the starting point of the left sphere and the finishing point of the movement on the right side—and the 3D software has interpolated the inbetweens linearly across the entire sequence.

An interpolation calculates in-between values using various methods, the simplest being a linear connection between two main points. One can also interpolate curves.

Figure 2-9: A linear movement

2.7.2 Showing Acceleration or Deceleration

These interpolated linear movements don't look too realistic, though, because in the real world, all objects have mass and confront attempts to change their position with inertia. These factors cause acceleration and deceleration.

With the appropriate programming, the computer can also handle the movement type you see in Figure 2-10, which would be quite difficult to achieve by hand. The distance between the spheres changes at the beginning and end of the movement, and since the time between the images is the same, the result is movements of varying velocity.

Figure 2-10: A motion with acceleration and deceleration

Using your computer it's easy to insert or remove keyframes without destroying an animation or completely rebuilding it by hand. In Figure 2-11 we inserted an additional keyframe in the middle of the animation, which pushed the sphere higher. The computer program then interpolated gradually between the three key positions.

2.7.3 Other Animation Methods

There are other ways in the field of computer graphics to move an object besides keyframe animation. For example, *path animation* will create movement along a curve-defined path, and movement can be calculated based on physical simulations. Still, keyframe animation remains one of the most popular and accessible methods. Furthermore, keyframing makes it possible to do some things easily that would require much more effort with alternative methods.

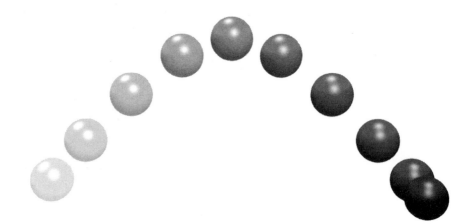

Figure 2-11: An additional keyframe included

With keyframing you can not only animate position, orientation, and scaling of objects but also their color or even the thickness of fog in a scene. A good program allows the animator to control and change virtually all scene parameters with keyframing.

2.8   Rendering Images

There are several ways to render a 3D image, and the quality of their output varies significantly. The quality of the rendered image, however, depends on both the expended processing time and the skillful implementation of the method.

2.8.1   Raytracing

Raytracing is used to render realistic reflections and light diffraction (as in glass objects). Despite ever-faster processors and various improvements, raytracing remains time-intensive and comparatively expensive when producing longer animations.

2.8.2   Scanline Rendering

Raytracing's predecessor is called *scanline rendering*. In its simplest form, called *raycasting*, scanline rendering shoots an electron beam onto the scene for each point in the image to be rendered. If the beam meets a surface, a point is placed on the screen.

When using the scanline method, the resulting image is always essentially black-and-white, with color rendered from the surface color and the lighting. Therefore, rendering the lighting beforehand is necessary. The scanline method can get as complicated as you wish, especially if you include transparencies, blurred motion, shadows, and so on in the rendering process.

Once the images are rendered they are played in quick succession to give the impression of fluid motion—thus producing the animation. The human eye perceives a motion as fluid at around 20 images per second. By way of comparison, a motion picture shows 24 images per second; video and television use 25 to 30; and computer video plays at around 15 images per second.

3

QUICK START

No matter what your experience with using 3D modeling programs, you'll have to overcome a few hurdles before you can use Blender. Although Blender is internally consistent, it is so different from other 3D programs that it can make using other 3D programs at the same time quite difficult.

Perhaps you've already started using Blender and clicked around with the mouse a bit—only to find out that you couldn't even exit the program. In fact, some of Blender's basic functions are simply so different from anything you may have encountered before that such frustrations are almost inevitable.

This Quick Start will help you avoid these frustrating experiences by giving you a feel for how to work with Blender and its peculiarities. Even if you already have a lot of experience with 3D graphics, you should work through the hands-on instruction in this Quick Start—it won't take long. Experienced 3D graphics users will probably finish the Quick Start in a couple of minutes and will have built their first Blender animation; beginners won't have to wait much longer for their first successes. Don't worry if you don't understand some of the concepts or terminology in this chapter—all it does is walk you through your first Blender animation to introduce you to the program. Chapter 4 covers the basic functions in more detail.

3.1   3 . . . 2 . . . 1 . . . Take Off

Blender installs the same way on all operating systems: download the compressed file from http://www.blender.nl (or copy it from the CD) and extract it into a folder of your choice. There's no time-consuming installation routine and you don't even need to restart your computer.

Depending on your operating system, you can start Blender from a command line or by clicking its icon. To start Blender in Windows, go to the Blender directory in Windows Explorer and click (either single or double, depending on your Windows version) either the Blender icon or blender.exe. (Note that Blender does not automatically put a shortcut in the Start menu or on the desktop. It's a good idea to set up one or the other for yourself if you plan to make a lot of use of the program.) If your system uses the command line, change to the Blender directory and issue the command

```
cw@mero ~/blender/ >./blender
cw@mero ~/blender/ >
```

Appendix E describes the installation process and different procedures for starting Blender in greater detail.

The first time it boots up, Blender copies a default file into your home directory or Windows folder. This file is the default *scene* (a scene is the "canvas" in Blender where all the data for your 3D world is stored), a large, almost empty window as shown in Figure 3-1. If you have a different system environment or window manager, your system's window decorations may look slightly different from those shown in the figure, but Blender itself looks the same in all operating systems because it uses its own interface. This aspect of Blender is a double-edged sword: a dyed-in-the-wool Windows user will find Blender's graphical user interface (GUI) unusual at first, but Blender operates exactly the same on all operating systems.

Pressing CTRL-X and then ENTER deletes the current scene and loads a new default one. If you get stuck, CTRL-X and then ENTER will always bring you back to Blender's default scene, though it will also delete the current scene.

3.2   Basic Functions

Figure 3-2 on page 26 shows the Blender screen (annotated to explain various elements) right after start-up. Don't worry if you don't recognize all the concepts yet; you'll learn about them as you make your way through the book. Here are some basic things to know about working with Blender.

3.2.1   Use Two Hands

Blender is designed to be used with two hands: one on the mouse and the other on the keyboard. This is one of Blender's great advantages: work proceeds quickly because you hardly ever have to move your hand from the mouse to the

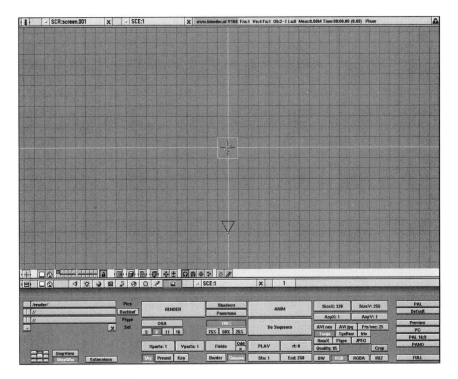

Figure 3-1: Blender's default scene

keyboard. And since the most important and often-used keyboard commands use single keys, you won't have to engage in any "finger acrobatics."

3.2.2 Selected Objects Are Displayed in Violet

Selected objects in Blender's 3D windows (the windows where objects and scenes appear) are always displayed in violet. The plane in Blender's default scene (shown in Figure 3-1) is selected, which is why it appears as a violet square in the 3D window.

In the default scene's 3D window (the large window), you see the default scene from above (a top view). The black triangle in the 3D window is the camera, which is looking—that is, turning the side with the open face, not its point—in the direction of the selected plane.

3.2.3 Active Window

Mouse and keyboard actions always relate to the active window. A window is active when the mouse pointer is in it (the window does not need to be clicked).

3.2.4 Using the Mouse Buttons

Unlike most software, Blender has you select items with the *right* mouse button. For example, right-clicking the camera selects the camera and turns it violet.

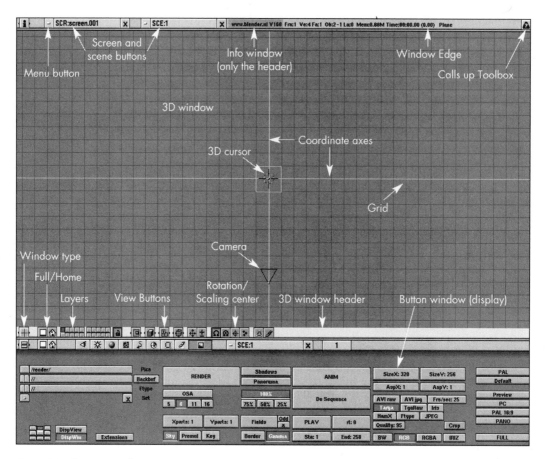

Figure 3-2: The annotated Blender *interface*

Clicking the *left* mouse button places the 3D cursor (the crosshair cursor with the red and white circle). The 3D cursor lets you precisely place objects in space even without views from all three sides. New objects are always placed where the 3D cursor is.

3.2.5 The Toolbox

The Toolbox (shown in Figure 3-3) is Blender's most important tool. To access it, press the spacebar or click the question mark icon in the upper right-hand corner of the Blender screen and use the mouse to call up its menu items. Mouse off the Toolbox area or press ESC to close it.

3.3 Loading a Scene

To load a saved scene, press F1 from within Blender and either middle-click the file in the file list (if you have a three-button mouse) or left-click the file and press ENTER to load it. Let's get started on your first Blender animation by loading basic_scene.blend (in tutorials/chapter03 on the CD-ROM).

ADD	Mesh	>>
VIEW	Curve	>>
EDIT	Surface	>>
OBJECT	Text	
OBJECT	MetaBall	
MESH	Empty	A
CURVE		
KEY	Camera	A
RENDER	Lamp	A
DIV	Ika	A
	Lattice	A

Figure 3-3: The Toolbox

NOTE

To change to a file directory on your hard disk, CD-ROM, or other media, click and hold the left mouse button on the Menu button (in the upper left of the File window) to call up a menu of paths (or drives in the case of Windows). The directory entry ".." changes to the next higher directory or drive and the Parent button (the button with the "p" on it) does the same thing.

NOTE

You can replace Blender's default scene with your own customized one and make it Blender's default scene to be loaded on start-up. Using your own default scene will speed up the start of a new construction since you won't have to build a complete modeling foundation every time. In Section 4.13 I'll describe how to customize Blender to your own way of working and how to configure your default scene accordingly.

The scene basic_scene.blend contains a grid that is already lit by two light sources. After loading it, Blender should look like Figure 3-4, with its interface divided into three views: a top view (the scene from above, in the large 3D window), a camera view (in the small window in the upper right), and a side view (the scene from the side, in the lower right-hand section of the window).

The camera (symbolized by the pyramid) looks down obliquely toward the ground (see the camera view window in the upper right). The side view makes it easy to see the camera angle.

3.4 The Object

Call up the Toolbox and choose Add • Mesh and left-click Mesh to show its menu options. Select UVsphere and click OK in the two dialog boxes that follow to accept the defaults of 32 segments and 32 rings.

NOTE

Confirm queries in Blender by clicking OK or pressing ENTER. If you're unsure, press ESC or mouse off the query to cancel the action.

You have just created your first Blender object—a sphere that appears where the 3D cursor was, shown in different views as a wireframe model with yellow vertices. If you didn't move the 3D cursor before creating the sphere, the sphere should take up almost the entire camera view and be displayed with filled-in faces. It should appear as a wireframe in the other views.

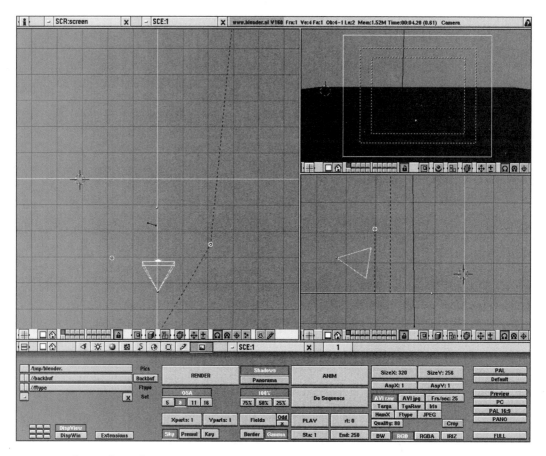

Figure 3-4: The Quick Start basic scene

Once you've created an object in Blender, the program enters *EditMode*. Now leave EditMode by pressing TAB; the sphere should appear as a violet wireframe showing that it's selected.

NOTE *Using the Toolbox quickly becomes second nature, so from now on I'll abbreviate the procedure for making a selection in the Toolbox menu. To describe the procedure for the sphere, for example, I'll write "Add • Mesh • UVsphere."*

3.5 Adjusting the Sphere's Size

Our sphere isn't quite right (see Figure 3-5): It's too big and poorly positioned in the scene, so let's translate (move) and scale (resize) it.

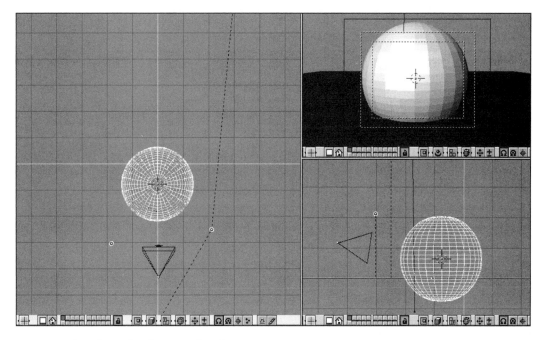

Figure 3-5: The sphere when first created (in three 3D views)

1. To edit the sphere you first have to select it. If it is not already selected, mouse over the sphere in the top view or side view and right-click once. If you got it right, the sphere will turn violet (that is, selected).

2. Move the mouse into the large 3D window and press S on your keyboard. (The sphere should now appear as a white wireframe.)

3. Use your mouse to adjust the sphere's size by moving it toward the sphere (to make it smaller), or away (to enlarge it), keeping the mouse within the 3D window the entire time. (The size change is simultaneously displayed in the other 3D windows.) Right-click to restore the sphere to its old size (right-clicking cancels a function).

4. Press S again and move the mouse toward the sphere until the sphere is just over the green line in the side view, then set this new size by left-clicking.

NOTE *The closest thing Blender has to an undo function is pressing the U key in EditMode, which restores the condition before entering EditMode.*

3.6 Changing the Sphere's Position

The steps for translating or moving an object are similar to the scaling procedure described above.

1. Select the sphere.

2. Place the mouse pointer over the wireframe display of the sphere and press G on your keyboard. The sphere will change to a white wireframe and can now be translated by moving the mouse.

3. Left-click to set a new position; right-click to restore the sphere to its original position.

NOTE *Object movement is limited to one plane in a translation. For example, if the mouse is in the top view and you press G, you can move the sphere to the left or right but not to or from the surface in the side view. Similarly, if you translate in the side view, you can move the sphere to and from the surface and along the camera's line of sight. This limitation is necessary because the mouse can move in only two directions. Thus movement in three directions always consists of two translations, each in a different view.*

4. Now place the sphere so that it's clearly visible in the camera view. (Note that the outer broken line in the camera view is the edge of the camera's field of vision.)

5. Press F12 to create the first image of the sphere (press F11 to hide or redisplay the image); it should look something like Figure 3-6. In contrast to the preview shown in the camera view, the sphere now casts a shadow, the two light sources produce separate reflection points on the sphere, and the sky and ground have changed colors. This process of creating a realistic 3D scene out of a simple description of the scene is called *rendering*.

NOTE *You may also render an image by selecting the large RENDER button in Blender's Button window (at the bottom of the screen). The Button window contains several important Blender function groups, which will be especially important in the next section.*

6. Finally, save your scene (if you like it; remember, there are few ways to undo mistakes in Blender) by pressing F2 or choosing File • Save File as in the Toolbox menu to call up the File window; choose the destination for your file by clicking with your mouse and then name the scene to be saved. After typing in the name, press ENTER twice—once to confirm the name and once to save the scene and close the File window.

3.7   From Rough and Gray to Smooth and Bright

The rendered image still clearly shows the individual faces used to create the image of the sphere so we'll need to fix that. To make the sphere look round, we could use a whole bunch of really small faces, but the sheer number of faces needed would demand a lot of power and memory from the computer. Fortunately, a simple mathematical trick can smooth out the sphere without adding more faces.

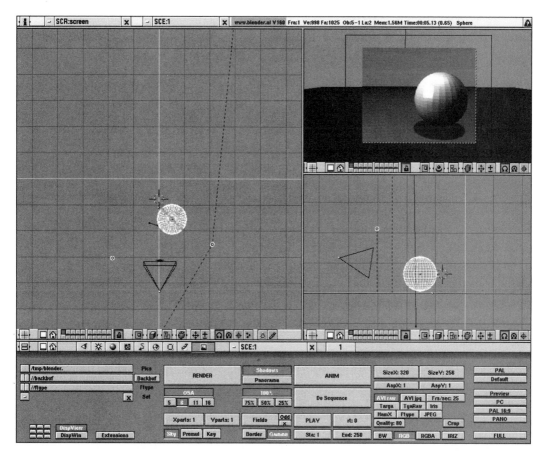

Figure 3-6: A rendered scene in the camera view

1. Right-click the sphere to select it and then press F9 or the Edit buttons icon in the Button window *header* (a bar in every Blender window that, depending on the type of window, contains different buttons and information) under the 3D views (see Figure 3-7); note the new menu options that appear in the Button window.

Figure 3-7: The Button window header

2. Click Set Smooth in the Button window (at the bottom of the third column from the left). The sphere should now appear smooth in the camera window and in the rendered image.

If you like to experiment, go ahead and try all the icons in the header. However, since Blender displays different buttons depending on the type of active object, some icons won't give you very many buttons at this point.

3.7.1 Gray Is Boring: Adding Color with a Material

But even though our sphere is now smooth, it's still a bit on the drab side, so let's spruce it up with a material.

1. Call up the Material buttons for the selected sphere by pressing F5 or the corresponding icon in the Button window header.

2. Left-click and hold the Menu button in the Button window header and choose ADD NEW from the pop-up menu that appears to create a material called Material.001 and call up the material settings (Figure 3-8).

Figure 3-8: Material buttons

The Menu button is unique to Blender and surfaces often. When you use it, remember to hold the mouse button down to give yourself time to see the menu options.

RGB sliders

3. Define the material's color using the sliders for each of the three primary (RGB) colors (red, green, and blue) found at the left side of the Material buttons, in the third column (see margin). (For an introduction to Blender's color system, see Section 2.1.2.) Let's produce a red and white marbled material. First we'll set the material's primary color to white (R,G,B = 1.0); do so by left-clicking the small knobs on the controls and dragging them to the right to increase the value. (You can, of course, set any other color; gold, for example, is R = 0.9, G = 0.8, and B = 0.) Don't worry about the red for the moment—we'll get to that shortly.

3.8 Surface Structures: Texture

Now let's produce a marbled effect using a *texture*. A texture is a pattern that determines an object's surface appearance. In addition to simple color textures, *procedural textures* can control other parameters such as transparency or illumination. And beyond procedural textures, which are mathematically generated, a texture can also be an actual image—for example, a photograph of a rock face or a pile of jelly beans—that is "wrapped" around a sphere.

To create a new texture, do the following:

1. Select the sphere and click the Texture buttons icon or press F6.

2. Add a new texture using the Menu button (just as you did for the new material)—left-click and hold the Menu button in the Button window header and choose ADD NEW from the pop-up menu.

3. Choose Marble from the list of texture types to create a procedural texture with a marbled look (Figure 3-9).

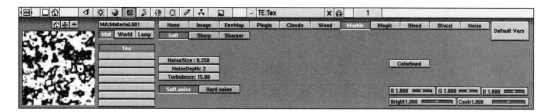

Figure 3-9: The Texture buttons

4. Use the default settings for the other parameters, or, depending on your taste, increase the turbulence (to 15.0, for example) to create a more marbled texture. To increase the turbulence, left-click and hold the Turbulence button and move the mouse to the right or left to increase or decrease the value, respectively. The texture preview to the left will update when you release the mouse button.

NOTE *This method of clicking and dragging to change the numerical value of a button is common in Blender. To enter a value directly with the keyboard, click and hold the left mouse button in the button with the numerical value, right-click, let go of both buttons, and type in the numerical value you want. This procedure is awkward to describe on paper, but it's easy in practice. If you have a two-buttoned mouse, try holding SHIFT and left-clicking.*

5. At this point, a test rendering with F12 should produce a white and violet marbled sphere.

6. To change the texture color, switch back to the Material buttons with F5 (Figure 3-8) and set the texture color controls (to the right in the Material buttons) to a red (R = 0.6, G = 0, B = 0).

At this point, your image should look like the one in Figure 3-10.

Figure 3-10: A finished image from the Quick Start scene

3.9 Bringing Movement into the Game: Animation

We'll now construct a very simple animation using *keyframes*—frames between which Blender automatically calculates an animation. (Chapter 8 will cover the diverse animation possibilities Blender offers in more depth; this is just a taste of what the program has to offer.)

1. Make sure the frame slider is set to one. If it isn't, move it to the left until you see the "1" in the window, as shown here:

NOTE *You can flip through an animation frame by frame by using the left and right arrow keys. The up and down arrow keys move ten frames forward and backward, respectively.*

2. Press G in the top view to move the sphere to the spot where you want the animation to start (you can control the positioning best in the camera view). To have the sphere come slowly into the frame at the beginning of the animation, place it to the left so that it's outside the outermost broken line in the camera view. Left-click to record the position change.

3. With the sphere still selected, press I and choose Loc (location) from the pop-up menu to create the sphere's first keyframe in Frame 1.

4. Using the mouse (or the arrow keys) set the frame slider to 51. (If you hold CTRL while adjusting, the value in the control will increase by tens.)

5. Now move the sphere to the desired end position for your animation (for example, outside the camera's field of vision to the right and nearer the camera). Figure 3-11 illustrates the two suggested keyframe positions.

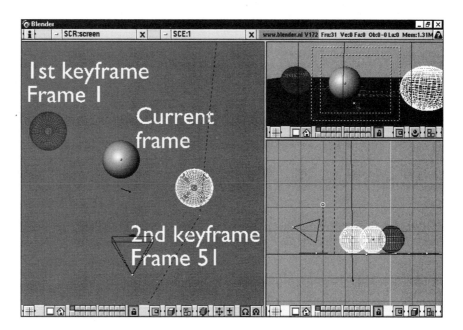

Figure 3-11: The two keyframes and the sphere's current position

6. Press I to add a keyframe for the sphere's end position and choose Loc again from the menu.

3.9.1 Playing the Animation Preview

To preview your animation based on the keyframes selected above, set the frame slider to Frame 1. ALT-A plays the animation in the active 3D window (where the mouse is); SHIFT-ALT-A plays the animation preview in all views. Press ESC to stop the animation preview.

In 50 frames, the sphere goes in a straight line from your defined start position to the end position and then stops, with the current frame number indicated by the mouse cursor. After Frame 250 Blender begins playing the animation from Frame 1 again (the sphere sits at its final position from Frames 51 to 250 and then returns to its starting position at Frame 1).

3.10 Rendering the Animation

Even though computers become faster and cheaper every day, they are still not powerful enough to render a convincing animation in real time. In particular, finely tuned lighting, reflective or transparent objects, and various other special effects (like smoke and fog) overwhelm even today's most powerful and expensive computers.

For this reason, individual frames are rendered separately (in a process that can take hours, depending on the scene), after which the frames are played back in sequence, at the desired speed. Figure 3-12 gives you a look at five of the frames that produce the animation we've been working on. This playback is recorded by the computer and can be output to video or even exposed on film to produce the animation.

Figure 3-12: A few frames from the animation

Let's render our animation.

1. Switch to the Display buttons by pressing F10 and enter the first and last frame to be rendered using the Sta:1 and End:250 buttons. Since our animation is set for 50 frames, use the mouse to set End:250 to 51 (counting begins with 1). (If you have trouble setting the value precisely, hold down SHIFT to let you enter the exact value with the keyboard.)

NOTE *Depending on your computer's power and your patience, you may use the 100%–25% buttons in the middle of the Display buttons to render a smaller version of the animation. Use the SizeX and SizeY buttons to set an exact resolution.*

2. Tell Blender where to save the frames using the field at the upper left of the Display buttons window; left-clicking in this field allows you to enter the destination path with the keyboard. The end of the path requires the frame name, and Blender will add to that the relevant frame number. (Clicking the gray button near the path brings up the familiar File window.)

Path for saving frames

3. Click the big ANIM button to render the animation, display the finished frames, and store them on your hard drive.

4. When the animation is finished, preview it by pressing PLAY; press ESC to stop the preview.

Depending on the setting in the Display buttons, the rendered animation will be saved as a numbered frame sequence or as a digital video file. In this example scene, the uncompressed, standard AVI file format (readable by every program that supports AVIs) is selected. (Note that Windows requires a fairly new player or Apple's QuickTime version 4 to play compressed JPEG AVIs, so choose your format with care.)

Press Q to exit Blender.

4

BLENDER BASICS

Like many other 3D programs, Blender uses the OpenGL
software libraries—the industry's most widely used and supported 2D and 3D graphics application programming interface
—to display 3D graphics during its modeling phase. It also uses
OpenGL (or Mesa, a free implementation of the OpenGL software
libraries) for its GUI (graphical user interface).

Blender's use of OpenGL to draw its entire GUI differentiates it from all
other systems I'm familiar with, and makes it an extremely compact program
that looks and acts the same across its eight supported platforms. It also lets
you scale its interface buttons and lay out its interface almost any way you wish.
But this flexibility has a disadvantage too: If you're used to using Windows or
Macintosh interfaces you'll have to learn a lot of new tricks to use Blender successfully. Several of Blender's buttons, controls, and other interface elements
do not correspond to elements found in other GUIs.

As I've mentioned, Blender is designed to be used with both hands (one
for the mouse, the other for the keyboard). And you need both—although
many functions can be activated only with the mouse, the keyboard is an
extremely important part of modeling with Blender.

This chapter teaches you the basics of Blender operation, including how
to use the mouse and keyboard. I also cover important functions like loading
and saving scenes, operating and navigating in 3D windows, selecting objects,
and performing the most fundamental edits and manipulations.

With this foundation and the Quick Start (Chapter 3) behind you, you
should find it easy to follow the tutorials in the next few chapters.

4.1 The Mouse

Blender's use of the mouse is fairly uniform throughout the different program components. Here are the basic functions.

4.1.1 The Left Mouse Button

- In general, left-clicking operates switches, buttons, and controls.

- Combining clicking with holding and dragging often enables additional functions (such as changing the value in a number field).

- Left-clicking in a 3D window places the 3D cursor, determining where new objects are created.

- Used in combination with the keyboard (for example, with CTRL, to add a new vertex to an object), left-clicking can trigger even more functions (which I'll describe in more detail in the following section on Blender's interface and in the individual tutorials).

4.1.2 The Middle Mouse Button

Blender was born on operating systems that support or even require a three-button mouse. If you have a Windows system without a three-button mouse, press ALT and left-click to substitute for the middle mouse button. (Or better yet, pick up a three-button mouse!) The middle mouse button is very important to Blender, as you'll see in the following chapters.

In general, the middle mouse button is most important when you *transform* (that is, translate, scale, or rotate) an object. Middle-clicking can also limit a change to only one axis or line of movement. When you're in the 3D windows, the middle mouse button translates, turns, or zooms in on and out from the views.

4.1.3 The Right Mouse Button

Unlike most other programs, Blender uses right-clicking to select and activate objects or vertices. Here are some general notes:

- Holding SHIFT and right-clicking lets you add to your selection.

- Right-clicking on a selected object deselects it.

- Selected objects are displayed as violet in the 3D windows.

- If several objects are selected, the last one selected is light violet and is the *active* object—the one to which subsequent actions apply.

4.2 The Keyboard

In contrast to keyboard commands in other programs (usually the result of key combinations), many of Blender's functions are called up by pressing a single key, thus sparing you complicated hand contortions. Furthermore, these function keys are connected to important options.

The following keys call up the same actions in all windows. (See Appendix A for a more complete list.)

4.2.1 Basic Functions

You'll use these keys and key combinations often: to back out of a menu choice, call up the Toolbox, or to load or save a scene.

ESC	Cancels an action and returns to the previous condition.
Spacebar	Brings up the Toolbox—Blender's main menu. You can also call up the Toolbox by clicking the Toolbox icon.
TAB	Begins or ends EditMode.
F1	Loads a scene file; the window containing the mouse becomes the File window, from which it is also possible to load VRML-1 (ASCII) and DXF (ASCII) files.
SHIFT-F1	Loads individual elements from a scene file. Here you can navigate in scenes just as in directories. In addition, you can also use the Library function, which generates a link to an external scene.
F2	Saves the scene; the active window becomes the File window, where you can declare the path and file name.
CTRL-W	Quick save without the File window.
Q	Quits Blender (after you verify you want to quit).
CTRL-U	Saves the current scene as the default (see Section 4.13) for new scenes and Blender's boot-up scene as .B.blend in the home directory or Windows folder.
CTRL-X	Deletes the current scene in its entirety and starts over with the default scene.
F3	Saves a rendered image in the format set in the Display buttons. The active window becomes the File window.

4.2.2 Changing Button Windows

These function keys toggle through the various button windows within Blender. Each window offers its own particular set of themed buttons tied to a particular function group.

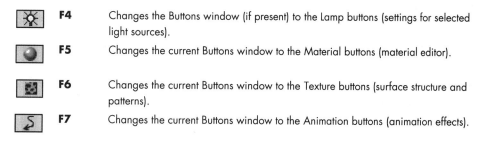

F4	Changes the Buttons window (if present) to the Lamp buttons (settings for selected light sources).
F5	Changes the current Buttons window to the Material buttons (material editor).
F6	Changes the current Buttons window to the Texture buttons (surface structure and patterns).
F7	Changes the current Buttons window to the Animation buttons (animation effects).

F8   Changes the current Buttons window to the World buttons (global scene settings).

F9   Changes the current Buttons window to the Edit buttons (object-specific edits).

F10   Changes the current Buttons window to the Display buttons (the rendering control center).

4.2.3 Rendering Hotkeys

You'll use these keys often when rendering.

F11   Moves the Render window to the front or back.

F12   Renders the current image.

4.2.4 Stepping through Animations

Use these keys to step through your animations.

→	Advances one frame in an animation.
SHIFT-→	Displays the last frame (set in the Display buttons).
←	Goes back one frame.
SHIFT-←	Goes to the first frame.
↑	Advances ten frames.
↓	Goes back ten frames.
ALT-A	Plays the animation preview in the active window (the one containing the mouse cursor). The mouse cursor displays the frame numbers; ESC stops the animation.
SHIFT-ALT-A	Plays the animation preview in all windows.

NOTE   *Pressing a key always applies to the* active window *(the window the mouse pointer is in).*

4.3   Operating and Navigating in the 3D Windows

Blender's default scene starts with a 3D window that shows an orthogonal projection of the scene from a top view—you see the scene from above with a small, square plane and a camera. The plane is selected and therefore violet. Figure 4-1 gives you a look at a scene in various views.

4.3.1 A Tour through the Keyboard Commands in 3D Windows

Let's begin our tour.

1.   Start by pressing PAD 1 (the "1" on the numerical keypad) for a front view of the scene.

Figure 4-1: Various views of a scene

2. Press SHIFT-PAD 1 for a view from behind (the SHIFT key functions analogously in the other views). We are now looking at the camera from behind (the arrow above the camera indicates the camera's alignment).

3. Press PAD 7 to redisplay the top view.

4. Use PAD + and PAD – to zoom in or out.

5. Press PAD 3 for a side view of the scene; you should see the camera, symbolized by a pyramid with its base pointing toward the object.

6. Press PAD 0 to turn the 3D window into a view from the camera's perspective. Since the camera and plane are elevated, we see only a line—we're looking straight on at the plane's edge. The camera's field of vision is represented by the outer broken line.

7. Press PAD . to center the selected objects and zoom in on the objects until they fill the view.

8. Press PAD / to display just the selected objects, which can then be edited separately.

9. Now press PAD 7 again to switch to the top view, or load the default scene with CTRL-X.

10. On their own, the 4, 8, 6, and 2 keys on the numerical keypad rotate the view; with the SHIFT key they translate the view. Press PAD 4 four times and then PAD 2 four times to rotate the scene so that you are looking down on it at an angle. Experiment a bit with the keys to rotate, zoom, and translate the view.

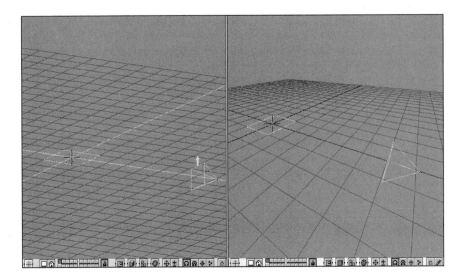

Figure 4-2: Orthogonal and perspective views in the 3D windows

11. You'll notice that the three-dimensional impression created by the grid in the 3D window is weak or even confusing—the orthogonal perspective does not produce a genuine 3D view (Figure 4-2). Pressing PAD 5 switches to a perspective view that conveys the sense of depth much better (which is especially clear with the grid, as its lines now run together in the distance).

4.3.2 Operating 3D Windows with the Mouse

You can also execute the commands introduced in section 4.3.1 with the mouse, which is often more practical because you can leave your hand on the mouse instead of reaching for the keypad.

Middle-clicking the mouse begins mouse operation in the 3D window. By default, Blender is set so that holding the middle mouse button while moving the mouse rotates the 3D window with either the trackball or turntable method, depending on the TrackBall button's settings in the Info window, the window that has many of Blender's default settings (see Section 4.13). The turntable method rotates the window around its main axis only and is somewhat easier to use, but the trackball method is more flexible—and it's easy to master, with a little practice.

- When Viewmove is activated in the Info window, middle-clicking translates the window's contents. (I activate this setting in my scenes since I translate a window's contents much more often than I rotate them. Holding SHIFT then lets me rotate the window.) By default, holding SHIFT translates the view.

- Press CTRL, middle-click, and move the mouse to zoom in or out, just like a zoom lens on a camera does with a telephoto or wide-angle lens.

You can call up Blender's most important 3D window functions from the 3D header, shown in Figure 4-3.

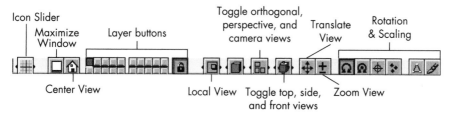

Figure 4-3: The 3D window 3D header

- The Icon Slider (a type of Blender button with a value you change by clicking and dragging) on the far left in the 3D header changes the window type (here, of course, set to a 3D window). The icons next to the Icon Slider maximize the window (the screen icon) and center the view (the house icon) on all objects.

- The next buttons, up to and including the lock icon, set the layers. (I'll explain them in more detail in the next section.)

- The Local View button, to the right of the layer settings, allows you to concentrate and work faster on an object by displaying the active object in the window by itself (you can also switch to the Local View of a selected object with PAD /).

- The next Icon Slider toggles between the orthogonal, perspective, and camera views.

- The Icon Slider after that toggles between top, side, and front views.

- Left-clicking the two buttons with crosses (the Translate View and Zoom View buttons) while holding the left mouse button and moving the mouse translates or zooms in on or out from the view.

- The remaining buttons on the Icon Slider set the rotation and scaling functions—I'll explain them in Section 4.7.

4.4 The Layer System

You can think of *layers* as a stack of overhead transparencies of Blender's 3D objects. When you *deactivate* a layer you remove an overhead transparency from the stack, so the objects on the transparency become invisible—but they're still available for use; you haven't thrown them away.

Blender's layer system lets you organize your work and achieve a better overview of a scene by hiding objects on separate layers. Objects in deactivated layers are not rendered or displayed, which considerably quickens your work (especially modeling) with complex objects. You can also store intermediate modeling steps or backup copies of objects on deactivated layers. Layers also play a role in selective lighting (Section 7.3.4) and in generating reflections (Section 6.8.3). In Section 4.12 I'll discuss even finer scene divisions.

4.4.1 Layer Basics

Layer buttons

The Layer buttons appear in the 3D window's header or footer. A depressed button symbolizes an active layer. Left-clicking selects an active layer, and holding the SHIFT key lets you select multiple layers.

NOTE *When the lock icon is deactivated (open), you can work with layers and their settings will not be taken into account when you render a scene.*

- The upper row of layer buttons corresponds to layers one through ten; the bottom row to layers eleven through twenty. The number keys on the main keyboard (above the letters) may also be used to select the layers, with the keys 0 through 9 corresponding to layers one through ten. Holding SHIFT here, too, lets you select multiple layers. Use ALT-0 through ALT-9 to select layers eleven through twenty.

- The last layer you select is the active layer and further work applies to it. The last layer is also where Blender puts new objects you create.

- To move objects between layers, activate the relevant layers with the mouse or number pad (either using the Edit buttons or the pop-up menu called with M), and then click OK or press ENTER to confirm your selection. Moving objects between layers lets you make an object active and visible in more than one layer.

NOTE *To organize your work, you should begin using layers as soon as possible. In particular, separate the lamps and ground of the default scene so that they won't disturb your modeling.*

4.5 Loading and Saving

Loading and saving scenes and objects is a critical part of 3D modeling—you'll often have projects in various stages. You initiate Blender's loading and saving functions with F1 and F2 or through Toolbox • File.

Figure 4-4 shows the File window used to load Blender's scene files.

4.5.1 Loading Files

- File names with yellow squares next to them are files that Blender can load. Middle-click a file to load it.

- Left-click a file to transfer its name to the file name line, then press ENTER to load it. If you wish, you can change or append the file or directory name before pressing ENTER.

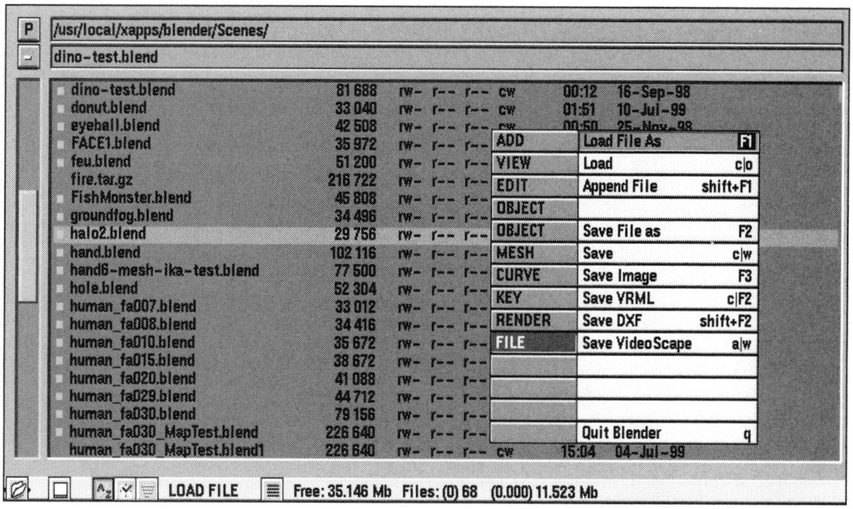

Figure 4-4: The File window with Toolbox

- When loading images, right-click individual files to make multiple selections; use the A key to select or deselect all files in the current directory.

- Load individual elements (objects, material, and so on) from a Blender file with SHIFT-F1 or the Toolbox menu option Append File. Left- or middle-clicking the file lets you navigate it as if it were a regular directory—individual object groups (materials, objects, and so on) are treated as subdirectories from which one or multiple individual elements may be loaded into the current scene.

- Select Link instead of Append (from the Toolbox menu) to create an unchangeable copy of an object, allowing multiple animators to work on a scene, or a company to make a companywide material library.

- Load 3D files supported by Blender with F1 (the active window turns into a File window from which you can load scenes). Blender recognizes the file type and converts it to its own internal representation. (See Appendix B.1 for an overview of supported file formats.)

NOTE *Before Blender overwrites a file, it asks for confirmation. You can confirm this dialog by clicking it or pressing ENTER, or you can cancel by pressing ESC or moving the mouse pointer out of the pop-up menu.*

4.5.2 Saving Files

- When saving files, press PAD + or PAD – to add a version number to the file's base name (before .blend), and to increase or decrease that number, respectively.

- Save individual rendered images with F3 or Toolbox • Save Image. The image will be saved in the format set in the Display buttons.

4.5.3 Managing Files and Directories

- Click the first line of the File window to enter a file path. If you type in a directory that doesn't exist, Blender will create the directory (after issuing a warning).

- The button with the P on it changes to the next higher directory. The directory entries ".." and "." are of special importance. Clicking the ".." entry changes to the next higher directory (like the Parent button). The "." entry marks the current directory; clicking it refreshes the directory's contents (particularly helpful when another program has written new files into that directory).

- Click and hold the Menu button at the upper left of the File window to see recently selected directories, or drives in Windows systems. (The data on recently viewed directories is saved in the .Bfs file in the user's home directory or in the Windows folder and can be edited with a text editor.)

- The status header lets you sort files alphabetically, chronologically, or by size. The button next to the status header lets you switch between a detailed file list (for example, file size, access permissions, and date) and an abbreviated one (file name only). The status header also indicates the amount of free space on the hard drive or partition, the size and number of selected files (in parentheses), and the total number of files in the current directory.

- With functions such as loading images, right-clicking lets you make multiple selections, and the A key selects or deselects all the files in the current directory.

4.6 Selecting Objects

- Right-click an object to select or deselect it. Hold SHIFT and right-click to make multiple selections.

- When multiple objects are selected, the last one selected is the active one and the target of all actions or processes applicable to individual objects. When multiple objects are selected in wireframe mode, the active one is a somewhat lighter violet.

- Use the A key to select or deselect all objects.

- Press B to introduce a selection box that can be expanded by clicking and holding the left mouse button. Release the mouse to select all objects that are either partially or completely inside the box.

- Press B twice in EditMode to select vertices (an object's control points) with a circle. Left-clicking makes the selection and middle-clicking deselects. PAD + and PAD − let you change the selection circle's size.

4.7 Manipulating Objects

The most common modeling and editing actions are moving (translation), turning (rotation), and resizing (scaling). Every movement through space (animation) and creation of an object (modeling) involves a combination of these fundamental manipulations.

4.7.1 Translating

Working in different views and with the 3D cursor is quick and above all precise. The objects you select follow the mouse without jumping to the mouse pointer. Instead, they keep their relative positions, making it easy to place objects in relation to a reference point. The only difficulty is that you have to translate selected objects or vertices only on the plane of the screen. To translate into depth you must make a second translation in another view because mouse movements are limited to two axes.

NOTE *The current version of Blender doesn't support input devices that can move in more than two directions (mice with wheels, 3D mice, and so on).*

- Press G to turn on object translation.

- Left-click or press ENTER to set the translation.

- Right-click or press ESC to cancel it and return the objects to their original positions.

- Use the arrow keys for fine positioning.

- Middle-click when you start a translation to constrain the object's movement to the main direction the mouse is moving in (either the vertical or horizontal axis); thus minor variations in the way your hand moves won't affect the positioning of the object.

NOTE *Depending on the grid settings in the User menu (Section 4.13), holding CTRL during a translation activates the grid; holding SHIFT then lets you achieve very fine positioning.*

4.7.2 The Grid

Blender is not a CAD program, but it does offer a bunch of functions for exact modeling. Also, you can load 3D models from CAD programs and thus combine the strengths of each (CAD for precise construction; Blender for fast and realistic visualization).

One simple procedure for creating precise constructions uses the 3D cursor (new objects are always placed at the 3D cursor's position). Left-clicking puts the 3D cursor in a 3D or camera view, and so even though the mouse only moves the cursor in two dimensions, you can reach every point in a 3D world by using combinations of the different views.

SNAP menu

The SNAP menu (SHIFT-S) lets you place the cursor on selected objects (Curs -> Sel) or the nearest grid point (Curs -> Grid). You can also use the SNAP menu to place selected objects on the 3D cursor (Sel -> Curs) or nearest grid point (Sel -> Grid).

SNAP menu

SNAP
Sel -> Grid
Sel -> Curs
Curs -> Grid
Curs -> Sel

Moving objects along the grid line

If you translate a selected object with G, holding CTRL moves the object stepwise along the grid—but not necessarily along the visible grid line. To make the object move on the grid line, you must first place the object on the grid line with SHIFT-S • Sel -> Grid. This may seem awkward at first, but after you get used to it, it will become clear that there are in practice two grids (the visible grid and a grid at an arbitrary set distance from the visible one), and that you can also move an object off the grid at a set distance (offset) from the grid lines without having to change the grid or disable it completely.

Adjusting the grid

Any grid settings apply only to the corresponding 3D window (the one the View buttons belong to). This feature allows each 3D window to have its own grid settings.

- You can adjust the grid with the View buttons. (SHIFT-F7 or the corresponding icon in the Icon Slider calls up the View buttons in the current 3D window.) The Grid parameter determines the distance between grid lines. The GridLines parameter determines the number of grid lines in the perspective view, and thus together with Grid determines the grid cell size. If you set GridLines to zero, no grid cells will appear in perspective views, which is especially advantageous in the camera view.

- The grid is always present in orthogonal views (top view, side view, and so on), so GridLines does not have any effect in these views. If you zoom out so far that the distance between grid lines becomes too small, Blender displays every tenth grid line, drawing them as broken lines to avoid confusion.

- In the orthogonal and perspective view grids, the coordinate axes are colored (the x-axis is red, the y-axis green, and the z-axis blue).

4.7.3 Enter Exact Values with the Number Menu

The Number menu is an important tool for quickly transforming an object or vertex. As shown in Figure 4-5, you can directly enter numerical values for the position, rotation, and scaling of an object. These values are absolute values—

Active Object: Cube
OK: Assign Values

LocX: 0.00
LocY: -5.00
LocZ: 2.00
RotX: 45.00
RotY: 0.00   OK
RotZ: 5.00
SizeX: 1.00
SizeY: 2.00
SizeZ: 1.00

Figure 4-5: The Number menu gives you precise control

position and rotation refer to world coordinates and scaling refers to the object's initial size. The rotation angle is given in degrees (0° to 360°). Left-clicking OK records the change; pressing ESC or mousing off the menu cancels the action.

Rotation centers

4.7.4 Rotation

Depending on which button is activated in the window header, the center of rotation can be the midpoint of a bounding box, the center of gravity of the selection, or the 3D cursor, or each object can rotate around its own midpoint (a small, violet sphere). The axis of rotation is always the axis perpendicular to the screen.

- Press R to turn on rotation. You can rotate one or more selected objects.

- Moving the mouse around the center of rotation rotates an object; the grid settings function as set in the User menu (Section 4.13). Left-clicking records the change and ESC or right-clicking restores the condition before entering rotation mode. Middle-clicking switches to simultaneous two-axes rotation.

- Pressing X, Y, or Z during rotation mode switches the rotation to the x-, y-, and z-axes.

4.7.5 Scaling

- Press the S key to scale selected objects.

- Move the mouse pointer away from the selection to enlarge objects and toward the selection to shrink them. The mouse pointer's distance from the center of scaling determines the rate at which the size changes, making the size change easy to control precisely.

- Use SHIFT for finer scaling, and CTRL (depending on your defaults) to activate the grid.

As with rotation, you can set the center of scaling in the 3D window's icon header. If you middle-click during scaling, you'll limit the scaling to one axis, thereby enabling asymmetrical scaling of objects.

Mirroring an object

Mirroring objects (scaling with a negative sign) is a special case of scaling. To mirror an object, press S to change to scaling mode and then use the X and Y keys to mirror the object on the x- and y-axis, respectively. To avoid undesired size changes, either use the grid by holding CTRL or do not move the mouse.

If you mirror an already rotated object, the object may become deformed in an undesirable way. As a backup, record the rotation and size of the object with CTRL-A (Apply size/rot) before mirroring the object.

4.8   Changing Objects in EditMode

Blender's *EditMode*, used to create new objects, also allows you to change an object's geometry. To start or quit EditMode, press TAB.

When you transform (for example, translate or rotate) an object outside of EditMode, you affect the object as a whole, but when you're in EditMode, you can edit an object's individual control points (vertices). Let's try it.

1. Press CTRL-X to return to the default scene. The plane in the middle of the window should be selected; if it isn't, select it with the right mouse button. A translation (begun with G) moves the entire plane. Now, with the plane still selected, press TAB to switch to EditMode.

2. Vertices should now appear on the plane's corners. Select one of them by right-clicking it, turning it yellow (when you select vertices, the rest of the object turns black). Now press G and translate the point.

3. Press the U key to undo all changes, or confirm your translation by left-clicking.

4. Press TAB to leave EditMode—the plane should look different. (You can scale and rotate vertices in the same way.)

We'll cover additional EditMode features in the tutorials and different things you can do with faceted objects in Chapter 5.

4.9   Buttons, Controls, and Switches

Among Blender's various buttons, controls, and switches, there are a few that operate in ways that you may not have encountered before. Here's a rundown of all the generic types of Blender controls and how to use them.

BUT

This is a normal button (one that you simply click), usually beige, that starts a designated process.

 TOGBUT

This toggles between two conditions; active when displayed as depressed.

TOG3BUT

This button can be toggled between off, positive, or negative. When switched to negative, the text turns yellow.

ROWBUT

A row of buttons with mutually exclusive options, so that only one button can be active at a time.

ICONSLI

This provides a range of options on one button. The Icon Slider is recognizable by its two small left and right arrows. Left-clicking on the right or left of the icon switches to the button's next or previous option. To quickly move through the options, hold the left mouse button and move the mouse horizontally across the button.

NUMBUT

This button is for displaying and entering numerical values. There are three ways to set a value:

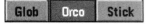

- Click and hold the left mouse button on a NUMBUT, then move the mouse to the right or left to increase or decrease the button's value; holding CTRL changes the value in intervals; SHIFT allows for a more precise setting.

- Click and hold the left mouse button, then middle- or right-click; the button becomes a field in which you can type new values (SHIFT-left-click also works). ENTER records the value and ESC cancels the change.

- Left-click at the right of the button to increase the value or at the left to decrease it. This method is especially advantageous for whole number values.

NUMSLI

A normal slider. Set its value by left-clicking and dragging its knob, or left-click the displayed value to select it so you can type in a new one.

`- | MA:Material | X ⊕`

MENUBUT

The Menu button usually consists of several elements. Left-click and hold to bring up a pop-up menu from which you may select an entry or create a new one with ADD NEW. The name of the entry appears next to the button; click its name to modify it. Click the X to delete an entry. The button with the car, if present, automatically names an entry.

4.10 Windows

Windows are an essential part of Blender's user interface. All information pertaining to the current scene is displayed in windows, and the integrated file manager also uses windows for its display. And Blender's windows are customizable, making it possible to change their size and layout to fit your needs.

Every window has a *header* (technically, either a header or footer, depending on your configuration—right-clicking on a header switches it to a footer), which, depending on the type of window, contains different buttons and information. At the far left of the window header is the Icon Slider, which displays the window types and switches between them.

4.10.1 Window Borders

When you mouse over a window's border in Blender, the cursor turns into a double arrow that can perform various functions, all of which apply to the window surrounded by the border. When the mouse cursor appears as a double-headed arrow, you may:

Translate windows by left-clicking

Left-clicking and holding the left mouse button translates a window border. The window borders move in steps of four pixels, ensuring precise positioning and making it easy to join windows.

Divide windows by middle-clicking

Middle-clicking a window border initiates a split. A pop-up menu appears asking "OK?-Split"; if that's what you want to do, left-click to confirm. A new

Window borders

window border appears, holding a copy of the divided window. You can move this new window with the mouse (see Figure 4-6), set it with a left-click, or press ESC to cancel.

The window holding the mouse as it approaches the new window border is the important one—it is this window that is divided.

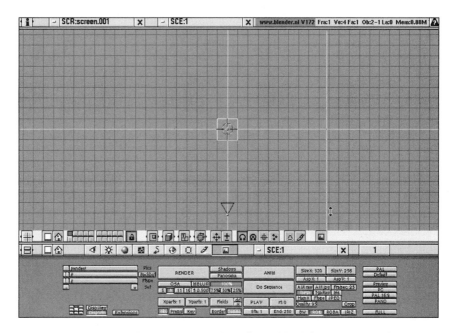

Figure 4-6: Determining where to split a window after middle-clicking the window border

Merge windows by right-clicking

Right-clicking a window border brings up the "OK?-Join" pop-up menu. Clicking Join combines the two windows divided by the border. With this function, too, the direction the border was approached from determines the window that is kept; that is, the window the mouse was in as it approached the border is the window that will take up the larger, combined window.

4.10.2 Window Types

Blender has ten window types, as shown in Figure 4-7. The Icon Slider displays the type of window occupied by the mouse at the far left of the window's header (the window type can also be changed with this slider). These windows are:

Info window

Blender's information bar is shown in the Info window header. You can set the defaults for file paths, the copy function, backups, and so on in the Info window itself.

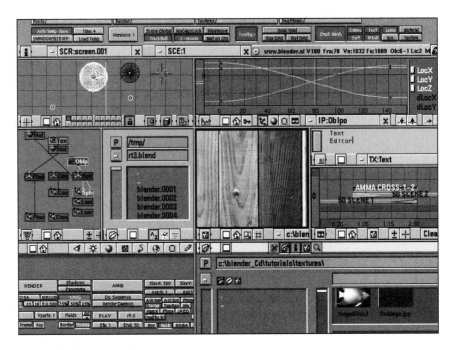

Figure 4-7: Blender window types

 3D window

Windows with 3D and camera views.

 IPO window

Animation curves for objects, materials, worlds, and so on.

 Oops window

Visualization of Blender's internal object structure and the relationships between objects.

 File window

Blender's file management tools; select files to load, save, copy, and delete, and create directories.

 Image window

Images for functions like the Sequence Editor.

 Text window

A text editor for creating texts and scripts.

Sequence window

Blender's cutting room, used for the postproduction of animations and films and to add effects like blurring, editing scenes together, changing colors, and so on.

 Buttons window

Displays a variety of object-related buttons. Depending on the selected object and mode (EditMode or ObjectMode), this window has different buttons that are subdivided according to function group and subgroup. The function keys or the Buttons window's icon header call up the functions.

Image Select window

Displays image files and their thumbnails.

4.10.3 Mission Control: The Buttons Window

Blender is object-oriented, which means that it offers you different functions depending on the object or function you select. This object orientation, in turn, results in context-sensitive menus and options that relate to the task at hand: Buttons for editing curves appear when you're working with curves; material parameters appear when you are working with materials. This principle is especially relevant to the Buttons window (see Figure 4-8).

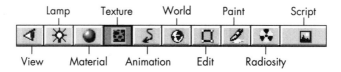

Figure 4-8: The Buttons window icons

An icon header in the Buttons window switches between various function groups depending on your current activity. For example, the Material buttons or the Edit buttons display the material or edit functions, respectively, when you are working with 3D objects. These are the individual function groups:

View buttons (SHIFT-F7)	3D window settings (gridlines, background image for roto-scoping, and so on) for the corresponding 3D window.
Lamp buttons (F4)	Settings for the active light source.
Material buttons (F5)	Blender's material editor; displays the settings for the active object's material.
Texture buttons (F6)	Blender's texture editor.
Animation buttons (F7)	Animation settings for the active object, particle animation, and so on.
World buttons (F8)	Settings for the environment (world) of the active scene.

Edit buttons (F9)	Settings and modeling options for the active object.
Paint buttons (F10)	The editor for coloring (painting) polygon objects.
Radiosity buttons	Radiosity rendering.[1]
Script buttons	Assign Python scripts to objects.
Display buttons	Rendering and output settings.

4.11 Screens

Your personal settings for the Blender window's layout are saved and managed in *screens*, which are saved with each scene. These screens let you create customized work spaces to fit the different tasks you might perform on a scene. Since screens are saved with each scene, you can customize your window layout to each scene so that you get the appropriate environment whenever you open a scene.

Use the Menu button (in Blender's main window header) to switch between different screens, create new screens, or delete screens. Click the screen name next to SCR to enter a name for the individual screen in a text field. Click the Menu button or press CTRL- ← or CTRL- → to switch between screens.

SCR:screen   **X**

Screen browser

NOTE   *Some operating systems or window managers under the X window system use this key combination (CTRL - ← or CTRL - →) for their own functions.*

Blender's default scene (`.B.blend`) defines these three screens:

- `screen.001` for working in 3D windows

- `screen` for working with IPOs (animation curves)

- `screen.002` for animation postproduction in the sequencer

I've defined even more screens for my personal work environment. One of them (Figure 4-9) emulates a file manager and can copy, delete, and move files and also offer image previews. I also have a special screen for writing scripts.

4.12 Scenes

Another concept fundamental to Blender is the use of more than one scene in a file. Thus it is possible to save several views of a 3D world in one file, differing in rendering resolution or quality. For example, if an animation for a multime-

---

1 Radiosity is a way to account for the diffuse reflection between objects, whereby all energy emitted or reflected by every surface is accounted for by its reflection from or absorption by other surfaces. The rate at which energy leaves a surface is called its radiosity.

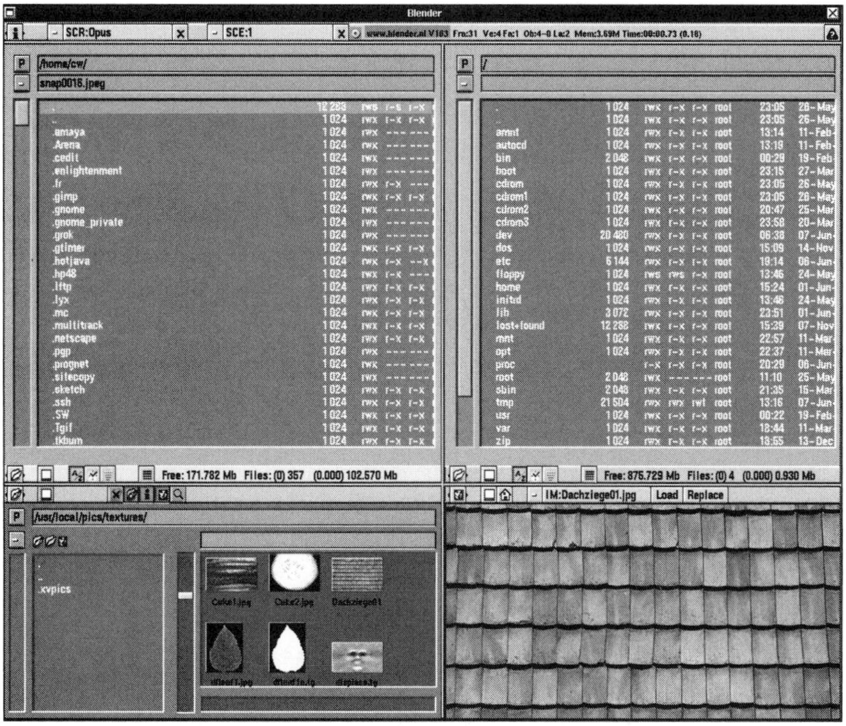

Figure 4-9: My Blender file manager

dia CD requires image resolution of 320x240 pixels while the same image for
the CD cover requires 4000x4000 pixels, you can use two images and switch
between them with a click of the mouse.

Using Blender's built-in video editing system, it's also possible to store cuts
and dissolves between scenes in one file and to render them in one go, without
having to bother with an external program. The ability to save more than one
scene in a Blender file allows you to organize your work even further as well as
quickly create test scenes—scenes you can play with and change without affecting the default scene. The Info window header (usually the uppermost header
in Blender) has a menu button that, like the SCR button, switches between different scenes, creates new scenes, or deletes scenes.

When you create a new scene with ADD NEW, a pop-up menu appears with
the following options:

Empty   Creates an empty scene.

Link Objects   Links the objects in the new scene. Object changes are transmitted to
                   the other scene, but layer or selection settings are set locally. The origin
                   point of a linked object taken from another scene is colored blue.

Link ObData	Links object data to the new scene and copies the position and rotation. A change in the position or rotation is not transmitted to the original scene, though the object's mesh or curve data are—that is, changes in EditMode appear in both scenes.
Full Copy	Creates a complete copy of the original scene.

> **NOTE** *Click the scene name next to* SCR *to change the text button to an entry field where you can name your scene.*

4.12.1 Linking

Linking scenes or objects is ideal for trying out ideas without having to modify or lose the original scene. Display button settings are always local for a new scene, so, for example, a simple mouse click can switch between different resolution, format, and quality settings for video output and individual GIF images for an animation. Linking does not increase the size of the scene because it does not create new object data.

4.13 Customizing Blender to Work Your Way

I hope that the methods described in this section will help you to create a work environment that suits you. You can save your adjustments in a normal scene file that Blender loads upon booting up.

You'll learn Blender's functions in the step-by-step tutorials that follow. And at the same time, as you experiment you'll be making your own default scene that will serve as the basis for all the scenes you make. (The file I use is on the CD-ROM under `tutorials/B.blend.carsten.blend`.)

For your default scene I recommend a plane and at least two light sources for your predefined objects so that you can quickly render your experiments. You should also save often-used materials. And, since Blender saves scenes and window layouts in screens in its normal files, you can also save this information in your default scene.

> **NOTE** *When saving a scene, Blender removes objects (objects in general, not just 3D bodies) from the scene file if they aren't used in the scene.*

Once you have a default scene that you like, save it with CTRL-U to make it the default scene (`.B.blend`). Blender will save it in your home directory or Windows folder.

If you enlarge the Info window by clicking and pulling on the window border, you'll find the *User menu* (that is, Blender's defaults—see Figure 4-10). The most important settings here are the font paths and texture and sequence plugins; left-clicking turns them into text fields where you can enter a path or name.

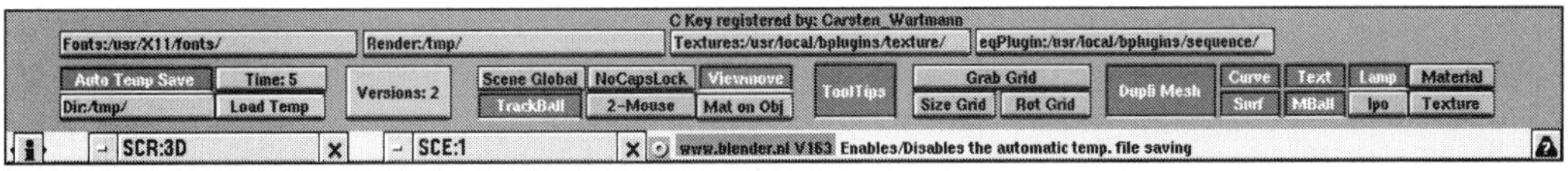

Figure 4-10: The Info window and User menu

The next buttons (on the left under the font field) help guard against lost work. Blender can make backup copies of a scene every minute as well as keep previous versions of a saved scene.

Viewmove reverses the function of the middle mouse button so that clicking and holding the middle mouse button translates a view and does not, as in the initial default setting, rotate it. This setting accommodates my personal way of working better than the initial default setting since I translate views more often than rotate them.

When creating objects, the Mat in Obj setting makes a material a property of the object as opposed to a subordinate form as in a polygon frame or curve. This simplifies working with objects that come up several times in one scene—they don't require additional memory since this way each instance of the object can have its own material.

The Tooltips button activates the Tooltips, short descriptions that appear in the status header when you mouse over a GUI element.

The next settings define the grid settings for translating (Grab Grid), scaling (Size Grid), and rotating (Rot Grid). The grid is exceptionally helpful for quickly constructing precise variations of an object. I recommend using the grid for rotation to make undoing rotations quick and easy.

No grid is used in the initial default settings—changes are made on a continuum. SHIFT activates a kind of "gear box" for more exact control (that is, in a "low gear" you could move the mouse a long distance but the cursor would move only a short distance), CTRL uses the large grid intervals, and SHIFT-CTRL the small grid intervals. If you activate the Size Grid or Rot Grid buttons, the normal change uses large grid intervals, SHIFT the small intervals, CTRL is continuous, and SHIFT-CTRL uses the gears.

The settings for copying and linking in Blender are located in the right of the Info window. Because of its internal object-oriented representation of connections, Blender can reuse datablocks (for example, wireframes or materials). Reusing datablocks requires much less memory, and when you edit the base object, all other linked objects change as well. These buttons determine which object properties and components are really copied when copying objects with CTRL-D.

4.13.1 The Info Window's Status Bar

The Info window status bar displays the following information: the Blender version number; the current image number; the number of vertices (3D or control points) and faces in the current scene; the number of objects, selected objects, and lamps; the amount of memory being used by Blender; the last time something was rendered; and the name of the active object. In EditMode, it displays the number (total and number selected) of all the vertices and faces of the selected object. If Tooltips is activated in the User menu, mousing over icons and buttons brings up short descriptions of them in the status bar.

5

MODELING TUTORIALS

There are two fundamentally different ways to model objects in Blender: with polygons and with formulas.

Polygonal models, which are made up of closed two-dimensional surfaces stretched between points in space (like the numbered faces on a die), are appropriate when you need complete control over every point of the object you're creating. You would use a polygonal model to create a room in a house, for example, that had to fit exact dimensions.

Mathematical models, which are the product of mathematical formulas describing curves and surfaces, allow you to quickly construct complex, rounded faces and objects that appear to be organic. For example, you would use a mathematical model to suggest natural forms in a random landscape that did not need to be precisely measurable.

While polygonal models allow for more precision, mathematical models allow for more variety within a given file size—they require much less memory and may be successfully compressed. (Compressing an object made with polygons often results in a lower-quality image—a by-product of the compression algorithm's needing to shrink the relatively large polygonal construct.)

The tutorials in this chapter take you through a few simple example scenes that will introduce you to Blender's basics for working with both approaches. As you work through the tutorials, experiment with the examples to refine and expand upon them.

5.1 Polygons

The *vertex* is the smallest element in Blender's polygon modeling that can be selected and edited in EditMode. When you connect two vertices you create an edge; three form a triangle—the simplest polygon or *face*.

When you connect multiple faces you create a *mesh* that determines an object's form and contains information about the object's outer shell. (An object's inner structure is undefined, so try to avoid making holes in an object's geometry!)

Blender has nine built-in polygon *primitives* (basic shapes used in modeling) that you can place in a scene; they are accessed from the Toolbox (Spacebar • Add • Mesh). These are the objects at your disposal:

Plane   A square face consisting of four vertices; an ideal starting point for all sorts of polygon modeling.

Cube   A three-dimensional object with six squares as faces. A cube is a good starting point for creating boards, stones, and so on.

Circle   A circle composed of vertices and edges (without faces). A good starting point for extruding objects.

UVsphere   A sphere that consists of longitude and latitude lines like the ones on a globe. Its symmetrical structure makes a good starting point for further modeling.

Icosphere   A sphere made up of isosceles and equilateral triangles distributed symmetrically over its surface. Looks smoother than a UVsphere with the same number of polygons.

Cylinder   An apparently solid rod that makes a great starting point for columns, tree trunks, and so on.

Tube   An open, hollow cylinder you can easily extrude into a tube with thin or thick walls.

Cone   A good starter shape for sharp points and so on. You can create a truncated cone by scaling one end of a cylinder.

Grid   A flat surface that allows you to define any number of regularly spaced vertices across its surface—like a piece of graph paper.

The different objects are shown in Figure 5-1. I used the GIMP (an image editor and Linux graphics program mainly derived from Photoshop) to make both the shaded surfaces and wireframe structures visible.

5.2 Working with Vertices in EditMode

Once you've created an object, Blender enters *EditMode*, where you can edit individual vertices. Press TAB to exit EditMode and edit the object as a whole; vertices should appear, displayed as small violet points in the wireframe or shaded view (SHIFT-Z).

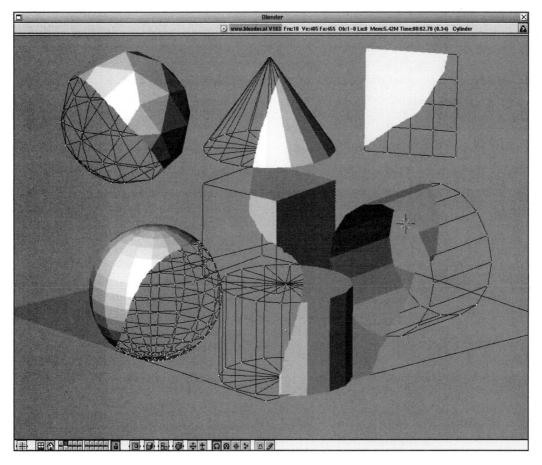

Figure 5-1: Blender's polygon primitives (wireframe and shaded display mounted in The GIMP)

- Right-clicking a vertex selects it and turns it yellow; holding SHIFT enables multiple selections. To deselect an inadvertent selection, hold SHIFT and right-click the selected vertex.

- Pressing A selects or deselects all vertices, and B introduces a selection box (BorderSelect).

- Activate CircleSelect by pressing B twice, then left-click to select all vertices inside the circle or middle-click to deselect them. Right-click cancels the function; PAD + and PAD – change the size of the selection circle.

In general, you can perform all of the same operations in EditMode on vertices as you can on complete objects. Thus you can translate (G), rotate (R), and scale (S) vertices, and even copy selected vertices with SHIFT-D.

For example, if you want to model a truncated cone, start with a cylinder, select all the vertices on one end and *scale the vertices down* (that is, move them closer together) until you achieve the size you want. But you can get much fancier than simple pencil-sharpening like this—Figure 5-2 illustrates the sort of games you can play with a sphere.

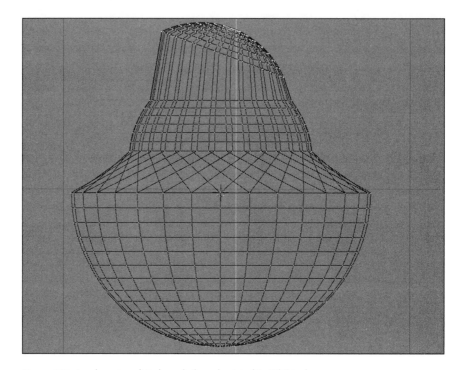

Figure 5-2: A sphere translated, scaled, and rotated in EditMode

5.2.1 Deleting and Creating Vertices

To create new vertices, switch to EditMode, then hold CTRL while left-clicking.

When first created, vertices are simply individual points. Combine or delete them as follows:

- Press F to turn two selected vertices into an edge or three or four vertices into a face.

- Press X to call up the Erase menu for EditMode, where vertices, faces, edges, and so on can be deleted.

NOTE *If you make a mistake while working with vertices—easy to do, as objects have so many of them—press U to restore the object's condition before entering EditMode. It's a good idea to drop out of EditMode fairly often when you're working on something complex, so as to reduce your potential losses. Unlike undo in some other programs, Blender's U will jump you back to a starting point—there's no way to automatically go back just one step.*

5.3   Smoothing Polygons

Objects composed of polygons are never smooth when first created because they are made of individual faces. (As you'll clearly see when rendering a polygonal object or viewing it in the shaded view.) To fix this problem, we need to smooth them.

5.3.1   Smoothing Simple Objects

If your object is relatively simple (no sharp angles, simple construction), consider using Blender's automatic smoothing. To do so, use the Set Smooth button in the Edit buttons; use the Set Solid button to create the opposite effect (turn the smooth objects back into angular ones, that is, show the objects in solid mode).

5.3.2   Smoothing Complex Objects

If your objects have sharp angles, automatic smoothing may not function correctly on its own. To get the effect you want, you'll need to specify the faces to smooth. To do so:

1.   Enter EditMode and select the vertices of the face to be smoothed. You can use either BorderSelect (press B) or CircleSelect (B-B) to make your selection.

2.   Press Set Smooth to smooth your selected faces.

The cylinder in the middle of Figure 5-3 shows the result of correctly applying smoothing by selecting vertices, as does the right-hand half of the sphere in the figure. In contrast, the cylinder at the left was smoothed as a whole, without specifying vertices, producing the odd result shown: Blender selected the vertices and tried to smooth the edges that join the ends and the cylinder's surface. Oops!

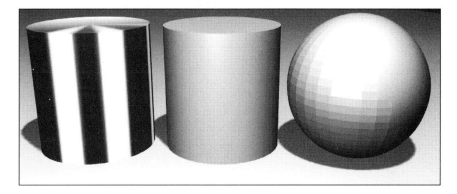

Figure 5-3: Incorrect and correct smoothing of polygon objects

To achieve the desired result, you need to separate the faces of the cylinder's two ends from its surface. (Don't worry—this separation does not create more objects!) Just follow these steps:

1. In EditMode, select the vertices at one end of the cylinder.

2. Press Y or choose Mesh • Split in the Toolbox menu to separate the end from the cylinder.

3. Left-click or press ENTER to accept the change proposed in the dialog box that appears.

4. Press A to deselect all vertices.

5. Repeat the procedure for the cylinder's other end.

6. Press Set Smooth to smooth the cylinder.

 When you leave EditMode, the cylinder should appear correct in the shaded mode (the mode showing Blender's faces as filled in) or as a rendered image.

NOTE *The process described above may seem like overkill for simple objects. Still, automated processes fail so often, it's better to routinely use Blender's ability to manually control the smoothing process rather than have to go back and fix incorrectly smoothed polygons.*

5.3.3 Automatic Smoothing with Auto Smooth

Although exercising manual control over the smoothing process gives you great flexibility, you'll sometimes want to automate the process to simplify your work. (This is especially important when importing 3D objects that were modeled in other programs, since you'll often find models with no smoothing whatsoever.)

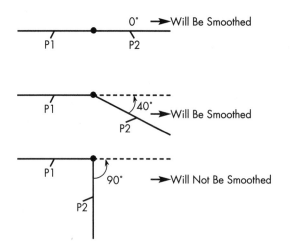

Figure 5-4: The Degr parameter set to 45° and its effect on which planes get smoothed with Auto Smooth

Blender's Auto Smooth button in the Edit buttons (F9) provides the necessary automation. Use the Degr parameter to define the largest angle at which faces can intersect with one another and still be smoothed (see Figure 5-4). You can correctly smooth the cylinder shown in Figure 5-3 by choosing Set Smooth, and then Auto Smooth. In contrast to normal smoothing (standard smoothing with Set Smooth), the effect is visible only in the rendered image.

5.4 PET

Blender's PET (Proportional Editing Tool) feature is another interesting modeling tool for vertices. It works like the magnet tools found in similar programs —but with more features.

With PET, a selected vertex affects other vertices proportionally within a definable distance, as if the selected vertex were a magnet—thus, its similarity to magnet tools. And, like magnet tools, PET lets you create a wavelike object by selecting a row of vertices from a surface that's been divided several times, and then moving the selection over the surface, as shown in Figure 5-5. But—unlike magnet tools in other programs—PET also works with rotation and scaling.

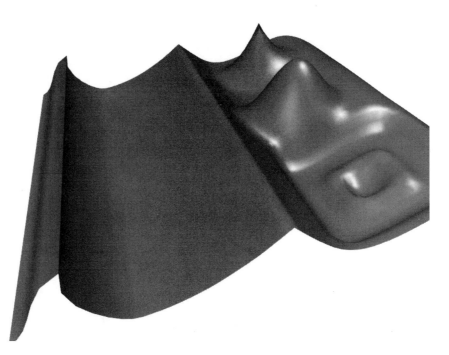

Figure 5-5: A surface edited with PET

When PET is selected, the two buttons that appear next to its icon determine how gradually or steeply its effect slopes toward the edges. You can easily see the difference between the two buttons by selecting one and pulling a single vertex out of a face, using it, and then repeating the action with the second button. The first setting produces a sharp point, and the second a soft tip.

As long as you're in the correct mode, (translation, rotation, scaling), you can change the size of the area affected by PET by pressing PAD + and PAD –. Changes are shown simultaneously in the 3D Windows, enabling precise control of the effect.

5.5 Extrude

When you extrude something, you pull vertices out from the object. The Extrude button, grouped with the Edit buttons, extrudes selected vertices or faces, letting you create objects like the ones shown in Figure 5-6.

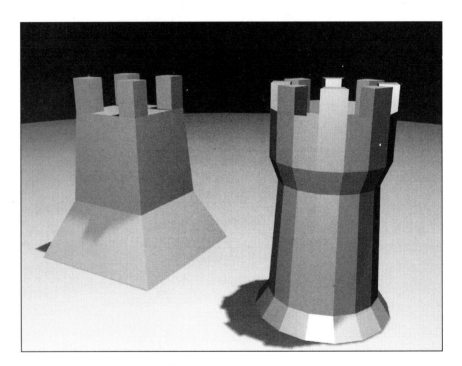

Figure 5-6: Some objects created by extrusion

Here's how to create the round tower shown in Figure 5-6:

1. From a top view, create a circle with sixteen segments by choosing Add • Mesh • Circle.

2. With the vertices selected, change to the Edit buttons and press Extrude. If you're working in more than one window, the mouse pointer should become a question mark. Click the question mark in a front or side view.

3. Extrude the vertices by moving them with the mouse. Unless you want to build the Tower of Pisa, middle-click as you extrude the vertices upward to change to single-axis movement mode. (This will make sure you move only the vertices along the vertical axis, something that's surprisingly difficult to do with the unaided mouse.) If you're caught going in the wrong direction, press the middle mouse button again. Move the vertices up until they form the foot of a tower.

4. Left-click to record the change.

5. Press S to enter scaling mode, then scale the top circle's vertices together a bit to form the base of the tower.

6. Use the same procedure to construct the other sections of the tower. (Use the E key instead of the Extrude button as a shortcut.)

Now let's create the battlements:

1. Extrude the top circle from its vertices again, but this time right-click just after beginning the extrusion to stop the movement mode. The vertices should be at their starting points.

2. Press S to switch to scaling mode and scale the vertices down (that is, move them closer together) to produce an appropriate wall thickness.

3. Select the base of a battlement-to-be from a top view using BorderSelect or CircleSelect.

4. From a side or front view, deselect the vertices at the bottom of the tower using B and the right mouse button; you may now extrude a battlement in a side view. (You have to do this for each battlement—though you can spare yourself some work by simultaneously selecting every second battlement and then extruding them together.)

5.6 Spin, Spin Dup

Blender offers two spin options: Spin and Spin Dup. *Spin* rotates and then connects open polygons (vertices connected by edges) or faces to make a continuous rotation body, while *Spin Dup* merely duplicates the object. For example, see Figure 5-7—the object at the left was modeled with Spin, as was the one at the bottom, while the one on the right was modeled with Spin Dup. Appearances notwithstanding, both methods produce cohesive objects. (The spaces in the object at the right are an illusion; it's all one thing as far as Blender is concerned, even though you can see gaps between the vanes.)

To spin an object, select the relevant vertices in EditMode and place the 3D cursor at the center of rotation. Select Spin to turn the mouse cursor into a question mark, and then click in a window to set the view for the rotation. The axis perpendicular to the screen will be the rotation axis.

Figure 5-7: Various objects created with Spin and Spin Dup

Here's how to construct the top two objects in Figure 5-7:

1. Create a plane in a front view (PAD 1).

2. In a top view, place the 3D cursor to the right of the plane.

3. Enter the rotation angle at Degr (an angle of 180° will create half a rotation body).

4. Select Spin (or Spin Dup) in the Edit buttons and click the question mark cursor in the top view.

5. Staying in EditMode, select all the vertices by pressing A and choose Rem Doubles to remove the double vertices that appeared on the object's seam (unless your rotation was less than 360°).

NOTE *Use* Steps *to specify the number of intermediate steps that will be taken to generate the object—which will, in turn, determine the smoothness of the object. For example, setting* Steps *equal to 4 produces a square.*

The shaft in the foreground of Figure 5-7 was made with an open polygon that was rotated with Spin. Here's how to do it:

1. Create a plane and delete three of its vertices in EditMode.

2. Select the remaining vertex and then press CTRL and left-click to place new vertices, which will automatically be connected with edges. (You can see an example of such an object on Layer 4 of the scene polygons/spin.blend on the CD-ROM.)

5.7 Screw

Blender's Screw option turns an open polygon around the 3D cursor, creating threadlike (or screwlike) structures. The corkscrew in Figure 5-8 was created using Screw (on the CD-ROM under polygons/screw.blend); Layer 2 of this scene has some open polygons that will be good for experimenting with Screw.

Figure 5-8: A corkscrew created with Screw

NOTE *The easiest way to create an open polygon is by deleting the vertices of a plane in Edit-Mode and then pressing CTRL while left-clicking to place a vertex that is automatically connected with the most recently set vertex.*

Let's experiment with Screw:

1. Place the 3D cursor on the form's origin by selecting the relevant polygon.

2. Call up the SNAP menu with SHIFT-S, then select Curs -> Sel.

3. Switch to EditMode and press A to select all the vertices.

4. Select Screw in the Edit buttons and "screw" by clicking the question mark cursor in the front view. (You must click in a front view for Screw to work.)

NOTE *To close a polygon so you can't inadvertently use it with* Screw, *select both endpoints and press F to connect them with an edge. To fill in the polygon with multiple faces, select all the vertices and press SHIFT-F.*

5.8   Bend Objects with Warp

Warp is an interesting Blender effect that allows you to deform objects. And since it is used on selected vertices in EditMode, it's possible to use Warp to deform only part of an object rather than the whole thing. Also, Warp is not limited to polygon objects—it works with curves and NURBS surfaces, though to apply it to text you must first convert the text to curves with ALT-C.

Let's experiment a bit with Warp:

1. From EditMode, create a plane in a top view, then divide it four times with Subdivide.

2. Place the 3D cursor under the plane in a front or side view, bearing in mind that the distance from the 3D cursor to the object will determine the object's bending radius. (If some of the vertices are no longer selected, press A to select them all.)

3. With the mouse in the side or front view, press SHIFT-W to warp. The plane should bend 90° to the 3D cursor. (A 360° warp would turn the plane into a tube.)

4. To change the warp angle, move the mouse vertically, then left-click to record the change (or right-click to cancel it).

NOTE *If the range of available angles is insufficient, zoom out of the view before you warp—Warp's intensity is directly related to the size of the view.*

Since you can see the warping effect simultaneously in all the 3D windows, it's easy to control Warp when zoomed out extremely far.

Carry out the above steps on the warped plane a couple more times in other views to add more bending axes. Try experimenting a bit with 3D bodies and vertices, too.

5.9   Subdivide Smooth

The Subdivide Smooth function divides a polygon frame and then rounds its edges a specified amount. Let's try this with a cube:

1. Create a cube and press A to select all the vertices in EditMode.

2. Press W and choose the Subdivide Smooth function from the pop-up menu.

3. Blender will ask you how strong an effect to use. Note that percentages over 100 produce raised banks on the edges. The effect is immediate.

Figure 5-9 shows an object that was created with *Box Modeling* and then finished with Subdivide Smooth. Here, the basic figure (right) was modeled from a simple primitive (a cube that was extruded and subdivided). Extruding planes, scaling, and translating were also especially useful. After modeling, I used Mesh Smooth and Smooth on parts of the object and the object as a whole until I got the effect I was looking for. It takes some practice to turn a blocky basic figure (like the one at the right) into a smoothly sculptured final version (like the one on the left)—but I recommend giving it the time it needs to get a reasonable duplicate of the figure. The resulting skills will be very useful as you work with Blender.

Figure 5-9: Nessie before and after plastic surgery with Set Smooth

5.10 Instant Landscapes

Noise is another interesting Blender effect (applicable to polygon objects only) that lets you translate an object's vertices along the object's axis. The result is determined by the object's texture color.

Try this experiment with Noise:

1. Make a plane in a top view with Add • Mesh • Plane and change to the Edit buttons (F9).

2. Now we'll subdivide the plane so that you have enough points to make the effect visible. Press A to select all of the plane's vertices, then click the Subdivide button in the Edit buttons to double the number of planes.

3. Click Subdivide five more times to produce more than 4,000 polygons (which should be enough for now).

Now we need to create a material to fill the space between the displaced vertices. Any texture will do, though each will produce its own kind of effects. For example, a white patch will produce the strongest effect and a black one none. The Marble texture will give you a wavelike surface, Stucci a dented-looking surface (like a stucco wall), and a radial color change from black to white will give you a round hill. You can also use normal images or photos as materials: Their light contrasts can create interesting relief effects.

1. Change to the Material buttons (F5) and create a new material by clicking and holding the Menu button and selecting ADD NEW.

2. Change to the Texture buttons (F6) and use the Menu button to create a new texture for the material (we'll use a texture from the CD).

3. Select Image for the texture type and then Load Image. Select the texture on the CD-ROM under textures/highlands.tga (see Figure 5-10).

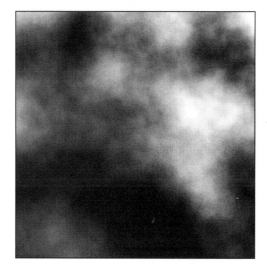

Figure 5-10: The texture for this tutorial

If a texture interferes with the effects of a rendering, you can disable it by toggling Col *in the Material buttons. (The* Noise *function will still work without the display of texture-generated colors.)*

4. Switch back to the Edit buttons and press A to select all the vertices.

5. Press the Noise button until you achieve the desired jaggedness in the landscape.

A test rendering with F12 should display a mountain landscape like the one in Figure 5-11. (If the individual faces are still clearly visible after the rendering, you can smooth them with Set Smooth.)

Figure 5-11: A landscape created with Noise

To create a body of water, color a smooth area blue, then position it appropriately to change the scene into an ocean landscape or group of islands, depending on the water level.

5.11 Boolean Operations—Mesh Intersect

When performed on 3D objects, *boolean* operations melt objects together, pull them apart, or intersect them—resulting in a new or modified object. For example, you could use boolean operations to create a drill hole in a cube by subtracting a cylinder from the cube, or to create a lens by taking the intersection of two spheres (as shown in Figure 5-12). Blender's boolean function is called Mesh Intersect.

Figure 5-12: Two spheres edited with Mesh Intersect

Mesh Intersect is tricky to master because Blender works with polygon objects that are not really solid, but which are a layer of faces that describe a thin surface. Such layered objects require complex mathematical descriptions and often that leads Blender (and similar programs that dare to perform boolean operations) to undesired results.

NOTE *In fact, the Mesh Intersect function was removed from earlier versions of Blender because it was considered too difficult to use. There was such strong demand for it, though, that the programmers have put it back, but you can't necessarily count on it. Sometimes it just doesn't work or even crashes Blender.*

But let's take a risk using an Icosphere and a cube—simple polygons that shouldn't cause much of a problem. Follow these steps:

1. Create an Icosphere and a cube.

2. Stick the corner of the cube into the Icosphere.

3. Press CTRL-J to combine the polygons (using Mesh Intersect).

4. Change to EditMode and press A to select all the vertices.

5. Start the process by clicking Intersect in the Edit buttons (F9). This process will take a few seconds, depending on the speed of your computer and the complexity of the objects you're working with.

6. You may now see newly created vertices where the objects touch. Press A to deselect all the vertices, then place the mouse cursor on a vertex of one of the original objects.

7. Press L to select the vertices connected to this vertex and select or delete the parts resulting from the boolean operation to achieve the desired result (see Figure 5-13 for an example).

Figure 5-13: The result of Mesh Intersect on a cube and sphere

Follow these tips for a successful Mesh Intersect:

- Avoid having intersecting faces on the same plane.

- Individual faces should intersect as little as possible. If this is a problem, try subdividing objects before running Mesh Intersect for better results.

- Avoid using objects of the same type. For example, instead of using two UVspheres, use a UVsphere and an Icosphere, or another subdivision of a sphere.

- Rotating the object a fraction of a degree almost always helps.

- Save your file before performing the Mesh Intersect or quickly leave EditMode and then reenter it by pressing TAB-TAB so that you can use the undo function (U).

5.12   Lattices

Lattices are three-dimensional frame objects, which, when deformed, deform their child (subordinate) object as well. Lattices can be used on polygon objects, surfaces, and particle clouds (see Chapter 10), as well as in modeling and animation. (See Chapters 8 through 10 for more information on parent and child objects, and Chapter 8 for animating with lattices.)

Here's a quick exercise with a sphere and lattice:

1. Create a UVsphere in the camera's field of vision.

2. Leave EditMode and create a lattice right on the sphere's center with Add • Lattice.

3. With the lattice selected, change to the Edit buttons (F9).

4. Increase to 3 the values for the lattice object's resolution (the number of vertices) in all three dimensions—U, V, and W.

5. Scale the lattice just enough so that it includes all of the sphere.

6. While holding down SHIFT, select the sphere and then the lattice and press CTRL-P to turn the lattice into a parent object. The sphere is the child of the lattice.

What have you done? You've created a parent (lattice) with a child (sphere). As a result, when you change the lattice you deform its child object (the sphere—see Figure 5-14). Thus you can create constrictions or bottle necks by selecting, in EditMode, an entire plane of control points (vertices) from the lattice and scaling them down. Or you can make dents by translating a vertex.

NOTE   *Unfortunately, if you need to increase the lattice's resolution later, you'll lose all your lattice deformations, so make sure that you use the right resolution when working extensively with lattices.*

Here are some lattice parameters:

Outside   Displays only a lattice's outside vertices, making it easier to see what you're working with if you're using lattices of high resolution. When the Outside button is used, lattices that aren't displayed can no longer be edited and are automatically rendered or interpolated by Blender, and changes to the control points are also lost.

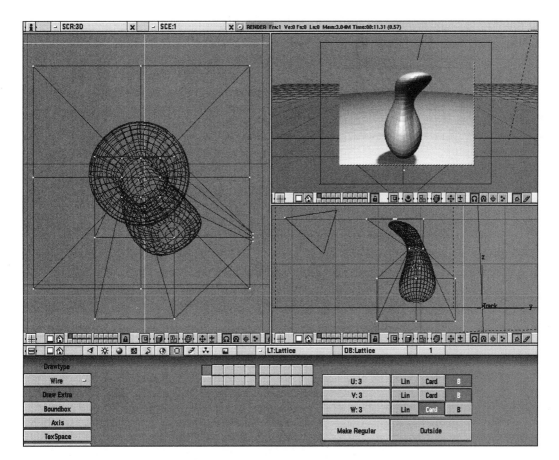

Figure 5-14: A sphere deformed with a lattice

Make Regular	Resets (undoes) lattice deformations.
Lin, **Card**, and **B**	This row of buttons (next to the lattice resolution buttons) defines the deformation's interpolation model for the corresponding dimensions. The buttons stand for linear interpolation, cardinal spline interpolation, and B-Spline interpolation. B-Spline interpolation produces the softest deformations.

5.13 Mathematical Curves and Surfaces

Polygons will do only part of the modeling job for you. As noted at the beginning of the chapter, Blender also works with mathematically described curves, and the surfaces composed of these curves. The primitives of these mathematically defined curves or surfaces are either NURBS or Bezier curves. With the help of these curves you can create subtly curved, organic-looking objects. Each curve consists of a series of control points. In addition, curves can be pulled into depth and also beveled (that is, rounded). The advantage to working with mathematically described objects is that they require little memory and you can change their resolution dynamically. *Rendering* these surfaces breaks them up into polygons, whereby you can set the resolution to achieve finer subdivisions or fast render times.

Curves are usually two-dimensional: Their vertices all lie on one plane, and movement is in two directions only.

Three-dimensional curves are used for surfaces and animation paths. Because they are automatically filled in from the front and back, it's easy to detect a hole in closed 2D curves.

Try to avoid intersections, which can result in undesired fill.

5.13.1 Bezier curves

Bezier curves are the best-known mathematical curve type (there's hardly a program that doesn't support them), and they are an ideal way to create letters and logos. Each vertex of a Bezier curve consists of one control point where you can grab handles. By rotating and moving the handles on a Bezier curve you can generate almost any curve.

You can define each curve's resolution in the Edit buttons with DefResolU. The higher the number, the smoother the curve. Bear in mind that complex animations require a lot of computer power and memory.

Figure 5-15 illustrates the four different types of vertices you can use with a Bezier curve.

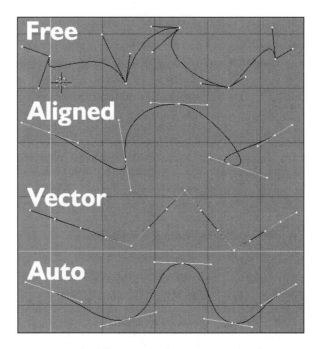

Figure 5-15: The different types of Bezier curve control points

Free handle

The two handles at each vertex are independent of each other and are displayed in black.

Aligned handle

The handles lie on a straight line. They can be any length and are displayed as dark violet (unselected) or light red.

NOTE *Press H to toggle selected vertices between free and aligned handles.*

Vector handle

Press V to align the handles with the next or previous vertex; translating vector handles does not change this arrangement. Vector handles are displayed as green or light green.

Auto handle

Selected handles are automatically rendered with SHIFT-H. Auto handles are displayed as yellow; when moved, an Auto handle becomes an Aligned handle.

NOTE *After you create a curve, Blender goes into EditMode.*

5.13.2 NURBS

NURBS (Non Uniform Rational B-Spline) *curves* are three-dimensional curves represented by a class of equations defined by nonuniform parametric ratios of B-Spline polynomials. (That's probably more than you wanted to know, but there you have it.) A three-dimensional surface represented by a NURBS equation is called a *NURBS patch*.

NURBS can be used to define very complex curves and surfaces and, unlike Bezier curves, NURBS curves do not go directly through control points. With a little practice, the many parameters of NURBS—controlled via the button panel shown in Figure 5-16—will allow you to produce forms that are mathematically correct, yet still round and organic.

Convert	Make Knots		DefResolU: 6	Set
Poly	Uniform U	V		
Bezier	Endpoint U	V	Back	Front	3D
Bspline	Bezier U	V		
Cardinal	Order U: 4	V: 0	Width: 1.000	
Nurb	Resol U: 12	V: 12	Ext1: 0.000	
Set Weight	Weight: 1.000	1.0	Ext2: 0.000	
			BevResol: 0	
	sqrt(2)/4	0.25	sqrt(0.5)	BevOb:

Figure 5-16: The NURBS parameters in the Edit buttons

NOTE *NURBS curves are commonly used as animation paths for objects. NURBS curves also let you create especially soft, fluid movements.*

Here are the most important NURBS parameters:

Knots

The following are the different types of knots:

Uniform   Uniform division between the control points, which is important for closed NURBS curves.

Endpoints   A NURBS curve that starts and ends on these points. These are the only points that lie exactly on the curve.

Bezier   Bezier interpolation between curve sections.

Order

The mathematical order of a curve calculation: 1 is a point, 2 is linear, 3 is quadratic, and so on. Always use the fifth order for animation paths.

Weight

Every point on a NURBS curve has a weight that determines how strongly the point influences the curve.

Figure 5-17 shows different NURBS of the same curve. The curve was not edited with its control points—only the parameters discussed above were changed in the Edit buttons (Figure 5-16).

- The curve at the upper left of Figure 5-17 is a NURBS curve immediately after being created with Add • Curve • NURBS Curve.

- Endpoint U was enabled for the second curve in the left column. The curve begins and ends exactly on the control points.

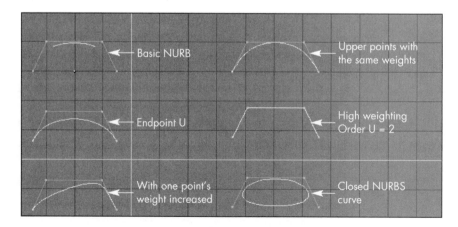

Figure 5-17: A NURBS curve adjusted with different parameters

- In the third curve on the left, the weight of the upper right vertex has been increased by entering (in EditMode) the weight for a selected vertex in the Weight field and then selecting Set Weight.

- To create a perfect circle, set all vertices to the same weight (that is, make sure their default weights in the Edit buttons are all the same). Press N and select a vertex to view its weight.

- The curve at the upper right was created by setting the upper left and right points to the same weight.

- For the middle curve on the right, Order U was lowered to a value of 2.

- Finally, the last curve was closed with C.

5.14 Make a Logo with Curves and Rotoscoping

The technique we'll use in this tutorial is called *rotoscoping*. Rotoscoping is a way of creating outlines of objects, or patterns of movement, using a rotated projection of a sequence of static images, which are laid into the background of a 3D window.

Think of rotoscoping as an efficient kind of "painting on movies." Prior to computers, an animation stand called a Rotoscope was used to project a sequence of action frames against a surface so that a set of animation frames could be traced or created. The same work can now be done with digital images and special computer software.

Rotoscoping is ideal for drawing logos that exist only on paper or in files as pixel data. In this tutorial we'll construct a yin-yang logo.

1. Load the yinyang.blend scene from the curves subdirectory.

2. Move the mouse cursor to the big 3D window (a front view) and change the window type to a Buttons window using the buttons slider or SHIFT-F7.

3. Left-click the BackGroundPic button in the Buttons window.

4. Click Load and select the image yinyang.tga from the tutorial's texture directory on the CD-ROM. This will give you the image shown in Figure 5-18, without the curve drawn over the left-hand side (which gets added later in the tutorial).

NOTE Size *and* Blend *let you enter the size of the image and the extent to which it is blended into the 3D Window. Leave these features at their default settings for this tutorial.*

5. With the mouse pointer over the window, switch back to the 3D window (SHIFT-F5 or the button slider) and you will see the loaded image in the window's background. You can now work in the window as usual; zooming or translating will affect the background picture as well.

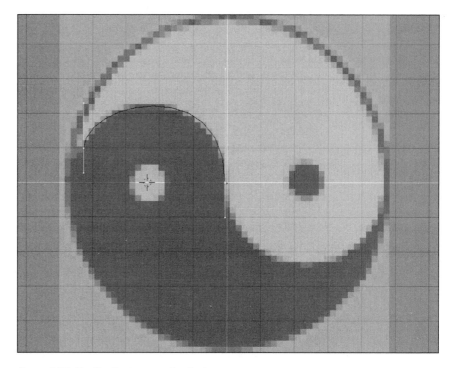

Figure 5-18: The first Bezier curve for the logo

5.14.1 Construct the Logo with Bezier Curves

Now we'll construct the logo. We'll use Bezier curves, which makes it easier to model the elements' sharp ends:

1. Create a Bezier curve (Toolbox • Add • Curve • BezierCurve) with two control points (handles) and place them as in Figure 5-18 with the handles aligned vertically.

2. Use the two upper handles (right-click a handle to select it and translate the handle upward with G) to set the curve so that it roughly corresponds to the image underneath.

5.14.2 Adjust the Curves

When all of the curves have been drawn, it's time to start the precision work:

1. Select the control point in the middle of the logo so that the three handles turn yellow.

2. While holding CTRL, click to set a third control point for the curve. Place this point on the outer right edge of the logo, and align the handles vertically.

3. Pull both handles down (together with the lower handle from point 2) until the curvature is correct.

4. Select the third control point and press CTRL and left-click to set another point next to the first. (Don't try to close the curve yet, though, or the point would be too sharp and could not be fixed by beveling.)

5. Using the handles, place the curve over the upper edge of the logo.

6. Close the curve with C, and zoom in a bit on your construction. Use the handles to make a small curve between the first and fourth points, so you wind up with something that looks like Figure 5-19.

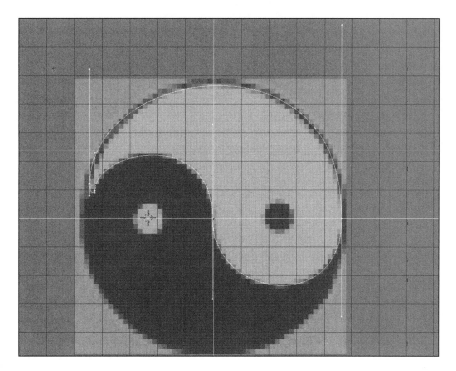

Figure 5-19: Finished Bezier curve

7. Leave EditMode with TAB. You should see a filled-in surface in the shaded view, though not in the view displaying the background image, so click BackGroundPic in the Buttons window (SHIFT-F7) to turn the background image off.

8. Return to the 3D window (SHIFT-F5) and you should see that the curves are not smooth. Remedy this by defining the curve's resolution: Select it and set its resolution with DefResolU in the Edit buttons (F9). A value of 30 should be sufficient (use Set to confirm the value).

5.14.3 Add the "Eye"

Next, with the object selected, change to EditMode so you can add the logo's "eye."

1. Turn the background image on again (BackGroundPic) to help with the positioning.

2. Create a circle with Toolbox • Add • Curve • NURBS Circle. (You could use a Bezier circle here, but NURBS circles are somewhat rounder.)

3. From within EditMode, scale the circle to the desired size. If for some reason some of the control points are not selected, place the mouse pointer over a vertex and press L to select the vertices connected to that vertex.

4. Leave EditMode when you've got the right position and size. Blender will automatically detect holes and take them into consideration when it fills the curve.

5.14.4 Mirror the Finished Section

To complete the logo, we'll mirror the finished section by creating a copy of the object using the same base curve. Thus, a change to one half of the logo will be mirrored in the other.

1. Press ALT-D to copy the finished section of the logo. Grab mode is still active, so end it by right-clicking.

2. Start scaling mode with S, being careful not to move the mouse.

3. Press X to set mirroring on the x-axis, Y to set mirroring on the y-axis, and then ENTER to record the change.

NOTE *To avoid inadvertent scaling with this procedure, you might want to use the grid during scaling (press CTRL).*

Since both curve objects have the same open curve as their basis, editing one open curve in EditMode changes both objects, so the two sections, which don't yet fit perfectly together, can now be adjusted to each other (Figure 5-20).

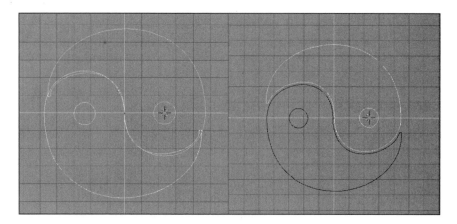

Figure 5-20: Adjusting the logo

5.14.5 Adding Depth

Now let's leave EditMode and touch up the logo with the buttons for extrusion (to add depth) and beveling (to round the edges), which appear in the Edit buttons (F9) when curve objects are selected, as shown in Figure 5-21.

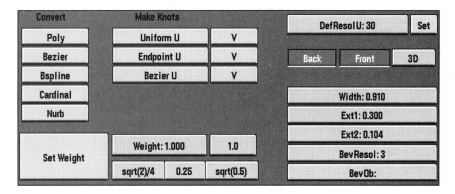

Figure 5-21: Edit buttons for curve objects (not in EditMode)

1. Use the Ext1 button (a Number button) to set the depth of a curve object. Left-click and pull it to set the depth (you can also use the grid settings with CTRL and ALT). Or left-right-click the mouse on the Number button to select it so you can enter a specific value.

2. Once you've defined the depth, use Ext2 to set the beveling intensity on the object's edges (set it the same way as you did Ext1). If the Ext2 value is too large, causing the objects' edges to intersect, correct it with Width.

3. Set the beveling resolution with BevResol (higher values turn the beveled edges into a curve). When used with Set Smooth, a BevResol value of 3 or 4 will give you a nice, rounded edge. (Higher values than these produce a lot of faces and demand more of your machine—thereby increasing the time it takes to create the objects—and don't really improve the object's quality.)

4. If you started with the basic scene for this tutorial (yinyang.blend), activate Layer 1 (which has a camera and two light sources) and then execute a test rendering. (If the logo is too big or incorrectly positioned, translate and scale the logo to make it look like Figure 5-22.)

5.14.6 Adding a Material

Our logo is still missing its black and white coloring. Here's how to add a material (Section 6.1 covers the individual material editor parameters).

1. Select one half of the logo and open the Material buttons (F5).

2. Click the beige OB button to make the material an object property (see Section 4.13). (If we were to assign the material to the base open curve, both sections of the logo would have the same color, since they both share the same open curve.)

3. Create a new material by clicking and holding the Menu button in the Material buttons and choosing ADD NEW.

4. Set the material's colors with the RGB sliders (at the left in the Material buttons) to black: R,G,B = 0. (To rename the material, left-click its name in MA:Material.)

5. Follow the same steps outlined above for the other half of the logo, but make its material white (R,G,B = 1.0).

6. Press F12 for a test rendering, which should produce a logo that is half black and half white, as shown in Figure 5-22.

Figure 5-22: The finished logo (with material)

5.15 An Animated Roller Coaster Ride

Beveling lets you create object edges on complicated curves and is most often used for creating tracks, tunnels, and similar objects. It lends itself especially well to modeling and animating a roller coaster, including the tracks and loops.

The animation produced in this tutorial will give you a taste of what's coming in Chapters 8 through 10 (where I'll describe the procedures in more detail). In addition to beveling, this tutorial also shows you how to quickly create and place many duplicates of the same object on a path.

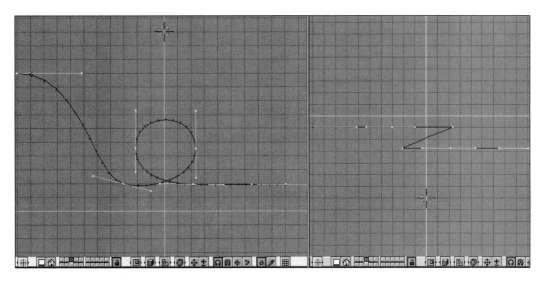

Figure 5-23: A Bezier curve for the roller coaster

1. In a side view, create a Bezier curve with a loop similar to the one shown in Figure 5-23. (Activate the 3D button in the Edit buttons so you can move the control points out of the plane.)

2. Create a new camera in the front view (PAD 0).

3. Select the curve by holding SHIFT and pressing CTRL-P to make the curve a parent to the camera.

4. Press ALT-O to put the camera and curve's origin points on top of each other (confirm the "OK? Clear origin" query).

5. Select only the curve and click the CurvePath and CurveFollow buttons in the Animation buttons (F7).

6. Press ALT-A to preview the animation. You should see that the camera follows the path but is looking or tipping in the wrong direction. Fix this by selecting the camera and choosing UpX in the Animation buttons.

7. Select the camera, place the mouse pointer in the camera view, and press ALT-PAD 0 to select the camera's view of the roller coaster.

8. Press ALT-A to take your first virtual roller coaster ride!

5.15.1 Bevel the Tracks

Follow these steps to bevel and widen the tracks:

1. Construct the track's cross section by creating a Bezier circle with Spacebar • Add • Curve • Bezier Circle.

2. Press V to turn the circle into a square, then rotate the square 45° and leave EditMode.

You can use whatever cross section you want for the tracks since the normal editing functions let you change the cross section at any time. I recommend using a square since it produces the fewest faces in the final beveling, letting you work faster with the scene.

3. Name the cross section by entering cross in the OB field (in the Edit buttons).

4. Left-click the roller coaster curve, then enter cross in the BevOb field (in the Edit buttons). Once you press ENTER to confirm your entry, you should see that the entire curve is beveled.

5. Select the cross section and scale it down (S) so that the tracks are the width you want. Left-click to confirm the scaling and view the change.

   Let's create the second track.

1. Switch to a top view in a 3D window (PAD 7).

2. Select the first track and copy it with ALT-D.

3. Translate the copy with the mouse until you get the proper track width. Left-click to confirm the translation.

4. The camera is now on top of the first rail, so translate it (G) between and a little above the two rails like the 3D view in Figure 5-24 to give yourself a better view of the ride.

In contrast to SHIFT-D, ALT-D creates a copy of the object that has the same base curve. This means that if you edit the original curve later, the copy will change as well.

5.15.2 Creating the Ties

Blender can automatically create objects without saving their geometries in the scene. This allows you to have many objects in a scene and still use little memory. Any change to such objects affects all the objects at once.

We'll use a method called *DupliFrames* to create the ties for the tracks. DupliFrames places a virtual copy of the object to be duplicated on each frame of the underlying animation system (for example, a path or keyframe animation). (I'll discuss a similar method, DupliVerts, in the next section.)

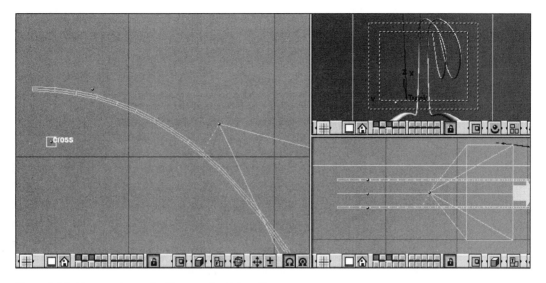

Figure 5-24: Cross section and rails created with beveling

To add the ties:

1. Select a rail and copy it with SHIFT-D (rather than ALT-D). We need to adjust the curve a bit, so we need an independent curve here.

2. From a top view, move this third curve between the two rails.

3. With the curve still selected, delete the name of the rail cross section (cross) in the Edit buttons; the curve should appear as a thin line.

4. Place the 3D cursor on the selected curve with SHIFT-S-4 (a shortcut through the SNAP menu).

5. Create a cube and scale it so it looks like a railroad tie.

6. Select the tie and the middle curve, and make the curve the parent by pressing CTRL-P.

7. Remove both objects' origin points with ALT-O.

So far, all we've done is animate the tie along the curve path (press ALT-A to see if you've done it right). Now the DupliFrames function comes into play:

1. Select the tie in the Animation buttons (F7) and activate DupliFrames to distribute the ties along the curve path, setting the number of ties with PathLen.

2. Now it's time to rotate and translate the tie. To do so, select the original tie (the others only appear to be there) in a side view, then move it until it's just under the tracks and perpendicular to them. You can also edit the original tie (to add bolts, for example) and the changes will be transmitted to all the other ties. Figure 5-25 shows a frame from the completed animation.

Figure 5-25: A frame from the roller coaster animation

As I hope you've seen, DupliFrames is a good way to quickly create different arrangements of objects. If the arrangement is supposed to be a part of a larger object, it's a good idea to make the virtual copies into real objects by selecting the base object and pressing CTRL-SHIFT-A. Once you confirm the action with the pop-up dialog box, all copies become individual objects and are no longer affected by changes to the original object or path.

5.16   Duplicate Objects with DupliVerts

DupliVerts duplicates an object on the vertices of another object, with one of its greatest advantages being that you can always edit the original model.

When using DupliVerts, the object to be duplicated may be a polygon, curve, surface, or even a lamp. The base object must be a polygon or a particle system. (Section 10.6 describes using DupliVerts with a particle system.)

Let's use DupliVerts to create a spiked ball:

1.   In a top view, create an Icosphere with a subdivision of 2.

2.   Leave EditMode and create a cone in a top view. Then leave EditMode again and scale the cone to about 0.2 (the size is displayed in the information bar).

3.   Select the cone and the Icosphere by holding SHIFT and right-clicking.

4. Press CTRL-P to make the Icosphere the cone's parent.

5. Now select the Icosphere by itself, change to the Animation buttons (F7), and select DupliVerts.

6. A cone should appear on every vertex of the Icosphere. If you render the scene, you'll see that the Icosphere is no longer rendered. (The Rot parameter in the Animation buttons turns the cones into normals of the Icosphere, and the cones will arrange themselves symmetrically on the sphere.)

7. Finally, select the cone and turn on the Track Z button in the Animation buttons; the cones will point away from the Icosphere.

With a few mouse clicks we've made an object that bears a striking resemblance to the end of a morning star.

Color Plate 3 shows a less warlike object modeled with DupliVerts. You'll find the file for this furball on the CD-ROM under dupliverts/furball_curves01.blend. But don't be surprised if, when you load it, your computer slows to a crawl—the scene has a ton of faces and vertices. You can even use curves to simulate growing hair (animations/mpeg/furball.mpg).

5.17 Gutenberg's Heritage: The Text Object

A *text object* is just a group of letters treated as shapes. To add a new text object to your work, choose Spacebar • Add • Text, then type in your text while in Edit-Mode. Special characters are created by typing in a base character, pressing ALT-BACKSPACE, and then entering the combination character. Table 5-1 lists some helpful ones.

NOTE *Blender supports PostScript Type 1 fonts only, and not all of those. While you will find plenty of PS1 fonts on the Internet or on font CDs, many are defective and will not work properly in Blender (even though they may be fine in two-dimensional programs). Experiment until you find a set that will work on your system.*

Table 5-1: Entering special characters

Key combination	Resulting character
ALT-**C**	© (copyright symbol)
ALT-**G**	° (degree)
ALT-**R**	® (registered trademark)
ALT-**X**	x (multiplication symbol)
ALT-**.**	• (bullet)
ALT-**1**	^{1} (superscript 1)
ALT-**2**	^{2} (superscript 2)
ALT-**3**	^{3} (superscript 3)
ALT-**%**	% (percent sign)

NOTE *You can save entire text files as* `/tmp/.cutbuffer` *and then add them, special characters and all, to a text with* ALT-V *(in EditMode).*

When you leave EditMode, the text will be flat and filled in. To set the beveling or depth of the text, use the Ext1 and Ext2 buttons, as you did with the beveled edges in Section 5.14.5. You can modify the text in several ways as illustrated in Figure 5-26. The following list details the action of the various buttons.

Figure 5-26: Text examples

Size	Sets font size.
Linedist	Sets distance between lines.
Spacing	Sets distance between characters.
Shear	Changes the text angle (negative numbers tilt the text to the left, positive numbers to the right).
X offset, Y offset	Moves the text a given distance from its origin point (especially important and helpful when used with TextOnCurve).
LoadFont	Loads a new PostScript font, which you can then select from the Menu button. You can configure the path to the fonts in the Info window (see Section 4.13).
ToUpper	Changes case.
Left, **Right**, **Middle,** and **Flush**	Changes alignment. Flush justifies the text.

TextOnCurve	Makes text follow the curve (either Bezier or NURBS)—just enter the curve name in this field. A little fine-tuning (that is, scaling) may be necessary to make the text follow the curve exactly.
ALT-C	Changes selected text into an open curve and lets you manipulate individual letters as if they were normal Blender curves. The reverse does not work.
ObFamily	Lets you use a series of objects (which can only be modified letters) as a character set and then write with these objects.

5.18 Metaballs

Metaballs are objects that interact with each other like liquid in zero gravity. Metaball objects are rendered by Blender according to mathematical equations, making it possible to detect intersections mathematically, and to add and subtract metaballs. (The blending concepts of metaballs originate from molecular bonding theories used in chemistry.) When working with metaballs in Blender, only one material is used per metaball system, and it is defined for the main metaball only.

The Blender logo in Figure 5-27 was modeled with metaballs and then changed into a polygon object with ALT-C.

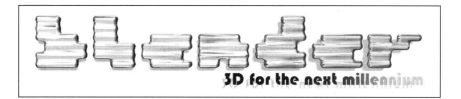

Figure 5-27: Blender's logo created with metaballs

5.18.1 Working with Metaballs

Metaball systems with different *base names* (the name without any numbers) in the OB field do not influence each other, while those with the same base names affect each other in a scene. Change this object name to create metaball systems that do not simultaneously affect each other.

To add a metaball, choose Add • MetaBall in the Toolbox. Once it's added, you should see the parameters shown in Figure 5-28 in the Edit buttons.

The settings at the left apply only to the metaball with the base name as follows:

Wiresize	Determines the size of the metaball wireframe as displayed in the 3D windows. Smaller values create frames with finer meshes, which produce a more exact representation of the metaball. (Keep in mind, though, that smaller values also take the computer longer to compute in the 3D windows, which can slow down modeling.)

Figure 5-28: Metaball parameters

Rendersize	Defines the resolution of a metaball when rendering an image.
Threshold	Determines how strongly the inner metaball's material coheres. Decreasing the threshold value enlarges the metaball and weakens its attraction to other metaballs. The result of the intersection of two metaballs with a low threshold is a metaball that is only slightly larger (due to the low level of cohesion). On the other hand, when the threshold is set high, metaballs behave like liquids and with even higher values they behave like mercury.

Use these three settings for recalculating metaballs in 3D windows:

Always	Complete recalculation *during* transformation.
Half Res	Calculates at half resolution.
Fast	Recalculates *after* a transformation.

When in EditMode, metaballs have the properties shown on the right-hand side of Figure 5-28.

Stiffness	Sets the stiffness for each ball and is connected to the global Threshold parameter.
Negative	Gives individual balls a reverse effect on other metaballs, producing holes and the like.

NOTE   *To animate individual metaballs, create one metaball, TAB out of EditMode, then create the second metaball, and so on.*

5.18.2 Metaballs Can Be Tubes

In addition to balls, you can also create tube-like objects that act as metaballs by setting TubeX, TubeY, and TubeZ in EditMode. The Len parameter determines the tube's length.

6

MATERIAL TUTORIALS

Materials and textures help make objects look realistic, and Blender's material and texture editors offer a variety of ways to generate a diversity of effects and materials. But the process of applying materials and textures is not an easy one to master. To be effective, you'll need a great deal of experience, and I encourage you, in the course of these tutorials, to perform your own experiments to gain experience. A good way to experiment is to use Blender to imitate materials you find around you, and to compare the results with reality. As you experiment you will discover how best to get Blender to imitate reality, and the quality of your projects will improve significantly.

6.1 The Surface

Figure 6-1 shows the Material buttons (F5). Let's take a look at the Material buttons by loading the scene `material/material01.blend`. Once it's loaded, create a material for the sphere by selecting it and then choosing Menu button • ADD NEW in the Material buttons (F5).

Figure 6-1: The Material buttons—Blender's materials editor

6.1.1 Playing with Color

Color is certainly the most eye-catching property of any material, and Blender allows you to set color using both RGB or HSV color systems (discussed in Chapter 2). To set color, use the buttons for each color system at the far left of the Material buttons. Experiment a little with Blender's color controls to get a feel for color mixing. (You can set the values for each system between 0.0 and 1.0.)

The Color field displays the color you set. Clicking the small Auto icon (the one with a little car on it) in the Material buttons header tells Blender to name the material automatically, based on the selected color.

Here's what the other buttons next to the Color field do:

Spec   Sets the color of the specular point. If you're creating a material with a metallic shine, be sure to choose a color for the specular point (the diffuse reflection of a light source on a surface) that is somewhat different from the material's color.

Mir   Displays the color of reflected light when reflection maps are used. (We will discuss these items in detail in Section 6.9.)

6.1.2 Reflected Light

Another significant factor that determines a material's appearance is the way it reflects light. The Ref, Spec, and Hard sliders govern reflection. (Ref and Spec work together.)

Ref (reflection)   Determines how much light the surface reflects overall.

Spec (specularity)   Determines the intensity of the specular point.

Hard (hardness)   The size of the specular point on the surface.

When setting the specular point properties, remember that plastic has a bright, small specular point, and metal a soft, less-bright one. (We will cover other parameters, especially those for transparent materials, in future sections.)

6.1.3 Emitted Light

The Emit slider controls how strongly a material emits light (though the material doesn't *really* project light the way a true light source would). In the context of Blender's radiosity renderer, however, the Emit value is important because the *radiosity technique* (a rendering technique that takes diffuse light reflected by objects into account) renders materials with an Emit value over 0 as true light sources (see Section 13.3).

6.2 Structures: Texture

Textures simulate the complex coloring of surface and material structures to make them look more realistic.

Blender offers three basic texture types, whose values may be combined:

Intensity Determines the intensity of a surface parameter (specularity, reflection properties, transparency, and so on).

RGB Determines color.

Bump Simulates a surface structure without the use of modeling.

Every texture you create with Blender will combine these three values. (We'll discuss textures in more detail later in this chapter.)

6.2.1 Adding Texture to a Material

Let's begin our exploration of textures by adding texture to the sphere from Section 6.1. Load `material/material01.blend` and assign a material to it using the parameters we discussed in Section 6.1.

Now let's use the parameters at the right side of the Material buttons to determine how a texture is placed on a material.

1. Select the sphere and click the Texture buttons icon or press F6.

2. In the Texture buttons header, create a new texture with Menu button • ADD NEW.

3. Choose the Marble texture from the buttons that appear, and the resulting window should look like Figure 6-2.

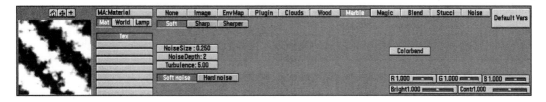

Figure 6-2: Marble texture in the Texture buttons

4. Name the texture or click the Auto icon in the header to let Blender do it for you. (It's a good idea to select the name yourself—a good naming scheme will simplify your work considerably, especially with complex scenes.)

5. Do a test rendering.

Your test rendering of the scene should produce a pink marble sphere, using the basic color you set earlier. You'll find the controls for setting the color of the marble texture at the right side of the Material buttons.

6.2.2 Setting Texture Parameters

Texture mapping (forming a relationship between a material and texture) may be used to add realism to computer-generated images by laying a texture onto an object in a scene.

In Blender, texture mapping occurs via a material's texture channels (the means by which a texture is linked to a material). The row of eight gray buttons at the upper-right of the Material buttons (see Figure 6-1) represents the texture channels. The first button shows the texture you just created and displays its name.

Each material has eight channels, which means it can combine up to eight textures at one time. You can set different texture parameters for each texture channel. To activate a particular channel, click its button, which will then remain "pressed," as shown here.

Texture mapping input coordinates

Generating texture coordinates

The green buttons under the texture channels define the way texture coordinates are generated for each texture. Called *input texture coordinates*, these coordinates determine, among other things, the way a texture is placed onto an object.

UV	The texture coordinates come from a NURBS surface and the texture fits directly onto the surface deformations.
Object	Identifies an object (whose name you can enter into the blank field to the right of the button) as the source of the texture coordinates. You can also create an empty object, which, if you rotate it, will rotate the texture.
Glob	Sets global texture coordinates that apply to the entire scene.
Orco	Standard setting; texture coordinates come from the object on which the texture lies, usually the bounding box—a cube that covers the object.
Stick	Allows for the exact placement of a texture on a 3D object, as if projected from a camera.
Win	Sets monitor coordinates as texture coordinates, which is especially suitable for integrating 3D objects in images or films.
Nor	Sets normal vectors of surfaces as the texture coordinates, allowing you to achieve reflective effects with prerendered images.
Refl	Sets reflection vectors of surfaces as texture coordinates. With a reflection map texture you can simulate reflections on objects.

Converting between coordinates

Textures that produce only two-dimensional coordinates, such as the texture type Image, must be converted from 2D to 3D coordinates when mapping images onto objects.

Flat	Cube	ofsX 0.000
Tube	Sphe	ofsY 0.000
		ofsZ 0.000
X Y Z		sizeX 1.00
X Y Z		sizeY 1.00
X Y Z		sizeZ 1.00

Coordinate transformation

Flat   Used for level surfaces like floors, walls, and so on.

Cube   Used for objects generally with right angles between the sides.

Tube   Used for cylindrical objects.

Sphere   Used for round, spherical objects.

The remaining parameters allow you to translate (ofs X,Y,Z) and scale (size X,Y,Z) a texture. You can apply these settings on the object interactively using the mouse by selecting the object and pressing T. The pop-up menu you get lets you choose between moving the object via the Grabber (normal translation) or resizing it via Size. Use the mouse to manipulate the texture cube (the space enclosed by the texture coordinates) accordingly.

The rectangle of twelve buttons shown in the margin control the conversion between coordinates. Each row represents the x, y, and z coordinates. The x coordinates are normally mapped onto x, y coordinates onto y, and so on. Selecting Y in the first row switches the y to the x coordinates.

The first unlabeled gray button turns the respective coordinate off. (See Section 6.8 for an example that illustrates the use of these parameters.)

Defining how material properties influence texture

The green buttons define which material properties are influenced by the texture. For example, if you use an image as a texture, the image can define the surface color (Col) and how much light it emits (Emit).

Col	Nor	Csp	Cmir	Ref
Spec	Hard	Alpha		Emit

Texture output coordinates

Some of these buttons have three states—on, off, and inverted. In the inverted state (which you get by clicking the button twice), the button label is yellow and the texture value is inverted.

These are the output coordinates and their effects:

Col (Color)	The texture determines the color of the surface points (as long as the texture supplies color information).
Nor (Normaps)	The texture generates relief-like structures without affecting the underlying object. Blender calls these structures *normaps*; other programs usually call them *bump maps*.
Csp (Color Specularity)	The texture determines the color of the specular point (Spec, in the Material buttons).
Cmir (Mirror color)	Determines the reflection color in the context of reflection maps.
Ref (Reflection)	The texture determines the value of the material's reflection parameter.
Spec (Specularity)	The texture determines the intensity of the specular point.
Hard (Hardness)	The texture determines the hardness value, that is the sharpness of a material's specular point.
Alpha (Alpha)	The texture determines the alpha value, or transparency, of a material.
Emit (Emit)	The texture determines the Emit value of a material, that is, how much light it emits.

You'll find these additional parameters under the texture output buttons:

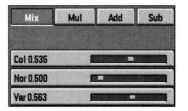

Texture parameters

Mix, **Mul**, **Add**, and **Sub**	Mix, multiply, add, or subtract texture values.
Col	Determines how strongly the color element of a texture is considered.
Nor	Defines the shaping of the bump effect.
Var (variable)	Influences one particular value of a texture, like the emit value if Emit is activated as an output.

NOTE *To control more than one parameter with a texture, use the IPO window (Section 8.1.1) instead of* Var.

The buttons under the texture datablock in Material buttons (see below) allow you to distribute textures onto various channels without switching to the Texture buttons. You'll find the controls for texture color under these buttons:

Texture datablock and color sliders

RGB	Sets a texture color if the texture itself has no color value.
No RGB	Replaces the existing color with one you set manually.
DVar	Lets you choose the strength of the effects on the texture channels.
Neg	Negates a texture's values and displays the negative of a color texture's actual color.
Stencil	Prevents a texture from a higher channel from covering one on a lower channel, since wherever a texture with an activated stencil has a value, another texture can have an influence. (You'll find an example of this type of material on the CD in material/stencil.blend.)

6.3 Texture Types

Blender offers various built-in texture types. You select a texture type with the Texture buttons (F6). These are the texture types and their effects:

Image	This frequently used texture type reproduces an image on an object in the image and animation formats supported by Blender (see Section 6.4).
EnvMap	An environment map simulates reflections and refraction (see Section 6.9).
Plugin	Once you've selected it, you can load a texture plug-in with the button Load Plugin. The plug-in's parameters appear after loading.
Clouds	Generates cloud textures that can also be used to produce smoke and fire effects. (Can also be implemented as a bump map.)
Wood	Generates woodlike structures in strips or ring form, either smooth or with turbulence.
Marble	Generates marbled structures.
Magic	Generates colorful structures that are honeycomb-like.
Blend	Creates colorbands that are linear, radial, and so on.
Stucci	Generates surface roughness with bump maps.
Noise	Adds noise, which is different in *every* frame of an animation. (You'll find an example in Section 8.1.2.)

You can also control the brightness and contrast of nearly all texture types by using Bright and Contr respectively (see Figure 6-3).

You can program even more texture types with Blender's programming interface for texture plug-ins. Some improved plug-ins include cloud textures, spiral textures, dots, and loads of Mandelbrot fractals. (You'll find many of these on the CD-ROM [see Appendix G] or on the Internet.)

6.3.1 Textures with Colorbands

With the Colorband switch (see Figure 6-3) in the Texture buttons (F6) you can add colorbands (used to create smooth color progressions) to many procedural texture types. Generally all procedural textures that produce a color value are suitable for colorbanding, including clouds, wood, marble, blend, noise, and many texture plug-ins (Clouds2, Dots, Musgrave, and Mandelbrot, for starters). Click Colorband to activate the settings and preview the effects immediately.

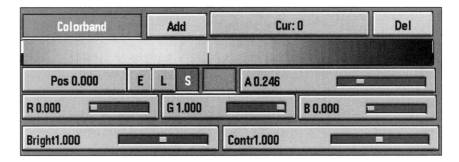

Figure 6-3: Colorband settings in the Texture buttons

Colorbands are generated from two or more colors. The active color is displayed in the colorband preview bar as a somewhat thicker, white line. By clicking on this line and moving it with the left mouse button, you can alter the color's position. (Pos displays this position numerically.) The Add button inserts a new color, while Del erases the active color (Cur). Use the RGB controls to set the active color.

A sets the alpha value of a color, enabling you to produce textures that influence transparency. The buttons E, L, and S—ease, linear, and spline, respectively—represent the interpolation level between colors. Of the three, S creates the gentlest transitions.

6.4 Building a Table with an Image Texture

Image textures are certainly one of the most frequently used texture types, and by integrating real or computer-generated images you can achieve a very realistic look. The textures can be in any format supported by Blender.

In this tutorial we will build a table and then make it look realistic by adding a wood image texture to it.

6.4.1   Building the Table

First, we'll build a table using simple objects, then we'll add a tabletop by either scaling a cube with the middle mouse button or by starting with a plane and extruding the four vertices. I used the latter method to build the table shown in Figure 6-4, and included a beveled edge on the side of the tabletop by extruding the four vertices three times by pressing E in EditMode, and then scaling them.

Figure 6-4: Building a table with a beveled edge

I built the table's legs from scaled tubes; a cylinder is not required since the ends may remain open. You can copy the legs with ALT-D, and the copies will all have the same polygon structure as the original. To modify all of the legs, select any one and change it while in EditMode—all four legs will change simultaneously.

Create the planks just as you did the legs: Make one plank and then make three copies with ALT-D. However, since all four planks are not of equal size, perform the scaling outside of EditMode. (This transformation is an object property that doesn't affect the polygon data common to all four planks.)

To change an individual leg at the polygon level, select an object and switch to the Edit buttons. The header should have a mesh datablock with the letters ME if the object is a polygon or CU for curves and surfaces.

−	ME:Sphere.004	2

Datablock

The datablock's name will be to the right of the letters. If the datablock is part of several objects, its Data button will be blue and the number of objects that use the datablock (referred to in Blender as *users*) will appear next to the name. To make a certain datablock local for the selected object, left-click on the number and answer the dialog box by clicking the "Single user?" option.

6.4.2 Adding Material

Let's add a material to our table.

1. Select the tabletop and switch to the Material buttons (F5), where you can create a new material by clicking and holding the Menu button and then selecting ADD NEW.

2. Switch to the Texture buttons (F6) and create a new texture with this Menu button. Select image texture as your texture type by clicking on Image.

3. In the file menu that pops up, click Load and select the texture planks.jpg from the directory tutorials/textures/ on the CD-ROM.

NOTE *The fields for entering paths allow relative paths, which can make a scene independent of the storage medium's location. As such, a texture with //textures/ as its path can be loaded from the directory textures in the current directory—that is, whichever contains the scene. Thus, you can move a scene (together with the texture directory) to a new location and point to a directory relative to that location.*

For example, the textures on the CD-ROM are in the directory tutorial/textures/. Using relative paths, a scene in the directory tutorial/chapter06/material/ with the path //../../textures/ can access the textures, regardless of the location of the drive containing the CD-ROM. (The double dots ".." indicate a directory one level higher than the current one.)

A test rendering (F12) should show the tabletop, complete with texture, but the wood is still much too shiny. Let's fix it.

1. Switch back to the Material buttons (F5) and change the parameter Spec to 0.200 and Hard to a value below 15. (If you want to zoom in on the tabletop with the camera, activate Nor on the right side of the material editor to simulate a certain surface roughness.)

2. Create a new material for the planks under the table, and cover it with the texture planks.jpg.

3. In the Material buttons, activate Cube for the coordinate transformation of the image, to ensure that the image will cover all four planks uniformly.

You can use a material for the legs similar to the one you used for the planks. But, because the legs have a cylindrical form, choose Tube for an effective coordinate transformation. Color Plate 4 shows you what the finished scene looks like (I've also added a monitor for the final touch).

6.4.3 Sources for Image Textures

There are many ways to obtain images for use as textures. The Internet is a great source for textures and background images, as are various CD-ROM collections. The Blender Web site (http://www.blender.nl/userlinks/index.php?textures= on) links to several texture collections, and comments on licensing policies. Professional textures are also available on numerous CD-ROM collections.

NOTE *Regardless of where you find your textures, whether online or on CDs, read the license agreements thoroughly before incorporating one into your project, especially if it is for commercial purposes. Many collections are intended for private use only.*

Sooner or later you will want to create your own textures, a process made much simpler today by the availability of high-quality, inexpensive scanners. You can scan flat objects directly with a flatbed scanner and the depth of focus is often up to a few centimeters.

A good 35 mm camera is the best way to acquire image material, and you can even have your film scanned to Photo CD relatively inexpensively. Digital cameras are much more available than they used to be and their quality can be quite good, but most don't offer high enough resolution for good textures. Though they offer the fastest way to get your own textures, their images typically require touch-up in an image manipulation program, which often comes bundled free with scanners and digital cameras (or which is available for download as shareware or freeware). You can find some general tips for image manipulation in Appendix B.

NOTE *The CD-ROM bundled with this book includes a selection of textures from Digital Design Box, published by dpunkt Verlag (of Germany), in the directory* DigitalDesignBox/. *These textures are JPEGs in a resolution suitable for monitor use. Higher-resolution versions in a print-quality resolution are available in the commercial product.*

6.5 Multiple Materials

Blender objects can use several materials, each of which can be assigned to different parts of the object using the Edit buttons (F9) in EditMode. Materials are assigned as a property of the vertices, which, in turn, affect the surfaces that they form.

To begin this experiment, create a scene with a cube, or open `material/multimaterial01.blend` on the CD-ROM.

Next, we'll allocate the material to the cube using the buttons shown below. The top button shows the name of the current material, and the box at the upper left indicates the material's color.

Assigning multiple materials

6.5.1 Adjusting the Material Index

The material index 1 Mat: 1 (next to the material color) shows the number of materials assigned to the object (the first number) and the current material index (the second number). To set the material index, click the left and right sides of its button.

To change the material index you must create other indices. Let's adjust the material indices for our cube.

1. Click New twice to increase the indices for the cube by two, raising the material index to 3 Mat: 3 (press Delete if you need to decrease the number). You'll notice that the material name does not change as you adjust the index: Blender has created two new links to the basis material, not two new materials.

2. Switch to the Material buttons (F5) and look for the material index again. The material name field in the header button should be blue, alerting you to the fact that the material is used several times. The number next to the material name shows the number of times the material is used.

`MA:Material    3  X  `

Material name and index

3. Change the material index to 3 Mat: 1 and click the number beside the material name. After confirming "OK? Single user", you will have created a separate material whose properties can be changed.

Follow the same steps for the other two materials, giving each a unique color and texture.

If you'd rather not experiment, you can use the numbers on the CD in `DigitalDesignBox/PhotoTypes/Newcomer/`, which were used to create Figure 6-5. If you use these numbers, activate CalcAlpha and NegAlpha in the Texture buttons to ensure that the base material remains as the background.

Now let's return to the Edit buttons (F9) to assign the material.

Figure 6-5: Cube with several materials

6.5.2 Assigning Material

At this point all surfaces should have the same basis material, so let's adjust the material assignments.

1. Switch to EditMode and select all four vertices of a visible cube face.

2. Set the material index to 3 Mat: 2.

3. Click Assign to assign the *second* material to this cube surface. (You should see the change immediately in the solid view 3D window, though shaded views require that you leave EditMode.)

4. Apply materials to the remaining cube faces.

When you are in EditMode you can use Select and Deselect to select and deselect vertices, which makes it easy to assign a material to additional surfaces, and also to create vertex groups. You can later return to EditMode to quickly access these groups.

6.6 Halo Materials

Halos are small, round light beams that are placed at the vertices of material-carrying polygons and particles. Because halos are treated like 3D objects and also use the Z buffer (which carries depth information), you can cover them with objects. Select Halo in the Menu buttons to access the options for halos and lens flares (Figure 6-6).

Color Plate 5 shows nine of a nearly infinite number of halo combinations.

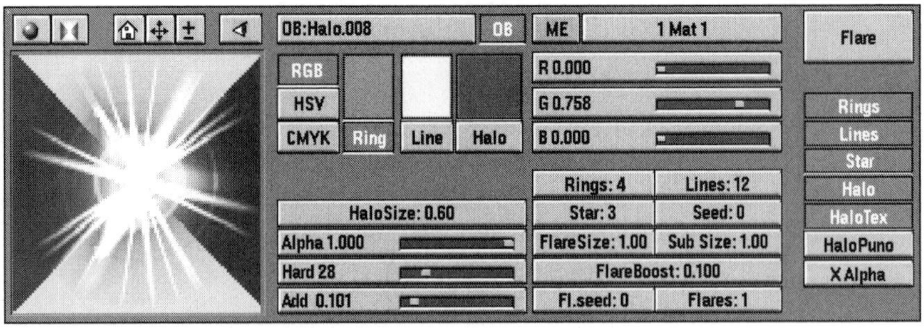

Figure 6-6: Options for halos and lens flares in Material buttons

6.6.1 Halo Settings

While there are various halo settings (as shown in Figure 6-6), the color settings are the most important ones for both the halo and its components (lines and rings). As with materials, set the colors with the RGB or HSV controls.

To set the number of lines and rings, activate the component display with the Lines and Rings buttons (in the Material buttons), then set the number of each with Rings: and Lines: (note the additional colon). Here's a rundown on the other parameters:

Star	Gives the halo a starlike form; Star: sets the number of points.
Seed	Sets the default value for the distribution (seeding) of the halo's rings and lines so that the halos on an object with several vertices will be different. If the object consists of only one vertex, Seed will directly influence the halo's appearance.
HaloSize	Sets the size of the halo.
Alpha	Defines the halo's transparency, with a value of 0.0 yielding a completely invisible halo.
Hard	Determines how the halo blends into the background. A high value creates a gradual transition; 0.0 creates hard edges.
Add	Determines the strength of a halo's light effect. A value of 0.0 means no light effect, which is important for halos with textures. Halos don't really shine onto other objects, but you can add a light source to each vertex with a halo if you want (DupliVerts, see Section 10.6).

6.6.2 Halo Textures

Halo textures are another very important effect. When HaloTex is active, each halo receives its own texture area and displays the texture completely; when inactive, the halo is colored by the texture of the object on which it lies.

For a better understanding of the effect of textures on halos, see the fourth layer of material/halo.blend, a subdivided surface with a halo material (select the surface then use the Edit buttons to access it). Render the image once with HaloTex deactivated and once with it activated to see the difference (see Figure 6-7). Also, take another look at Figure 6-6, which uses four halo materials. (Cloud textures make especially interesting halos, by the way.)

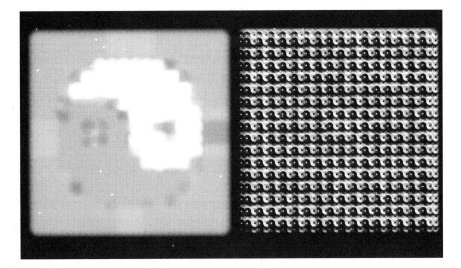

Figure 6-7: The difference between inactive (left) and active HaloTex

6.7 Nobody Is Perfect: Lens Flares

Lens flares are disturbances that appear in a camera lens when shooting pictures into the sun or very bright lights. Most photographers generally try to avoid these effects, but in 3D graphics lens flares are often used to create a more realistic impression.

Lens effects have often been applied wastefully, especially in science-fiction space animations. But, used sparingly and in the right spots, the lens flare can put the finishing touch on an animation and lead the eye and brain to believe that they are experiencing true reality. Lens flares can come in handy too for other special effects.

When working with lens flares, remember that, in reality, a light source causes lens flares. This means that if the object is close, you should probably put the light source in the middle of the object to get a realistic effect. Furthermore, a lens flare disappears when the object blocks the light source and the effect depends on the camera's perspective in relation to the lens flare object.

6.7.1 Basic Parameters

Like halos, lens flares are a material property. Once you assign a lens flare, you can no longer see the object it is attached to.

The halo parameters described in Section 6.6 apply to lens flares as well, once you've activated the Flare button. As with halos, you can alter the settings for rings, lines, and so on.

Lens flares take a few parameters not found with halos:

Flaresize and **Subsize**	Control the size of the lens flares and subflares. (Real subflares result from a series of lenses in the camera objective.)
Flareboost	Defines the lens flare's strength.
Fl.seed	Determines the distribution of the lens flares, as with halos.
Flares	Displays the number of flares and subflares, corresponding roughly to the number of lenses in the objective.

Color Plate 6 shows you just a few of the possibilities with lens flares; the scene material/lens_flares.blend has some lens flare objects on different layers.

6.8   Working with Transparent Materials

Since Blender does not support raytracing, transparent objects are tricky to simulate. When you're rendering glass or a similarly transparent material with Blender you must consider other properties besides transparency, such as reflection and refraction, which are difficult if not impossible properties for a renderer to simulate.

6.8.1   Setting the Transparency Level

The Alpha control (in the Material buttons) is the key transparency setting, and ranges from 0.0 (completely transparent) to 1.0 (not transparent). If you set Alpha under 1.0, you must activate the ZTransp option.

To experiment with transparency, try this exercise:

1. Create a sphere on the ground or load the scene transparency01.blend.

2. Cover the sphere with a material and set Alpha to 0.200.

3. Render the scene once with and once without ZTransp to see the effect. (With ZTransp active you should see a transparent sphere.)

4. Finally, change the color as you desire.

6.8.2   Making the Sphere Look Like Glass with Reflection

An important glass property is that the spot where a light source reflects off of it is practically opaque. You can simulate this property by raising the value of SpTr (Specular Transparency) to 1.0, and by increasing the parameters Spec and Ref to 1.0. (Remember that Spec is responsible for intensive specular points on the surface and Ref for the impression of reflected light.) Figure 6-8 shows a transparent object that reflects several light sources.

Figure 6-8: A transparent object

6.8.3 Using Reflection

Reflection maps are a powerful way to simulate an object's reflections in glass. Many chrome logo animations use them since the logos are often animated in a simple environment, like a black room with a single-color background. A true reflection would portray only this simple world, which would be quite boring.

If you are working with a chrome texture, you can use reflection maps to have a marble or a cloud texture reflect off of it. Or, if your glass object is sitting outside, you could have the image of a cloud-filled sky reflect off of it.

Let's create a reflection map.

1. Add a new texture to the sphere's material with the Menu button in the Texture buttons. Choose Marble for the type, set the Noise Size to 0.9 and the Turbulence to 16.

2. Change to the Material buttons (F5) and activate Refl for coordinate input.

UV	Object				
Glob	Orco	Stick	Win	Nor	Refl

Reflection coordinates

3. Set the texture color to white with the RGB control, activate Cmir and Ref, and adjust Col to 0.250 and Var to 0.5.

Coordinate output

The reflection map is now finished and a rendering should show more true-to-life glass.

NOTE *The fact that you are not reflecting the true surroundings isn't normally noticed in animations, and the more complex the surroundings, the less anyone will notice this trick.*

6.8.4 Working with Radial Blends

If you look at a glass surface, you'll see that it is almost completely transparent. But, if you look at a flat spot on the glass, you'll see that the glass reflects strongly.

The scene shown in Color Plate 7 (on the CD as `transparency05_env_map.blend`) introduces yet another trick for portraying glass called a *radial blend*, which controls the object's transparency and replicates this reflection property.

You can load the material with SHIFT-F1 or take a look at the (relatively complex) parameters for yourself. Here's a short overview of the settings you'll need when working with radial blend textures:

Texture buttons

- Set Blend for the texture type.

- Set Sphere as the Blend type.

- Set Bright = 1.800.

- Set Contr = 2.000.

Material buttons

- Input coordinates on Nor.

- Convert coordinates to x, x, y (from top to bottom).

- Set SizeX to 0.80, SizeY to 0.30 and SizeZ to 0.80.

- Deactivate output coordinates Col.

- Set output coordinates to a negative alpha value by clicking on Alpha twice.

6.9 Environment Mapping

Environment mapping is a way to simulate reflective surfaces without ray tracing. To that end you will either use a prefabricated texture to simulate a strongly diffuse reflection (especially suited to metallic objects), or you will render a texture on the fly. For an example, look at Color Plate 7, which shows one glass object rendered with reflection mapping (at left), and another rendered with environment mapping for comparison.

6.9.1 Automatic Environment Mapping

Automatic environment mapping renders from six different views, in all directions, starting from the position of the reflected object. The object itself is, of course, not rendered; the resulting images are then automatically mapped onto the object. Although the process is automatic, processing time is significant because a full six additional views must be rendered.

NOTE *Since the environment maps provide a realistic impression whenever there are surroundings that an object can reflect, the setting Real in the World buttons is very important.*

Once the maps are rendered, you can do a camera animation of the scene without re-rendering the maps. However, if you move the objects in a scene that has objects reflecting onto others, you will have to render a new map for each image.

6.9.2 Experimenting with Environment Maps

For our experiment, create a scene with a few objects, ground, and a sky, which can reflect off of each other in the environment maps. Or open the scene environment/env_map00.blend; its teapot will be the object of our experiment. Then do the following:

1. Select the teapot and add a new material with the Material buttons (F5).

2. Change to the Texture buttons (F6) and create a new texture for the material. Set the texture type to EnvMap.

3. Enter the object name for the environment map by left-clicking the Ob field and typing the name Teapot.

When you render the scene (see Figure 6-9) you should see Blender first render the six environment maps and then the actual image with the maps integrated into it. The rendered teapot will seem to have pictures pasted onto it. (The environment map from our example is shown in Figure 6-10.)

To achieve a truly realistic reflection, you have to adjust a few parameters.

1. Change to the Material buttons (F5). (To get a better idea of how the material looks, select the tiny red sphere directly over the preview window, to display the material on a sphere.)

Material preview

NOTE *The texture's input coordinates are automatically set to Ref, which ensures generation of the reflection coordinates.*

Figure 6-9: A teapot in render land

Figure 6-10: The environment map for the teapot example, automatically rendered by Blender

2. Deactivate Col and activate Cmir and Ref (in the Material buttons) to ensure that the texture will influence the material's reflection color (Cmir, for mirror color) and reflectivity (Ref).

Col	Nor	Csp	Cmir	Ref
Spec	Hard	Alpha		Emit

Mix	Mul	Add	Sub

Col 0.501

Nor 0.500

Var 0.501

Output settings for the EnvMap

3. Set Col and Var to determine how polished and clean you want your teapot to appear. (Don't set Col too high—almost no real objects reflect light perfectly.)

Now, return to the material's Texture buttons (F7) to have a look at some additional parameters (see Figure 6-11):

Static	Renders the environment map only once: when the scene is first rendered or when you change parameters. (Remember, if only the camera is animated, you don't have to re-render the environment map during the animation.)
Anim	Renders a new environment map for each image in an animation when activated.
Load	Loads previously rendered environment maps.
Save EnvMap	Saves environment maps. Here Blender supports all its standard file formats (with no animations), but the environment maps' dimensions must be correct.
Ob	Defines which object will serve as the position for the environment rendering; use an empty object to have your main object itself in the environment map. You can also implement this technique for transparent or hollow objects. With the layer settings you can keep objects on a particular layer off the environment rendering.
Filter	Displays how strongly the environment map is filtered, that is, how unsharp the illustration is. You can use this setting for rough surfaces.
CubeRes	Defines the resolution of one section of an environment map. Thus the entire map is six times as large (3 x CubeRes x 2 x CubeRes).
ClipSta and **ClipEnd**	Define the area around an object in which a rendering should take place. With these settings, you can keep very near or very far objects and surfaces out of the rendering.

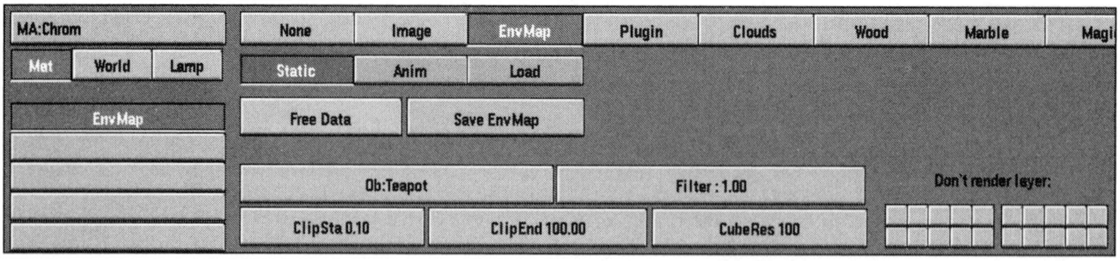

MA:Chrom		None	Image	EnvMap	Plugin	Clouds	Wood	Marble	Magi

Figure 6-11: Parameters for an environment map

7

LIGHT, SHADOWS,
AND WORLD TUTORIALS

Lighting plays a critical role in a good animation or static 3D scene, and thus deserves your full attention. The first part of this chapter provides you with a number of general tips and information to help you master the use of lighting in Blender. The second part of this chapter discusses how to use Blender's global World settings to set the scene attributes, including defining fog, color changes of the sky, stars, global lighting, and other related elements. Finally, we capture a scene with a virtual camera, which is set up in Blender like a real-life camera.

7.1 Lighting in Film and Video

Traditional films or TV productions frequently use a lighting scheme called a *three-point system* (see Figure 7-1). This scheme typically has one *key light* that simulates the natural light in the scene, usually sunlight or artificial overhead lighting. In general this light source is situated 30 to 45 degrees away from the axis between the camera and the filmed object and is also raised 30 to 45 degrees from the axis.

Fill light is commonly used to soften the shadows created by the primary light source. Fill light is less bright than the primary light, and is diffused to avoid throwing hard shadows. If the fill light is too strong, the scene will appear flat with minimal contrast. The fill light is commonly placed at the same level as the camera objective (the lens system).

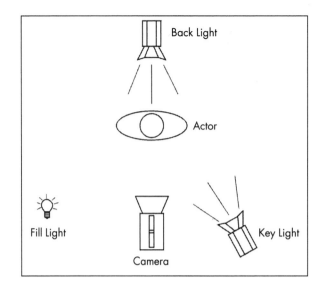

Figure 7-1: Three-point lighting

The *back light*, not to be confused with background lighting, is placed outside the camera's view, where it illuminates from behind and over the filmed object to emphasize the object's contours and to set it off from the background. The back light must not shine directly into the camera objective.

More extravagant lighting systems can contain a variety of other light sources, including:

- *Kicker light,* which is similar to back light but which is placed only on the ground, often opposite the key light.

- *Eye light,* which is focusable light. While originally intended to create twinkling reflections in the eyes of actors, it is also used to evoke reflections in other objects such as jewelry.

- *Background light,* which is used to illuminate the background.

By working with lighting, you can establish a number of useful effects:

- Lead the viewer's eye to the scene's important objects and areas.

- Create mood and atmosphere and increase dramatic effects.

- Create or enhance depth perception.

- Alter the existing light to portray a different time of day, season, or location.

- Underscore a character's personality; for example, by casting a clear, diffuse light on a hero and lighting a villain from below—the former will look honest and radiant and the latter full of sinister shadows.

To minimize processing times, computer graphics and animations use simplified mathematical models when rendering lighting. This limitation requires creative lighting solutions. For example, you can achieve a depth effect by using a series of slightly colored light sources. Or you can simulate diffuse light that reflects off of all objects that are not black. The radiosity renderer (see Section 10.3) is another tool for rendering diffuse light.

7.2 Types of Light in Blender

To add a new light source to your active scene, choose Add • Lamp from the Toolbox, then set the parameters for the light source in the Lamp buttons (F4). Use the Energy control for light intensity and the color controls for the red, green, and blue components.

When you add a new light source, Blender creates one with properties comparable to a standard light bulb, by default. Use these settings to alter the lamp type:

Lamp   A light source that emits light uniformly in all directions. Dist determines the light's reach. Sphere draws a line to show the light's radius and calculates how the light's intensity will decrease as the distance from the light source increases. Quad calculates a quadratic reduction in light intensity, which creates a more realistic effect.

Spot   A spotlight. At this writing, Spot is the only light source that can throw shadows (you must turn on Shadows in the Lamp and Display buttons). The rendering is effected with Shadowmaps, which enable you to render quickly without raytracing, but which also have limitations (see Section 7.3). SpotSi sets the width of the spotlight's beam and SpotBl defines its sharpness (with a high value producing a softer spotlight). Dist determines the light's reach, with the intensity reduced either in a quadratic (select Quad) or linear manner, commensurate with the distance from the light source.

Sun   A light source whose intensity is independent of distance, making its position irrelevant. You can control the light's direction by rotating it. A second dotted line indicates the direction.

Hemi   Creates a uniformly directed light that is emitted from an imaginary hemisphere (as in the light reflected by a cloudy sky).

7.2.1 Ambient Light

Besides the above light types, Blender also offers *ambient* light. In the real world, ambient light comes from the light reflected by objects, making the objects themselves light sources. Ambient light is what keeps real shadows from being completely black.

3D programs simulate ambient light by slightly illuminating each spot in the scene, but this trick makes the image appear flat. Therefore, wherever possible, apply additional, perhaps even lightly colored, light sources, rather than using ambient light.

You'll find the settings for ambient light in the World buttons (F8). AmbR, AmbG, and AmbB control the intensity of the three primary colors of the ambient light.

If ambient light plays a critical role in a scene, consider using Blender's radiosity renderer (Section 10.3), which renders light reflections mathematically.

7.3 There Is No Light without Shadows

To render shadows, Blender and other non-raytracing programs employ an algorithm called a *shadow buffer*. Essentially this algorithm renders from the perspective of the light source (a spotlight), but only the distance of the rendered pixel to the light source is saved in a 24-bit value. During rendering, the program compares the pixel distances to determine whether the point should be lit or in shadow. The shadow buffer is saved as a compressed file, which means that a 1024x1024 buffer requires only about 1.5MB of storage.

7.3.1 Clipping Line

The *clipping line* shows the range of a spotlight in the 3D window. (Set its starting and ending points with ClipSta and ClipEnd in the Lamp buttons.)

Notice the small black lines that move as you move these controls. All objects that, from the lamp's perspective, are situated in front of ClipSta are fully lighted, while all objects situated behind ClipEnd are in a shadow. Because the shadow buffer has a limited resolution, about 2500 pixels per square, set the values for ClipSta and ClipEnd carefully to achieve a high-quality shadow rendering, keeping the distance between them short: ClipSta should lie just above the objects in a scene and ClipEnd should lie just below them.

7.3.2 Potential Problems with Shadow Buffers

Rendering shadows with the shadow buffer can lead to two problems.

1. **Aliasing:** The shadow's edges appear pixilated and coarse (see Figure 7-2). To counteract this effect, increase the shadow buffer resolution BufSi, reduce the spotlight width with SpotSi, and increase the sample value with Samples.

2. **Biasing:** Surfaces that are fully bathed in light can appear dark with ribbonlike patterns. To counteract this effect, increase the Bias value and reduce the distance between ClipSta and ClipEnd.

You can view and compare settings for shadow-related parameters in the file light/good_shadow_bad_shadow.blend on the CD.

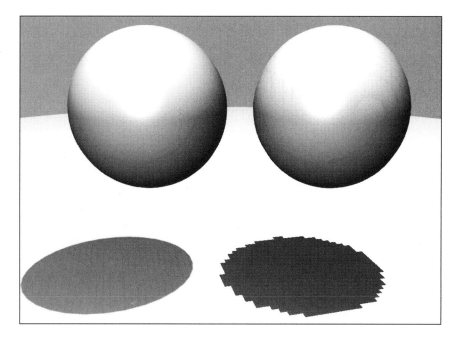

Figure 7-2: Good shadow, bad shadow

7.3.3 *Lighting Outdoor Scenes*

Blender's lamp type Sun is not yet able to generate shadows, which makes it especially difficult to find adequate lighting for outdoor scenes with a broad viewing area. Spotlights and shadow buffer rendering can only provide a shadow with restricted resolution, making lighting over a large area impossible.

A possible solution to this problem is to use a combination of both Sun and Spot lamp types. First create a spotlight and direct it, making it wide enough so that all objects will have a shadow, and bearing in mind the implications for the shadow parameter settings. Then select the same spotlight, copy it with SHIFT-D, and change the copy's type to Sun.

You should now have a very dark, abrupt shadow, which you should soften by decreasing the Energy parameter.

Because the sun is so far away, sunlight meets the Earth in an almost parallel fashion. Thus, place the shadow-throwing spotlight far enough away from the scene to avoid shadow distortions.

7.3.4 *Selective Lighting*

When you activate the Layer button in the Lamp buttons, light will affect only objects that lie on the same layers as the lamps. Select a lamp and then switch to the Edit buttons to set its active layers. If you press SHIFT and the left mouse button, you can activate several layers at once. The scene in Figure 7-2 uses this layer effect to illuminate the spheres differently in the same scene.

7.4 Halo Lighting

When in dusty or foggy environments, such as under water, one can clearly see the spotlight beam as a strong light source. Blender can simulate this effect using halos for the spotlight (see Figure 7-3). (Other 3D packages often call this type of light *volumetric light.*)

Figure 7-3: Halo, or volumetric, light

Load the scene light/volumetric_light01.blend from the CD and create a spotlight with Spot—the lamp should show up in the correct spot.

7.4.1 Aligning the Spotlight

To simplify pointing the spotlight, we'll align it along a track by directing it toward the dummy object "Target." To do so, follow these steps:

1. Select the lamp and expand the selection by pressing SHIFT and right-clicking on the object Target.

2. Press CTRL-T and answer the pop-up affirmatively to set the spotlight's path via a *track* with Target as its target.

If you created the lamp while in top view, the spotlight should be aligned correctly; if you created the lamp in side view, select it and press ALT-R to rotate it back.

The spotlight's track is permanent, which means that you can realign it at any time simply by moving Target (but don't forget to deselect the lamp before repositioning Target).

If you now do a test rendering, you should see a white splash of light on the ground from the spotlight. If you turn on the Halo option and try another rendering you should see a more defined light beam.

7.4.2 Penetrating a Wall

Now let's make an object (a letter or symbol) and have it penetrate a wall (as shown in Figure 7-4).

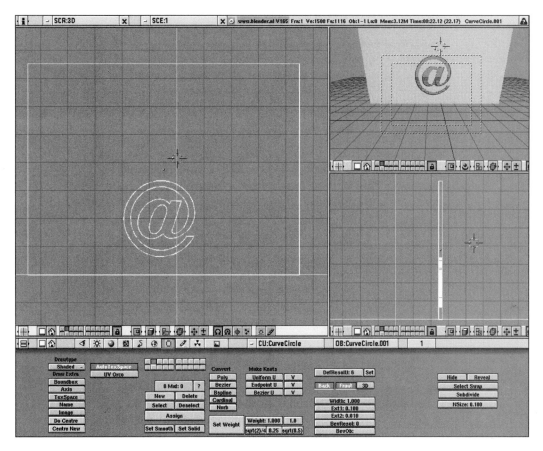

Figure 7-4: The penetrated wall

Create the object

We'll begin by using Blender's powerful curve tools (which can automatically recognize holes), rather than by creating a polygon object.

1. Change to the front view (PAD 1) and on a new layer create a Bezier circle with Add • Curve • Bezier • BezierCircle.

2. Press V to change the circle to a square that is rotated 45 degrees.

3. Use the middle mouse button to scale the square and turn it into a rectangular wall. Then press TAB to leave EditMode.

Create the text

To create the text object, follow these steps:

1. Choose Add • Text in the front view, delete the word "Text" that pops up automatically, and type in a symbol. (I chose "@" for this example because it is complicated enough to provide interesting effects.) Then press TAB to leave EditMode.

2. Scale the text object to about one-quarter the size of the wall and place it in the wall's lower half.

3. Set the resolution of the text curves to 15 (with DefResolU in the Edit buttons) and confirm it with Set. This will ensure smooth edges.

4. Convert the text object to a curve with ALT-C.

5. Right-click while holding SHIFT to expand the selection on the wall and then combine the two objects with CTRL-J to create a single object.

Adjusting the wall

A shaded view should show the wall with penetration in the form of the symbol you selected. Let's adjust it.

1. Apply a thick edge to the wall with Ext1, and round the edge with Ext2 (in the Edit buttons).

2. Now hold SHIFT and left-click to turn off the first two layers, and move the wall so that the spotlight shines through the penetration.

A test rendering at this point should display a light outline of the symbol on the ground, and a halo that maintains the form of the entire light beam.

Setting the halo light

To turn on shadow recognition for the halo light, set Halo set to a value greater than zero—lower values provide the most precision but take longest to process; 8 is a good compromise.

For an even better effect, adjust the values for ClipSta and ClipEnd according to the particular scene and reduce the halo's intensity with HaloInt (see Figure 7-5). The result will be a lightly colored light with an especially strong effect.

If, as in this scene, a halo light shines against the sky, turn off Gamma in the Display buttons, or the halo will be surrounded by a dark haze.

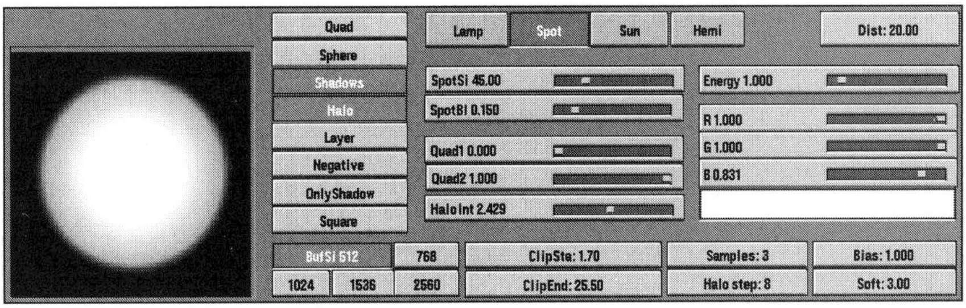

Figure 7-5: Setting the halo light

7.5 The World

The World buttons (F8) include settings for real reflected light (fog, stars, sky color, and ambient light), and allow for quick environment creation in an entire scene (see Figure 7-6).

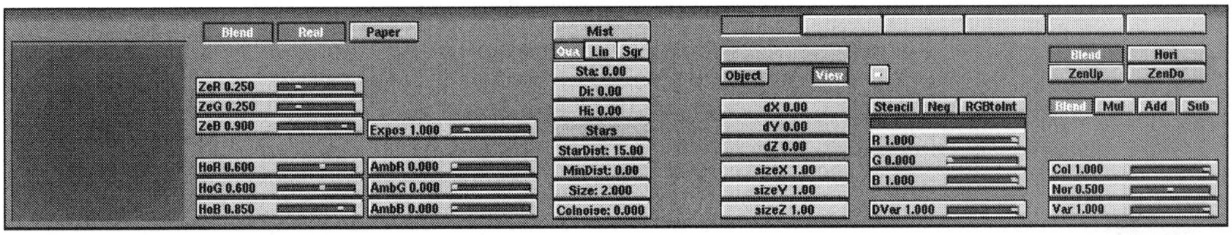

Figure 7-6: The World buttons

Let's create a new world so that we can experiment with it. Select ADD NEW in the World buttons Menu button. With Blend activated, this newly created world will be dark blue at the horizon and black at the zenith.

7.5.1 Adjusting Your World

The zenith color is determined by the RGB controls ZeR, ZeG, ZeB, and the horizon color by HoR, HoG, and HoB. For a cloudless sky, create a light blue horizon (R=0.6, G=0.6, B=0.85) and a bright blue zenith (R=0.25, G=0.25, B=0.9).

Also, turn on Real so that the horizon color truly starts at the horizon. (This starting point depends on the focal length of the camera and is rendered accordingly.) Furthermore, Real must be active for sky to show up properly on reflective surfaces during environment mapping.

7.5.2 World Textures

A world can wear a texture block, called a *world texture,* that is then projected into the sky. You can use procedural textures (like Cloud2) or image textures as world textures.

Image textures (such as a sunset—see world03_image_texture.blend) will produce more realistic results than procedural textures, but because they require high resolution, a visible edge will appear where the two textures meet.

If you find the disadvantages to image textures unacceptable, try a procedural texture. The texture plug-in "Clouds2," for example, allows for interesting effects, such as placing a blue to white colorband (using Colorband) on the clouds. You may also use up to six textures simultaneously for a world and overlap them to create nearly every cloud type.

NOTE *Although you can apply all of Blender's texture types to world textures, don't use a texture that produces only bump maps—world textures do not evaluate bump maps.*

Creating a world texture

To create a world texture:

1. Switch to the Texture buttons (F6) and load the appropriate texture.

2. Return to the World buttons and disable the two Blend buttons. Then activate Hori (horizon).

Blend	Hori
ZenUp	ZenDo

The Hori button

3. To render a scene with a motionless camera, activate Paper in the World buttons. When active, the entire texture will be displayed in the sky regardless of the camera's aim.

Blend	Real	Paper

The Real button

If you want the camera to move and change its viewing direction, activate Real and deactivate Paper. A test rendering at this point should show that the texture has slipped under the horizon; correct this with dY, which moves the texture vertically. If you use the image of the sunset from the DigitalDesignBox directory on the CD-ROM (sunset_big.jpg), a value of –0.90 is adequate (if the texture has slipped further under the horizon, use a larger negative value for dY). This translation depends on the location of the horizon in the texture image.

7.5.3 Fog

Fog and mist are key elements in adding realism to outdoor scenes and are created by clicking Mist in the World buttons. Fog effects apply to the entire scene, and their strength depends on the distance from the active camera.

Preview the fog settings in the 3D window by selecting the camera, switching to the Edit buttons (F9), and activating Show Mist. Adjust the fog settings this way:

Mist		
Qua	Lin	Sqr
Sta: 12.00		
Di: 16.00		
Hi: 7.00		

Fog settings in the World buttons

Sta and **Di**

Sets the fog boundaries (in the World buttons), displayed directly in the 3D window by two white points connected by a line (the line and points will rotate and translate along with the camera). Sta stands for the start and Di for the end.

Qua, **Lin**, and **Sqr**

Determine how the fog increases within its boundaries. Qua controls the quadratic, Lin the linear, and Sqr the inverse quadratic (square root). (You can test the effect of these settings in the scene world02.blend, in this chapter's directory on the CD-ROM.)

Create ground fog by entering a non-zero value in the Hi field. Hi controls the Y value of the fog in reference to the *coordinate origin,* which is the convergence of the three colored lines, or axes, in Blender's 3D window.

7.5.4 Stars

You can render stars with Blender's World buttons. The rendered stars are true three-dimensional, positioned objects—or more precisely, halo objects, making it possible to render a flight through the stars, just as you might see in a science fiction film.

NOTE *The scene world/SF_stars.blend on the CD-ROM shows a flight through stars. (The stars are rendered quickly to reduce the overall rendering time.) Motion-blur would normally be added to this sort of scene to give a more realistic feel to the animation. Note, however, that motion-blur increases, even quadruples, the processing time!*

Generate stars with the green button Stars in the World buttons (F8), then adjust them using one of these parameters:

Stars
StarDist: 8.19
MinDist: 0.00
Size: 1.040
Colnoise: 0.168

Star parameters in the World buttons

StarDist

Regulates the *star density,* the average distance of the stars from each other. Lower values create a denser collection of stars.

MinDist

Defines an area in global coordinates around the camera where no stars are located.

Size	Sets the average star size in pixels on the screen. You should set this parameter according to the resolution at which you render.
Colnoise	Lets you define a chance coloration for the stars, which they would show in the natural world as a result of atmospheric or inherent coloration. The value defines the intensity of the coloration between 0.0 and 1.0 (0 to 100 percent).

7.6   A Question of Perspective: The Camera

A Blender scene can include an unlimited number of cameras, but only the active camera is used for rendering. To render multiple takes of a scene, make the appropriate camera active and begin the rendering by hand. (You can also use the Sequence Editor to combine scenes or animations that involve different camera angles on a shared set of objects, as discussed in Chapter 11.)

7.6.1   The Camera View

It's easy to switch Blender's camera views. Pressing PAD 0 results in the camera view shown in Figure 7-7. Pressing CTRL-0 switches the current 3D window to the selected camera and makes it active. Pressing ALT-0 switches back to the previous camera.

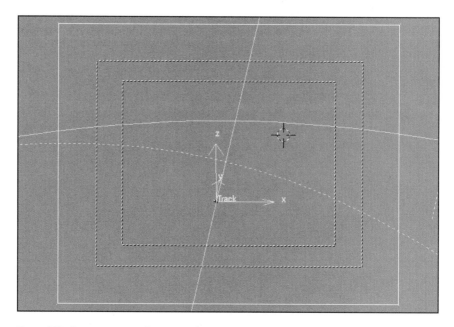

Figure 7-7: Camera view in the 3D window

This technique works with many other objects as well, meaning you can view and render the scene from the perspective of a light source (preferably a spotlight). This feature is extremely helpful in lighting a scene.

The camera view shows three boxes. The outermost one represents the camera itself and is used to select the camera in this view. The outer dotted line determines the area to render (sets its resolution in the Display buttons). The inner dotted line is the *title safe* area, the space that all televisions can display when a rendering is done in video resolution.

When in the camera view, press G and use the mouse to translate the camera on the camera level. Middle-click to switch the movement to affect viewing direction. Right-click to reject the changes; left-click to accept.

Press R to enter rotation mode, and the camera will turn on the axis of the viewing direction in the camera view. Middle-click to enter a mode that interactively changes the viewing direction.

7.6.2 Camera Parameters

Set the selected camera's parameters with the Edit buttons (F9). Here's how to use the various parameters.

Lens	Sets the camera's focal length. Focal length is the camera's most important parameter by far, and is set in millimeters. Lens functions as if you are working with 35 mm film: A 35 mm setting produces a slightly wide-angled lens, 50 mm corresponds to the view of the human eye, and 135 mm is telephoto.
ShowLimits	Shows the camera's *clipping area*, defined by ClipSta and ClipEnd, which also determines which areas are included in the rendering. You can save some processing time in complex scenes if you don't render hidden areas, like hidden walls in an architecture animation. (Keep the clipping area small so that the Z-buffer algorithm performs well.)
DrawSize	Defines the size of the camera symbol in the 3D window.
Ortho	Changes the camera projection from a central perspective to a parallel projection (see Section 2.6.1). The parallel projection lends itself to 3D effects on the Web, especially text elements with a 3D look. As opposed to central projection, parallel projection shows no rough edges and the font lines remain parallel.

8

KEYFRAME, PATH, LATTICE, AND VERTEX KEY ANIMATION TUTORIALS

Blender is a great modeling tool, but where it really excels is at animation. Its very fast renderer makes it possible to process even complex scenes in a reasonable amount of time, even on slow computers.

Blender's animation possibilities span everything from GIF animations of a few frames to animations played back on video or TV to thousands of frames rendered for and exposed on film.

8.1 Basic Animation Possibilities

There are three ways to create animations in Blender. The first two, keyframe and path animations, have some aspects in common and actually manifest their strengths best when combined. The third includes animations automatically rendered by Blender, including inverse kinematics and skeleton animations (discussed in Chapter 9) and particle, wave, and build animations (discussed in Chapter 10). For these animations, you provide the initial parameters and Blender then renders the animation.

Chapter 11 covers postproduction techniques and effects with Blender's Sequence Editor. And if you need still more effects, you can always program special effects with Python, Blender's scripting language (discussed in Chapter 12).

8.2 Keyframe Animation

Keyframe animation is based on traditional animation techniques. Master animators would define and draw the most important frames, or *keyframes,* to provide the foundation for motion. Apprentice animators would then fill in the intermediate frames, called *inbetweens.*

The earliest computer animation systems resembled conventional hand-drawn animation systems in which the computer served as an automated version of the apprentice animators. The positions of objects and the observer were specified at certain keyframes, and these positions were then interpolated to produce the frames between the specified points.

Let's make a simple keyframe animation.

1. Load the file animation/keyframes00.blend from the Chapter 8 subdirectory. (You can use your own scene, but the ready-made scene on the CD has a screen that's designed to work with keyframes.)

2. If you choose to create your own scene, create a cube, press TAB to exit EditMode, shrink your cube a bit, and then place it just outside of the camera's angle of view. (Make sure that the frameslider is on Frame 1.)

3. With the cube selected and the mouse in the 3D window with the top view, press I and choose Loc to make this frame a keyframe.

4. Press ↑ five times to advance to Frame 51. This puts you at a position corresponding to two seconds in a PAL video (25 frames per second), a bit shorter for NTSC (30 frames per second), and a bit longer for film (24 frames per second).

5. In the top view, press G and move the cube in a straight line to the right (using the middle mouse button), just outside of the camera's view. Now press I again and choose Loc to add the second keyframe.

6. Move the frame slider back to Frame 1 and press ALT-A in a 3D window; you should see the cube move in the chosen view.

In the camera view, the cube emerges on the left, accelerates, and then slows down, disappearing to the right.

You can use keyframes in this fashion to control the cube's rotation, but producing complex movements with keyframes alone is difficult. In particular, it is nearly impossible to control movement precisely because the interpolation between keyframes happens automatically.

This problem is solved by using IPO curves.

8.2.1 IPOs—Animation Curves

IPO curves (interpolation curves) let you control the animation of nearly every Blender element and parameter, including materials and world parameters, by controlling the keyframe interpolation. They are Blender's main animation control curves, letting you both visualize the animation and directly control it by manipulating the IPO curve.

Frame slider

Insert Key

Loc
Rot
Size
LocRot
LocRotSize
Layer
Avail
Mesh

Adding a keyframe

To display an IPO curve, change to the IPO window (SHIFT-F6) or, if you're using the keyframes.blend scene as your basis, switch to the screen SCR:IPO. If the cube is selected, you should see the animation curve for the translation along its x-axis in this window. To center the IPO window on the curves, select the Home button in the IPO window (see Figure 8-1).

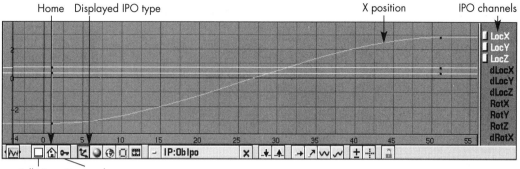

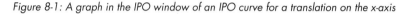

Figure 8-1: A graph in the IPO window of an IPO curve for a translation on the x-axis

An IPO curve plots the value of the parameter to be animated against the frames of the animation. As a result, the x-axis of the IPO window always represents the frames, while what the y-axis represents depends on the parameter being animated. In this case, the cube's path is plotted against time (in frames), and the slope of the curve represents velocity, with a steeper slope showing greater acceleration. Following the curve, you can see at a glance that the cube accelerates at first, reaches its highest velocity at Frame 25, and then slows at the end.

8.2.2 Manipulating IPO Curves

IPO curves are not meant simply for visualizing; you can also manipulate them in the IPO window, just like Bezier curves, to control the animation (see Section 5.13.1). For example, to make the cube move linearly without any acceleration, select the curve for the x-position (LocX), change to EditMode, then change the Bezier with the handles that appear on its control points.

Toggling the type of interpolation

You can control the type of interpolation for an entire IPO curve by selecting the curves and pressing T. In the pop-up menu you can then toggle between these options:

Ipo Type
Constant
Linear
Bezier

Ipo type

Constant The IPO curve always runs horizontally, jumping between various values on the y-axis. This IPO type is ideal for functions that describe only one condition; somewhat like "layers" for IPOs.

Linear Draws a straight line between IPO curve points. Consequently, there is no acceleration at the beginning and end of the movement. Together with the Cyclic option, Linear produces fast, continuous movements.

Bezier The default setting, Bezier produces a soft interpolation between IPO points.

8.2.3 Experimenting With IPOs

Let's experiment a bit on the IPO curve for the cube we created above.

1. Press A to select all the curve's control points and then press V to switch its handles into vector handles; the curve should now be linear. (You can undo this change by pressing SHIFT-H to switch the handles to auto handles.)

2. Compare both movements (with vector and auto handles) in the top view by playing the animation with ALT-A. Normal Blender functions like multiple selections, translation, and scaling (not rotation!) all work in the IPO window. The curves behave like normal Bezier curves.

3. Add a y component to the cube's movement by translating the cube in Frame 1 in the y direction and adding a new keyframe with I. The change appears immediately on the curve for the y position in the IPO window.

Try experimenting a bit with additional keyframes after Frame 51 or between the first two keyframes.

8.2.4 Hiding Channels

In Figure 8-2 I've added a couple more keyframes for translation, rotation, and scaling. As you can see, the IPO window is gradually beginning to get confusing, which is why Blender has a function for hiding channels in the IPO window. To clean up the window, click on a channel's name to display the channel and hide the other channels. Hold SHIFT to make multiple selections or hide an already displayed channel.

You can also select curves by clicking on the color fields next to the curves' names. And if View move is selected in the Info window, you can zoom just as in 3D windows by middle-clicking and dragging.

8.2.5 Animating Materials

Using a keyframe animation with IPOs, you can animate all of a material's parameters including its texture. In this tutorial we'll make an object disappear simply by animating the alpha value for its material.

1. Create an object in your default scene and assign it a material in the Material buttons (F5). (Since we want to animate the alpha value, ZTrans must be enabled.)

2. Use the frame slider or SHIFT-← to set the animation to Frame 1.

3. Place the mouse over the Material buttons and press I to add a keyframe. Left-click Alpha in the pop-up menu.

4. Change a 3D window to an IPO window and click the material IPO icon. A blue horizontal line, representing the alpha value, should appear.

5. Use the frame slider to advance the animation to its end or press ↑ to advance ten frames at a time to reach the desired frame.

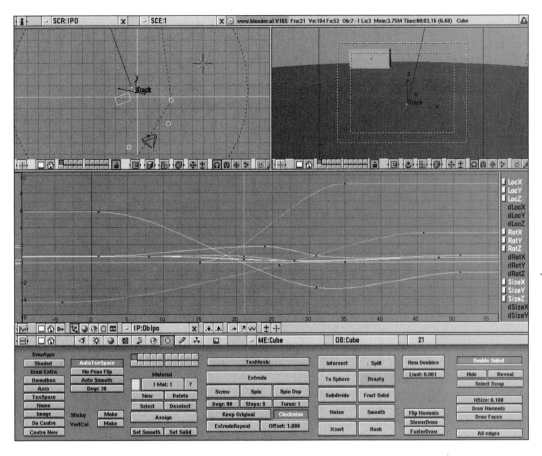

Figure 8-2: IPOs for translation, rotation, and scaling the cube

6. Change the alpha value to 0.0 (or a higher value if the object is not supposed to completely disappear) and click I once more in the Material buttons.

7. Choose Alpha in the pop-up menu as in Step 3. The straight line in the IPO window should now become a rounded curve indicating the change in the alpha value.

If you now render your simple material animation your object should become transparent during the animation. There's a problem, though: Because Blender's way of calculating shadows does not take transparency into account, your completely transparent object still casts a shadow.

You can solve this problem by using selective lighting to darken the lamp that's producing the shadow (enable Only Shadow in the Edit buttons), as you'll see in the scene material_anim02.blend.

8.2.6 Animating Textures

As I've already mentioned, you can also use IPOs to animate texture parameters. Let's give it a try.

1. Select the object in the material animation and create a Noise texture in the Texture buttons (F6). The Noise texture effect differs in each frame of the animation, which makes it ideal for depicting "snow" on TV screens and the like.

2. Change to the Material buttons (F5). Disable Col and enable Alpha and Emit in the texture's output settings.

You should now see noise on the object that gradually disappears as the object fades away. The object, however, has this noise from the start—it would be nice if the noise would come in later in the animation. Here's where animating texture parameters comes in.

NOTE *Because the* Noise *texture type produces a different image for every frame of an animation, don't use the* Noise *texture type as a bump map in an animation.*

Controlling the Noise with texture parameters

The Var parameter in the Material buttons lets you control the intensity of the noise.

1. Go to Frame 1 of the animation and set Var to zero.

2. Add a keyframe by pressing I and choosing All Mapping from the pop-up menu.

NOTE *This method is also used to add keys for the other texture parameters, but we won't worry about that for now since we aren't changing them in our animation.*

3. Advance to Frame 10 and add another key as described in Step 2 (without changing the Var value) to make the noise first appear in Frame 10.

4. Advance the animation to within 10 frames of its end and set Var to 1.0; then add a key for All Mapping.

5. Go to the last frame of the material animation (Frame 51 in this example) and set Var to 0.0, then add another All Mapping key.

The IPO curve you've just created should run almost horizontally on zero, rise up to 1.0, and then fall down to zero again. Rendering this animation should produce an effect with a striking resemblance to the transporter beams in *Star Trek*. See Color Plate 8 for a color image of a few frames. (The Scott_me_up.blend file on the CD-ROM is a somewhat more refined scene with this effect.)

8.3 Path Animation

Keyframe-based animation is great for many things, but what about orbital motion, or complicated flyby action? At some point, you may need to animate the orbit of a small moon around a planet, or the movement of an object around a complex path through a scene. A *path animation* is a convenient way to move objects in an animation by creating a precise path that describes the course of motion followed by an object. Blender has several ways of generating such paths.

8.3.1 Path Object Tutorial

Let's experiment with *path objects* (the actual paths objects in a path animation will follow):

Use Add • Curve • Path to add a path object to a scene. The default path object will let us create a smooth animation.

Once you've created the path you should see the path object, a NURBS curve with five control points, in EditMode. (The control points can be manipulated as described in Section 5.13.2.) Add control points by selecting an end point of the path then left-clicking while pressing CTRL to create a new vertex.

- To add a vertex between two existing vertices, select the two vertices and click Subdivide in the Edit buttons (F9).

- To obtain a cyclical path, select all the vertices (or at least the start and end points) and press C.

NOTE *In contrast to the standard setting for curve objects, the 3D parameter is already set for path objects, letting you freely position vertices in space.*

Now we'll create an object and animate it with a path animation:

1. Create a path if you haven't done so already (see Figure 8-3).

2. Press TAB to leave EditMode, and then add an object that will move along the path.

3. Press TAB to leave EditMode. Select the object and then the path object by pressing SHIFT and right-clicking.

4. Press CTRL-P to make the path the parent object of the object to be animated (indicated by a broken line between the objects).

5. Press ALT-A to play the animation in a 3D window.

Depending on the placement of the animated object, its animation should more or less follow the path. You can place the object right on the path by selecting both the path and the object and choosing Object • Clear origin from the Toolbox or pressing ALT-O, and then confirming the dialog.

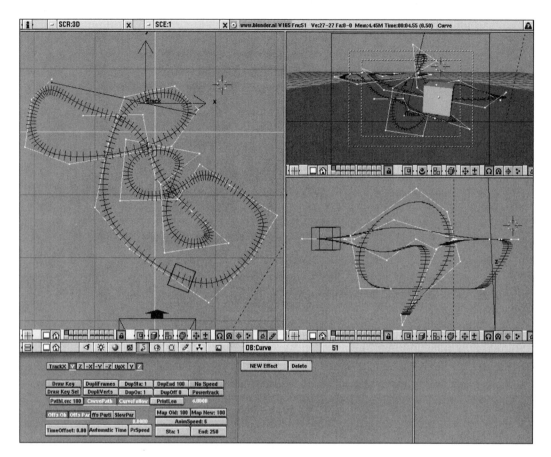

Figure 8-3: A crazy path with Cyclic and FollowPath selected

8.3.2 Speed IPO Curve

When you observe the object's movement, notice that, as with keyframe animations, Blender softly accelerates and then slows the animated object, and that the movement occurs in only 100 frames.

  These acceleration parameters are defined by a *speed IPO curve*. You can edit this curve by selecting the path, turning a window into an IPO window, and selecting the curved arrow for the speed IPO. The IPO indicates the position of the object to be animated at a given time, or distance over time, which defines the speed. The position on the path is indicated relative to the entire path on a scale of 0.0 to 1.0.

If you delete the speed IPO, PathLen (in the Animation buttons) determines the animation length. The animation then takes place linearly over the length of the path. Controlling the animation with the speed IPO is considerably more flexible, though, since it lets you animate the object cyclically or in the reverse direction on the path.

Figure 8-4 shows a speed IPO that slows an object down in the middle of the path, reverses it a bit, and then has it follow the path again. It also uses the Cyclic option for this path, which makes the object start again at the beginning of the path after 100 frames.

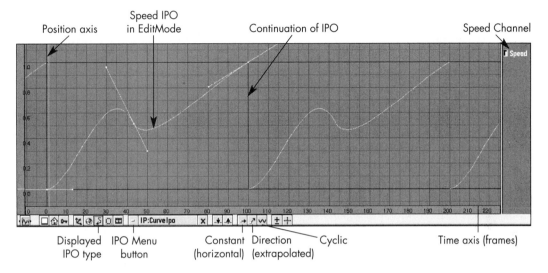

Figure 8-4: A speed IPO

> **NOTE** *The curves of cyclic paths have the same slope at their beginning and end so that there are no jumps in the animation.*

8.3.3 Curve Paths

In addition to path objects, any Bezier or NURBS curve may be turned into a path. Beziers are the best choice if you want to create a specific path for an object because they go directly through their control points. However, NURBS and path objects with an Order U of five or six produce smoother, more natural-looking animations.

The trick is to create the path as a Bezier and then convert it into a NURBS. The conversion will not be perfect, because the two curve types are based on different mathematical principles, but the resulting curve should give you a good starting point.

> **NOTE** *You can close or open a Bezier curve by selecting at least one control point and pressing C.*

1. Create a couple of basic objects as well as a Bezier curve for a path, similar to the small route shown in Figure 8-5, then disable Back and Front in the Edit buttons so that the curve will not be rendered.

2. Enable the 3D option so you can use the third dimension and see small hash marks along the path: The distance between the marks lets you estimate the speed along the path.

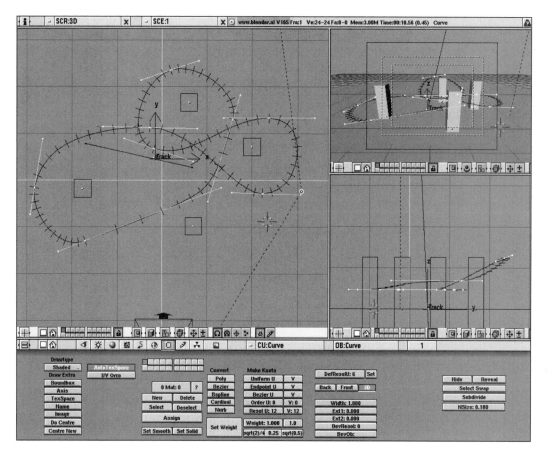

Figure 8-5: A path consisting of two Bezier curves

You should now be able to see some really blatant mistakes, like the abrupt jump in speed at the bottom-most point of the Bezier curve, which would lead to a corresponding jump in the animation. (You can correct this mistake with the editing functions for Bezier curves.)

Now let's make a simple path animation.

1. Create an object for the animation. Let's use a small rocket, like the one in the example files on the CD (see chapter08/animation/curve_path03.blend).

2. Select the rocket, then the path, and press CTRL-P to make the path the rocket's parent.

3. Set the length of the animation in frames with PathLen.

4. Turn the Bezier curve into a path by choosing CurvePath in the Animation buttons (F7). If you play the animation in a 3D window (by pressing ALT-A), you'll see that the rocket moves, but not along the path.

5. To correct this, select both the path and the rocket and clear the objects' origins with ALT-O. Then choose FollowPath in the Animation buttons.

Depending on the rocket's orientation when it was modeled, you may need to correct its position by selecting it and using the Tracking buttons in the Animation buttons (F7).

Tracking buttons

Controlling the axes

Press Axis in the Edit buttons (F9) to make an object's axes visible. TrackX, Y, Z, -X, -Y, -Z defines which of the object's axes should point in the direction of the path. UpX, Y, Z defines which of the object's axes should point upward (in the example UpX is selected).

If you were to choose Z, the rocket would revolve around its longitudinal axis during the animation, which can lead to undesired positions if the object does not rotate symmetrically. UpX prevents this type of rotation but you can explicitly define it for one of the points on the curve. To do so, select the path, change to EditMode, select the appropriate control point, and press T (for tilt). Moving the mouse will now set the tilt angle for this point on the curve. You'll notice the effects on the path and object immediately, and Blender will interpolate softly between the control points' individual tilt angles.

Unfortunately, the animation stops after one revolution. And in contrast to a path object, here no speed IPO was automatically generated, so you'll have to create a new IPO curve in the IPO window.

1. Make sure the path is selected, and then toggle a 3D window to the IPO window with SHIFT-F6.

2. Choose the curved arrow in the IPO window.

3. Create two control points in the IPO window by pressing CTRL and left-clicking. The position of these points is not important for now (you'll see how to enter exact values later in this chapter).

NOTE *Once a speed IPO exists, the* PathLen *parameter in the Animation buttons no longer has any function—the path length is controlled by the speed IPO.*

4. With the mouse over the IPO window, press TAB to enter EditMode and the IPO's Bezier control points should appear.

5. Right-click to select the left point (the first in time) and press N to call up the Number menu.

6. To set the IPO's first point at the beginning of the path and at Frame 1, enter 1 for LocX and 0 (zero) for LocY, then confirm the menu by clicking OK.

7. Repeat Steps 5 and 6 to place the second control point at the position LocX = 100 (or however long the animation should be) and LocY = 1.0.

8. Now select both control points and convert them to vector handles by pressing V so that the animation runs linearly.

9. Select the button that makes the IPO cyclical (a wavy line) so that the animation will continue to run until it reaches the last frame as defined in the Display buttons (F10).

NOTE   *To lengthen the animation, adjust the end frame with* End *in the Display buttons.*

A convenient way to edit the beginning and end points of a speed IPO is in the Animation buttons (F7), as shown in Figure 8-6. Here you can enter values for the x and y coordinates and record them with SET.

1.000	50.000	
Xmin: 1.00	Xmax: 50.00	
0.000	1.000	SET
Ymin: 0.00	Ymax: 1.00	

Speed: 1.90	SET

Figure 8-6: Another way to change the speed IPO

Reversing the direction of a path

To reverse the animation direction of a curve path or path object, select the path or path object, change to EditMode, and select at least one vertex. Press W to call up the Specials menu, and then choose Switch Direction.

8.4 Animation with Lattices

There are at least three ways to animate objects with lattices.

•   Animate a child object of a lattice through the lattice using a keyframe or path animation.

•   Animate the lattice itself using vertex keys (see Section 8.5). Or use *weighted* vertex keys to easily switch between or mix different deformations.

•   Animate a subordinate (child) particle stream to follow a lattice. (See the school of fish example in Chapter 10.)

The scene `lattice_anim/3_lattice_anims.blend` in the Chapter 8 directory on the CD-ROM has demonstrations of each of these three methods (the animation on the left of the scene uses a path animation, the one in the middle animates the lattice, and the one on the right is the particle stream).

8.4.1 Fitting a Cow through the Eye of a Needle

Question: How can a cow fit through the eye of a needle?
Answer: By using a lattice!

(The camel is actually the star of this saying, but I simply could not get hold of a model of a camel.)

Here is an example of how complex objects too can be made to undergo extensive changes using a lattice.

1. Load the scene `lattice_cow00.blend` and create a lattice object in the front view (PAD-1) by choosing Toolbox • Add • Lattice.

2. Change to the Edit buttons (F9) and set the lattice's resolution in the U dimension to 7.

3. Scale the lattice until it completely encloses the cow. You can also scale the lattice down by half in the x direction (see Figure 8-7).

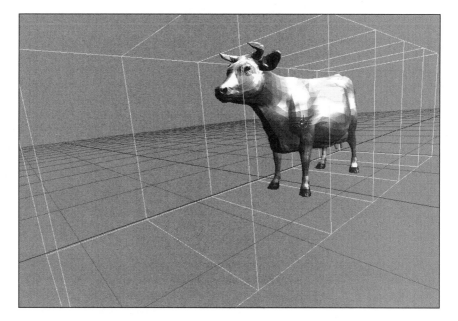

Figure 8-7: The lattice object for the cow

4. While holding SHIFT, select the cow and then the lattice and make the lattice the parent object by pressing CTRL-P.

5. To deform the lattice and its child, you must change it on the vertex level. Select the lattice and press TAB to enter EditMode.

6. You should see violet control points at the corners of the lattice's frame. Change to a side or top view, press B, and use the selection box to select the four vertices in the middle of the lattice. You should now see four yel-

low vertices in the camera view (only two will be visible in the top view because the other two are hidden behind the cow).

7. Press S and scale the selected vertices down to a constriction. (The cow's geometry will also be deformed in the active 3D window, so you can get a good look at the strength of the effect.)

8. Left-click to confirm the scaling; you should see the deformed cow in the other 3D Windows, too.

9. Finally, press TAB to leave EditMode, and then select the cow.

If you now translate (G) the cow along the lattice, you can observe the deformation interactively. A simple keyframe animation will render the deformation as an animation, as shown in Color Plate 9.

NOTE *If I could model a better spaceship, I would have used a spaceship accelerating to warp speed as my example instead of the poor cow. But I'm sure you can imagine how these types of effects are realized in films. Give it a try with your own spaceship model!*

8.5 Vertex Keys

Vertex keys are like keyframes, but for individual vertices rather than entire objects. They let you animate deformations in the geometries of polygon, curve, or surface objects as well as lattices.

The basics of constructing vertex keys is easy, but when you do, several things happen automatically in Blender (behind the scenes) that can cause confusion. In particular, Blender does not draw an IPO curve for every animated control point of an object, since doing so could result in thousands of IPO curves (depending on the object).

8.5.1 An Animation Using Vertex Keys

Let's make an animation using vertex keys.

1. Create an object to be animated. (I've used a surface sphere in this example because it's easy to generate major deformations on a sphere with just a few control points.)

2. Toggle a 3D window over to an IPO window, then choose the corresponding icon in the IPO window's footer to see the vertex keys.

3. Select the object and press I to create a key in the first frame of the animation. Choose the Surface option so you can create a vertex key for the surface object. If you're using a polygon or curve object instead of a surface object, your options will be either Mesh (polygon) or Curve. A yellow horizontal line, representing the first vertex key, should appear in the IPO window. This first key is also the reference key that determines the texture coordinates. A speed IPO curve is also created.

4. Advance several frames in the animation using ↑ or the frame slider and create another vertex key (which should appear as a blue horizontal line in the IPO window) with I • Surface.

5. Press TAB to enter EditMode and change a few control points to give the sphere a new form (see Figure 8-8). After leaving EditMode, the object should change when you move the frame slider between the two keys.

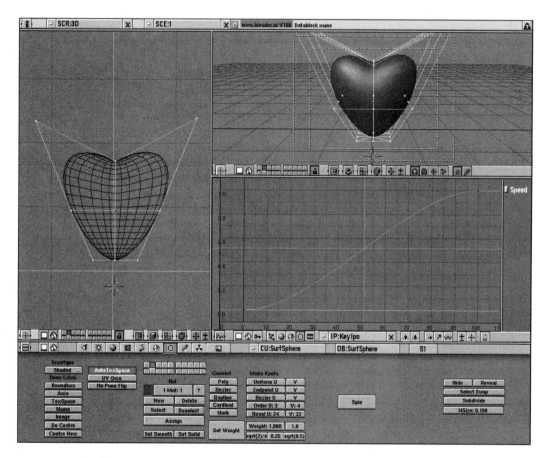

Figure 8-8: Defined vertex keys

Here are some general vertex key guidelines:

- Right-click a vertex key in the IPO window to select it and change the object accordingly in the 3D window. You can add more vertex keys in the same way.

- Make sure you leave EditMode before trying to select a vertex key—you can't select them in EditMode.

- The speed curve defines the speed of the transition between the vertex keys, with negative slopes merging smoothly into the previous key. Such a curve will let you, for example, make a heart pulsate (see vertex_keys/vertex_key05.blend on the CD-ROM).

- The vertex keys' vertical position in the IPO window determines when the corresponding vertex key is used. Use the Number menu for exact positioning by selecting a vertex key, pressing N in an IPO window, and then entering the position directly into the Number button.

8.5.2 Define the Interpretation Type

To define the type of interpretation between the vertex keys, select a key in the IPO window, press T, and then choose one of the following interpolation curves:

Linear Produces linear interpolation with a sharp transition between the keys; the key is displayed as a dotted line in the IPO window.

Cardinal The standard interpolation, characterized by fluid transitions; represented by a solid line.

B-Spline Produces especially fluid transitions; represented as a broken line.

8.5.3 Working with Vertex Keys

There are two basic ways to work with vertex keys. Your choice of method will depend on the situation and your preference. You can:

A. Work only in EditMode, add vertex keys in chronological order, and edit the object. To do so:

1. Select the object and press TAB to enter EditMode.

2. Press I to insert a reference key.

3. Advance to a predetermined frame number, press I to insert another key, and edit the object.

4. Repeat.

B. Insert the keys at their proper positions in the animation, outside EditMode, and then

1. Select the relevant key by right-clicking.

2. Press TAB to enter EditMode, change the object, and press TAB to leave EditMode.

3. Repeat.

Vertex keys are difficult to use when working with detailed objects and complex vertex animations. Nevertheless, you can still do a lot with normal vertex keys, depending of course on how complex the scene is (they work well on scenes that only require two states, for example). Here are a few tips to make working with vertex keys easier:

- Copy a vertex key by selecting the key in the IPO window (the object will then be deformed accordingly). Change to the frame where the key is to be inserted and insert a key in a 3D window by pressing I.

NOTE   *Always make sure you insert the key in EditMode. If you call up EditMode and haven't selected a key in the IPO window, all of your changes will be lost when you leave EditMode!*

- Remember that you cannot select multiple keys.

- When you're working with vertex keys with a different number of vertices, you'll find the faces will be somewhat chaotically arranged. Objects without faces (for example, halo materials or particle emitters) can, of course, be animated well with this method.

- Experiment with the Slurph value in the vertex keys' Animation buttons (F7). Depending on your settings, this value will delay the vertex keys, enabling lively transitions and also liquid-like honeycomb effects, especially with vertex keys for lattices.

- Vertex keys for curves and surfaces function exactly like those for polygon objects. Try deforming a bevel curve with vertex keys. This kind of animation will not be displayed in the 3D windows but will still be rendered.

8.6   Weighted Vertex Keys

It's easy to use vertex keys to create amazing effects for simple animation, but more complicated animations require so many vertex keys (all of which must be created by hand) that you need another solution. *Weighted vertex keys,* often called relative vertex keys, are the answer.

Normal vertex keys use only one IPO curve for all keys, but relative vertex keys assign an IPO curve to each vertex key that determines the key's effect on the entire deformation. This makes it possible to dissolve (add, subtract, and so on) between keys.

Relative vertex keys make more complicated animations, like animating facial expressions, extremely easy, since you need only define some basic facial expressions—further expressions are created by mixing the basic expressions. Animating between keys is also easy: A face can quickly go from a smile to an angry grimace. You even animate lip movements for speaking simply by modeling the lips for the vowels and then morphing between them for the rest of the text.

8.6.1 Basic Face Tutorial

The simple (and I mean simple) face in the scene vertex_keys/relative_
keys00.blend on the CD-ROM is good for demonstrating the use of weighted
vertex keys.

1. Select the face and add a vertex key with I • Mesh. A key and a speed IPO
    will appear in the IPO window.

2. Change to the Animation buttons (F7) and choose Relative keys. The key
    and speed IPO will disappear from the IPO window and the display on the
    right side of the IPO window will show the numbered key channels. The
    first strip (the one with the small orange box and the name – – – –) marks
    the object's basic pose. If you select this strip by left-clicking, the selected
    key will appear in the IPO window together with the speed IPO.

3. Move the mouse into the 3D window and press TAB to activate EditMode
    for the face object. You can now select individual vertices by right-clicking
    and then translate, scale, and rotate them. You can also select a complete
    object (like the mouth or an eyebrow) by placing the mouse pointer over
    an object's vertex and pressing L.

8.6.2 Create a Smiling Face

Now let's define a smiling face:

1. Pull the two outer vertices of the mouth upward.

2. Without leaving EditMode, add a key by pressing I • Mesh and then leave
    EditMode by pressing TAB.

3. A turquoise key should appear above the base key. Press G and translate it
    a bit onto the base key so that it's easier to select. Confirm the new key's
    position by left-clicking.

You can create different facial expressions by selecting the two keys in the
IPO window.

Add some more facial expressions in the same way and always move the
new keys over those created previously. If you want to use the base expression
or another expression as the starting object for a new expression, select the
corresponding key in the IPO window before changing to EditMode.

I defined the facial expressions shown in Figure 8-9. In the IPO window,
several blue lines, if you've arranged them as I suggested, represent the numbered keys from top to bottom. The orange base key represents Key 0.

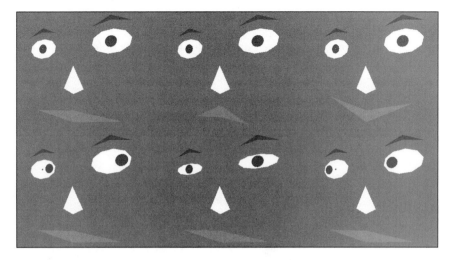

Figure 8-9: Various facial expressions; the base expression is in the upper left

8.6.3 Create a Smiling Face from a Neutral Face

Now let's make a smiling face from a neutral face:

1. Left-click to select the key strip with the number representing the smile (Key 2 in this example). The strip should now appear white and the others should disappear.

2. To make the smile appear within about a second, hold CTRL and click near the (0,0) coordinates (which represent the first frame) in the IPO window to create an IPO curve (since there is currently only one control point present). To position the point more exactly, you can zoom in on the IPO window, but exact positioning isn't that important here.

3. Define a second control point by holding CTRL and left-clicking near the coordinates (25,1).

    Flip through the animation with the cursor keys and you should be able to closely observe the face as it changes. SHIFT-ALT-A will play the animation in all views and clearly illustrate the connection between the face's expression and the IPO curves.

8.6.4 Controlling the Expression

The IPO curves let you determine how much of an expression goes into the resulting face. The range of values from 0.0 to 1.0 on the y-axis corresponds to an influence from 0 to 100 percent. You aren't limited to those values, though: A negative value creates, to some extent, the opposite expression (for example, a smile turns into an annoyed expression). Values over one yield an exaggerated expression, like a smile from ear to ear.

But the real strength of relative vertex keys lies in overlapping different expressions (see Figure 8-10). For example, a basic frown and smile will produce a slightly strained smile. To combine different facial expressions, select the relevant key strip and then create curve points by holding CTRL and left-clicking. If you select the resulting IPO curve, you can then translate or scale it. Furthermore, in EditMode you can edit the individual control points like Bezier curves. (When making edits like these, it's especially helpful to select the lock icon in the IPO header. That will make Blender show changes to the IPO curves directly in the 3D windows.)

The lock icon

Figure 8-10: Different facial expressions made by mixing the basic expressions

9

INVERSE KINEMATICS TUTORIALS

9.1   Inverse Kinematics (IKA)

When working with articulated figures, say a robotic arm that needs to grab something, you can use *inverse kinematics* (IKA) to calculate the angles the joints need to achieve to reach the desired end point. If you pull on the hand of a robot arm that uses inverse kinematics, for example, the other parts of the arm move according to how the joints are defined, thus animating the whole arm. To create such an animation with traditional methods, you would first have to move the upper arm, then the lower arm, and then the wrist. But if the hand's end position wasn't correct, you'd have to fix it by changing all other joints and then repeating the procedure for a new end position.

9.1.1 Articulating a Robotic Arm

Let's experiment a bit with inverse kinematics. To begin, make a simple robot arm like the one shown in Figure 9-1—or load the scene ika/robot_arm01. blend from the CD-ROM.

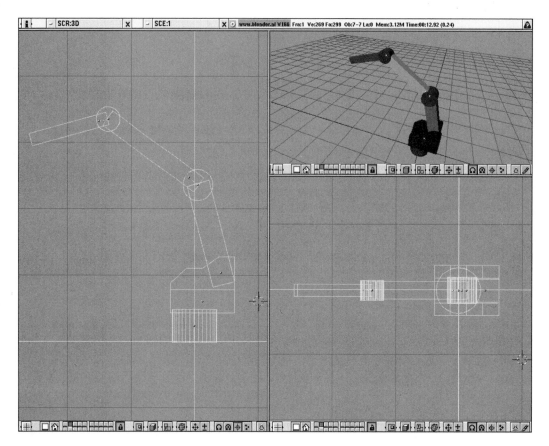

Figure 9-1: The robot arm's mesh

1. Construct your robot with an outstretched arm, and then rotate the joints around the 3D cursor to a slightly bent position.

2. Choose a base position at about the middle of the two most extreme positions as a reference position. This will prevent the joints from moving in undesired directions.

3. Connect the cylinders between the parts of the arm (the joints) with the parenting function (CTRL-P) to make them move with the arm.

9.1.2 Prepare for Rotation

We want the robot arm to rotate on its own axis and to be able to move the three joints. *Empties*, that is, objects that consist of one coordinate axis, will facilitate this, so let's create an empty now on the rotation axis of the robot's base.

1. Place the 3D cursor on the robot arm's base by selecting the base with the right mouse button, then pressing SHIFT-S • Curs • Sel to bring the cursor to the base's midpoint.

2. Create an empty here with Add • Empty to later serve as a grip for rotating the robot arm.

3. Place the 3D cursor on the pivot of the first arm segment (following the procedure in Step 1) and create an IKA on this point with Add • IKA.

4. Rotate and scale this IKA until the yellow vertex is in the second joint's center of rotation.

5. Set the first IKA limb by left-clicking; the second limb should appear. Position the second limb on the second joint (see Figure 9-2).

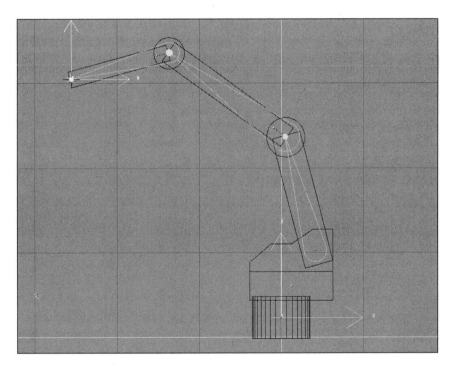

Figure 9-2: The IKA's position in the robot arm

6. After positioning the last limb in the robot's hand, press ESC to end the IKA session.

7. Position another empty on the arm's hand as a grip for directing the arm in the animation.

9.1.3 Connect the Parts with a Parent Chain

Next we have to connect the robot parts. While we could do so by melting the objects together (not the joints, of course), it's better to use the parenting function so that we will be able to change or position the individual parts later. You can also use this procedure to help you animate complex objects easily—first use simple objects to achieve fast interactive graphics and then later exchange these placeholder objects for more complex geometries.

When we connect objects we always follow the same model: Select the subordinate (child) object, press SHIFT and right-click to select the parent object, and then press CTRL-P to make the second object the parent.

We'll first create the parent chain for the IKA and the empties.

1. Select the IKA, then press SHIFT and right-click on the empty in the robot's base.

2. Press CTRL-P to make the empty the parent. Confirm the "OK? Make Parent" query by left-clicking the query or pressing ENTER. Answer no to the next question ("OK? Effector as Child") by pressing ESC or mousing off the pop-up menu.

3. Select the IKA and then the empty on the end of the arm and make the empty the parent of the IKA with CTRL-P. Answer yes to the "OK? Effector as Child" query by pressing ENTER or left-clicking.

4. To complete the IKA chain, select the empty on the robot's hand and then the empty in the base (hold SHIFT and right-click), and make the base empty the parent of the hand empty.

Save your scene, then try out the IKA chain by moving the empties; moving the base empty will affect the entire chain, even in a rotation. Be sure to cancel these movement experiments by right-clicking or pressing ESC so that the IKA will return to its old position.

9.1.4 Tweaking the Chain's Movement

But there's a problem: If the hand empty is moved in the top view, the IKA chain "tips" instead of following the hand empty in a rotation around the vertical axis. We'll use another IKA object to solve this problem.

1. Remove the connection between the hand and base empties by selecting both, pressing ALT-P, and clicking on Clear Parent.

2. Use the SNAP menu to place the 3D cursor on the empty in the robot's base and create an IKA with a limb in the top view, putting it directly under the arm and pointing it to the left (see Figure 9-3).

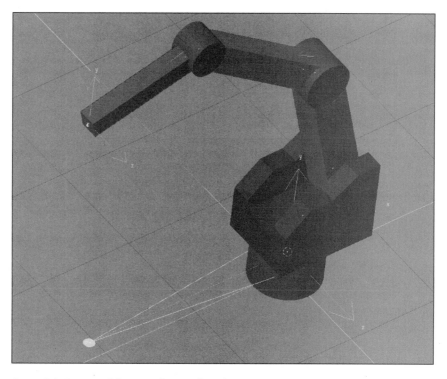

Figure 9-3: Position of the second IKA in the robot arm

3. Make the new IKA the parent of the base empty, choose the Use Limb option, and then, in the next menu, Limb 0.

4. With the new IKA still active, switch to the Edit buttons (F9) and set the XY Constraint to 0.0 to prevent the IKA from deviating from the local x-y axis.

5. Finally, right-click and hold SHIFT to select the IKA in the base and then the hand empty. Make the hand empty the parent with CTRL-P and choose Effector as Child.

9.1.5 Connect the IKAs to the Robot

If you now move the hand empty, the IKA chain should follow. Now all we need to do is connect the IKAs with the parts of the robot.

1. Right-click to cancel the hand empty movement and return the IKA to its original position.

2. Select the robot's body and then the base, and make the base the parent with CTRL-P. To complete the chain, select the base and then the empty, and make the empty the parent of the cylinder.

The robot body should now follow the movements of the hand empty. Now let's make the robot follow the IKAs:

1. Select the first part of the arm and then the IKA in the arm.

2. Press CTRL-P and choose Use Limb and then Limb 0 to link the first part of the arm to the first limb (the zeroth in Blender).

3. Do the same for the other two arm parts and adjust the limb numbers accordingly.

The robot's geometry should now follow the IKAs. Positioning the hand empty for a simple keyframe animation now lets you animate the entire robot.

9.1.6 *Setting the Limb Weight*

You can still set the limbs' weights in the Edit buttons. A limb with a high weight (near one) is harder to move, which means that its matching joint will not extend that much.

If you give the last limb (Limb 2 according to Blender) a high weight, it will be the stiffest limb when you try to move it. You can see the difference between the standard and adjusted weights in Figure 9-4, where the standard weight of 0.010 for all three limbs results in an undesired position for the robot arm.

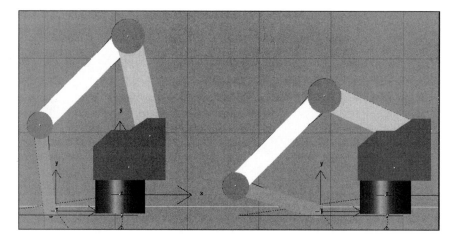

Figure 9-4: The robot arm with adjusted and standard IKA weighting

9.1.7 *Path Animation*

In addition to the keyframe animation using the hand empty that we've just created, you can also make a path animation.

For example, you could easily simulate the movements of a painter robot and then depict the spray paint's spray with particles or an animated texture created with a drawing program or Blender (see Color Plate 10). The advantage to using textures is that they can also be inserted along with bump maps, making it possible to simulate paint penetrating cracks in a wall. (The scene ika/robot_arm07.blend on the CD is a path animation of the robot arm and two particle systems that display the spray paint.)

9.2   Skeleton Animation with IKAs

Just as bones create a skeleton and control its shape, IKAs let you deform the polygon and surface objects around them. Called *skeleton animation,* this technique plays into character animation, which is still the supreme discipline in computer animation.

In addition to character animation, you can also use Blender's skeletons to deform other objects, like a coiled spring or a rubber buffer—objects for which a simple scaling isn't enough, and lattice and vertex keys don't offer enough flexibility.

9.2.1   What Is Character Animation?

In general, every moving object has a character and, as a result, every animation is a character animation. The trick is to give these inanimate objects the appearance of life by making them behave as though they had bones and muscles. For example, making bottles and cans move or cars talk is a common advertising trick.

The most complicated character animation is, of course, that of a living being. While we've never seen a hopping bottle in real life and thus have no real action to measure the animation against, we know how people move and thus we notice the smallest mistakes in the animation of a person's face.

9.2.2   Constructing a Skeleton

The scene ika/bottle00.blend has a bottle that's well suited for showing the main ways a skeleton animation works (though this requires a bit of imagination since normal bottles do not have skeletons). I chose to go with the skeleton shown in Figure 9-5.

We want the bottle's skeleton to let us make it bow like a performer on a stage. To produce this effect, we'll use the big IKA (the bottle's "spinal column") in the upper part of the bottle. The various empty objects serve as grips for better animating the IKAs.

The spinal column IKA begins at the empty that represents the pelvis. (The legs are also attached here and then end in the feet.) With this very simple motion apparatus, you can make the bottle walk (or rather waddle) and move at the hip.

Once the skeleton's parts have been created inside the bottle, we must link the joints and bones until the entire apparatus moves as a whole.

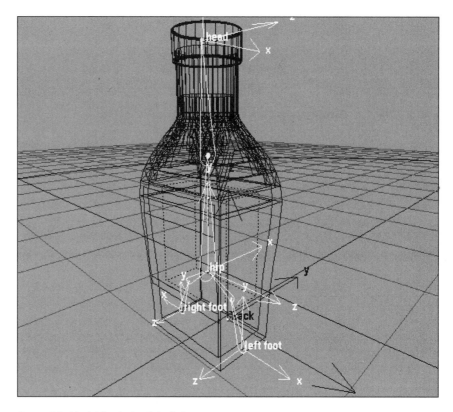

Figure 9-5: Model for the bottle's skeleton animation

9.2.3 Creating the Skeleton

1. Begin constructing the skeleton in a front view of the bottle; to get a better overall view, activate only the layer with the bottle on it (Layer 2 in the example scene).

2. Hold SHIFT and press 3 to activate a second layer so that the skeleton will be created on its own layer. Although not absolutely necessary, this step will make working with the skeleton a lot easier.

3. Place the 3D cursor on the bottle with SHIFT-S • Curs • Selection so that the skeleton lies within the bottle.

NOTE *If you move the skeleton to test it out, remember to cancel any transformations with ESC or a right-click so that the change will be undone.*

Create the legs

1. In the front view, place the 3D cursor on a corner of the bottle's base and create the first foot empty there (see "The first leg" below), then create the first IKA on the same spot with Toolbox • Add • IKA.

2. Use the mouse to scale and rotate the first leg limb and left-click to fix the position; the second limb then appears and can be positioned in the same way.

3. Finally, end the construction phase with a middle-click. (If you left-click by accident, another limb will appear—just press ESC to delete it.)

   Create the second leg in the same way.

NOTE *Although it looks sensible to construct the leg IKAs in reverse because the thick ends correspond more to the thighs, the procedure we've used makes sure that the feet stay on the ground when the hip is animated.*

Adding body parts

We'll now create empties as parts of the skeleton to be used as grips as well as body parts. The head empty will enable the bottle to turn and nod its head; the foot empties will let you point the bottle's feet.

1. Create the hip empty where the leg IKAs meet.

2. Change to a side view and create the spinal column IKA coming out of the hip empty. The first limb should be stretched to the bottle's "shoulder," and the second to the top of the bottle.

3. Create the head empty on the end of the spinal column IKA.

4. Switch to the layer holding the skeleton and link the skeleton's parts by selecting a leg and then the corresponding foot empty.

The first leg

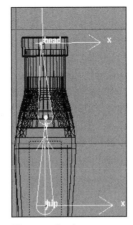

The spinal column

5. Use CTRL-P to make the empty the parent object of the leg. Answer yes to the "OK? Make Parent" question by clicking or pressing ENTER, and no to the "OK? Effector as Child" question by pressing ESC or mousing off the pop-up menu.

Follow the same procedure for the other leg.

NOTE *While the effector (the moveable end of the IKA) is the sharp end of the IKA, we answer no to this question because we want to connect the leg's base with the empty.*

If you now select a foot and translate with G, the leg should follow the foot's movement. (Don't forget to quit the translation with ESC or a right-click!)

Connect the legs to the hip

Now let's connect the legs to the hip so that the hip too will follow the foot's movement.

1. Select the leg and then the hip empty and make the hip the parent of the leg with CTRL-P. Answer yes to the "OK? Effector as Child" question by pressing ENTER, thus automatically setting the effector (the yellow vertex on the end of the IKA) on the hip empty's position.

2. Apply the same procedure to the other leg.

When you test the hip's movability again, it should follow the foot's movement.

NOTE *In the next steps you should either not move any skeleton parts or save the scene before making any attempts to move the skeleton: It will be very easy to misposition the skeleton.*

Let's connect the head to the upper part of the spinal column so that movements of the spinal column will transmit the rotation of the limbs to the head empty. Thus you can animate the head separately and still have it follow the body's movements.

1. Select the spinal column and then the hip, then press CTRL-P. Answer no to the "OK? Effector as Child" question.

2. Select the head empty and then the spinal column, then press CTRL-P and choose Limb from the pop-up menu.

3. In the next pop-up menu, set the Number button to 1 and click OK or press ENTER.

9.2.4 Defining the Skeleton

Now, using the IKA chain, we'll create a skeleton that deforms the surrounding geometry.

1. Select all the skeleton parts that should cause a deformation—either press A to select the whole thing or make a multiple selection.

2. Hold SHIFT and select one of the IKAs, then right-click it until it is displayed as light violet (the active object).

3. Now make the IKA into a skeleton by pressing CTRL-K and answering yes to the "OK? Make Skeleton" prompt.

4. Do the same for the other IKAs (do not deselect the other skeleton parts).

5. Switch to the layer with the bottle and select the bottle.

6. Hold SHIFT and select the spinal column IKA, then make it the parent with CTRL-P. Left-click the pop-up menu that appears and choose Use Skeleton.

7. Finally, save the scene in case something goes wrong with the skeleton, because now moving the empties and IKAs deforms the bottle!

Experiment a bit with the skeleton to get a feel for its range and limitations. In addition to translating, try rotating and scaling the skeleton parts too. Figure 9-6 shows the final skeleton.

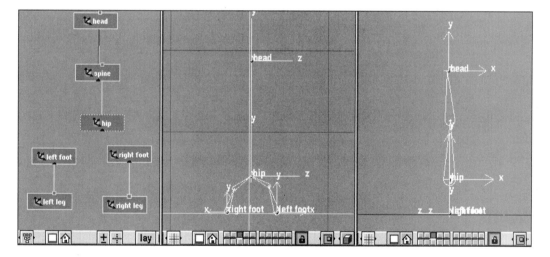

Figure 9-6: The skeleton

NOTE *To move the spinal column, you have to select the IKA itself. The best way to obtain a simple bow is to move the IKA in the side view.*

9.2.5 Setting the Parameters

When you now select an IKA in the skeleton, the skeleton parameters (shown in Figure 9-7) appear in the Edit buttons. Here you can set the IKA parameters for each skeleton part (next to the part's name) as described in Section 9.1.

	Limb Weight		Deform Max Dist	Deform Weight
Set Reference	Limb 0: 0.010	hip :	1.00	1.000
	Limb 1: 0.010	right foot :	1.00	1.000
Lock XY Plane		left foot :	1.00	1.000
XY constraint 0.500		left leg (0):	1.34	1.000
		left leg (1):	1.25	1.000
Mem 0.300		right leg (0):	1.30	1.000
Iter: 6		right leg (1):	1.26	1.000
		spine (0):	1.77	1.000
		spine (1):	1.65	1.000
		head :	1.00	1.000

Figure 9-7: The skeleton parameters in the Edit buttons

Deform Max Dist Defines the area of influence a skeleton part has on an object's geometry; its value is based on an object size of 1.0.

Deform Weight Sets the weight of the deformation in relation to the other skeleton parts.

Set the Deform Weight of the head empty to about 5.0 and the Deform Max Dist to about 2.0 so that moving the head empty moves the neck and deforms the bottle's top.

The values you choose for these parameters will depend on the size of the skeleton's parts and may have to be adjusted to your scene.

9.2.6 Animating the Skeleton

You can now animate the skeleton parts with the usual keyframe and path animation methods. Empties can be animated with respect to positioning (Loc), rotating (Rot), and scaling (Size).

> **NOTE** *If you move an IKA, choose Effector from the pop-up menu that appears after inserting a key with I.*

To make the bottle bow, follow these steps:

1. Select the spinal column IKA and insert a key in Frame 1 by pressing I • Effector.

2. Advance a few frames (depending on the speed of the bow), translate the spinal column in the side view to a bow, and insert another key.

3. Advance again a few frames, straighten the spinal column, and then insert the third key.

4. Finally, go to Frame 1 and play the animation with ALT-A; the bottle should take a bow.

If you advance several frames at once (with the ↑ and ↓ cursor keys or the frame slider) and the bottle's position (as rendered by Blender) does not correspond with the skeleton, move one frame forward and one frame back a couple of times with the ← and → keys.

Color Plate 11 shows a few frames from the bottle animation. You'll find the animation and the scene itself on the CD.

10

GETTING SMALL: PARTICLE
ANIMATION TUTORIALS

Blender's particle system is very flexible and powerful— you
can use it to create smoke, steam, fire, explosions, water fountains, fireworks, or even a school of fish. Halos or objects and
metaballs instantiated via DupliVerts can serve as particles and
any mesh can serve as a particle emitter. Particles can be affected by
global forces like gravity, wind, and currents, as well as by lattices, allowing you
to make them behave like natural clouds or crowds in your scene.

10.1 Playing with Particles

As a starting point for our work with particles, create a plane with Add • Mesh •
Plane in the top view of your default scene. Scale the plane down a bit and
place it just above the scene floor so it's completely visible. Each vertex of the
plane will serve as an emitter (see Figure 10-1). (In principle, an object with
one vertex would suffice for these experiments, but the plane's orientation
allows us to control the direction in which the particles are discharged.)

Leave EditMode and select the Animation buttons (F7), where you'll
assign the particle effect. Press the NEW Effect button and choose the Particles
effect type from the Menu button that appears to the right, and a whole load
of buttons and settings will appear (Figure 10-2). But don't worry: We'll create
the first particle animation in six steps!

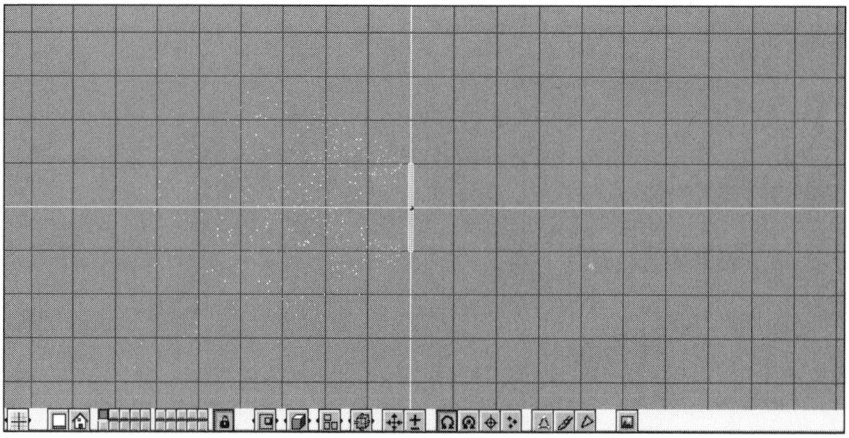

Figure 10-1: Particles emitted from a plane emitter

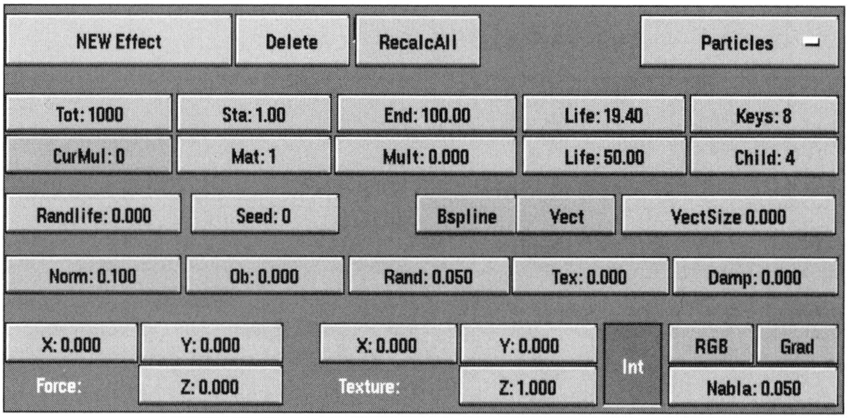

Figure 10-2: Particle effect settings

1. Click at the right of the Norm button to increase its value to 0.100.

2. Play the animation with ALT-A (preferably in the camera view), and a stream of particles should move away from the emitter plane.

3. Set the particles' life span with the upper of the two Life parameters. Decrease the life span so that the complete particle stream is visible in the camera view. To control the setting, advance to Frame 50, where you can set the lifetime interactively.

4. Now raise the Rand value to 0.050 and the particles will whirl around randomly.

With the settings defined in these first four steps, we've created a particle animation that resembles escaping steam or the like. But if you render an image or the animation at this point, you will see nothing in the rendered frames because the particles lack a material.

 5. Select the emitter plane and change to the Material buttons (F5). Choose ADD NEW from the Menu button to create a new material.

The Halo option is automatically selected for particles, even if you don't activate it in the Material buttons.

A test rendering of Frame 50 should show a homogenous, glowing mass where the particles should be. The halos are simply too big in the default settings to be individually seen given the scale of our scene.

6. Select the Halo button in the emitter plane's Material buttons to call up the settings for a halo material (Figure 10-3). Decrease the HaloSize setting to about 0.100 to adjust the size of the halo particles so they'll show up as individuals.

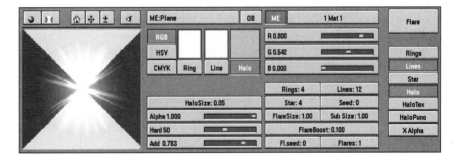

Figure 10-3: The particle material

 You can supply particles with lines or rings, for example, to create the sparks thrown off by a grinding disk. (The other parameters are explained in Section 6.6.) To get a feel for the parameters, render a small animation with different particle and halo parameters.

10.1.1 The Basic Parameters

Blender's particle system has a ton of features and I'll explain only the most important ones here. The other features and special effects are described in more depth in the following tutorials.

Blender renders its particle systems fast enough for you to quickly get a feel for its individual parameters with only a few test renderings. You can also preview the particle motion (without rendering) using Blender's excellent real-time display in the 3D windows.

Tot	Determines the total number of particles visible for each effect. You can assign up to 100,000 particles per emitter. If you need more, just add another emitter.
Sta and **End**	Determine the start and end of particle emission within the animation.
Life	Defines the lifetime of individual particles in frames based on the animation.
Norm	Determines the particles' initial speed. The direction in which the particles are emitted is determined by the particle emitter's plane normals (which are vectors that are perpendicular to the plane). Negative values produce acceleration against the direction of the normal.

NOTE *Norm functions only with planar objects. If you try using a sphere as an emitter you will see that the particles are emitted from the center of the sphere in all directions.*

Ob	Determines how the emitter's motion affects the initial speed of the particles.
Rand	Produces more or less random directions of movement in the particles. A value of 0 gives all the particles the same direction of movement, and a value of 2 produces completely random directions.
X, **Y**, and **Z** in **Force**	Determine a continuous force that acts on the particles. A negative Z value simulates gravity, and a positive one rising drifts of smoke. The X and Y values produce wind.
RecalcAll	Recalculates the particles' positions. This feature is especially useful when you have just animated an object and the particles in the 3D window are no longer correctly displayed. (A rendering, however, will always be executed correctly.)

10.2   The Scout's Word of Honor: Building a Campfire

Building a campfire is a popular way to test particle systems.

Let's think about a real wood fire to help us to create our computer-generated one. A fire's flames are born of the hot, gaseous by-products of burning wood. The hot gas rises because it is less dense than the air, and the flames, which are yellow-white in the middle, become redder toward their edges as they cool. The flames go out as they climb into the air because they run out of fuel.

Our knowledge of the physical conditions of a real fire will help us create a realistic animated fire based on a particle system, under these conditions:

- The gravitational force (in the z direction) must be positive, to make the particles rise.

- The speed of the particles starts at zero and is accelerated by the upward force.

- As we move from inside the flame to its outer edge, the material should change from yellow to red.

- The particles should become fainter and smaller over their lifetimes.

- The speed of the particles' upward motion should decrease at the end of their lifetimes.

10.2.1 Build the Basic Fire

To begin, use the finished scene `fire01.blend` as your basis, or build your own. If you choose to build your own, create a background for the fire: a wide area of ground, with world parameters that produce an ambient starry sky, and a lamp for pale yellow moonlight. Then frame the campfire with the classic ring of stones (to create the stones, try deforming an Icosphere with Fract Subd in the Edit buttons) and build the fire with a pile of logs in the center of the ring of stones. Finally, add a couple of weak red lamps in the center of the fire to produce its glow (set with Sphere and Dist so that they do not light the entire scene).

Now that you have your basic fire, let's get it ready for the particle animation.

1. Change to the top view and create a plane in the middle of the campfire to be the particle emitter.

2. Subdivide the plane by selecting all vertices and clicking Subdivide once in the Edit buttons. (The plane should fit completely within the ring of stones.) Since it will be best to have the flames come from the wood, place the individual vertices on the logs.

3. Press TAB to leave EditMode and, with the plane still selected, change to the Animation buttons (F7). Create a new effect with NEW Effect and change the effect type from Build to Particles with the Menu button. The particle effect settings should appear as shown in Figure 10-4.

NEW Effect	Delete	RecalcAll		Particles ⌐
Tot: 141	Sta: -20.00	End: 200.00	Life: 63.00	Keys: 8
CurMul: 0	Mat: 1	Mult: 0.000	Life: 50.00	Child: 4
Randlife: 0.100	Seed: 0	Bspline	Vect	VectSize 0.000
Norm: -0.008	Ob: 0.000	Rand: 0.016	Tex: 0.000	Damp: 0.107

X: 0.000	Y: 0.000	X: 0.000	Y: 0.000	Int	RGB	Grad
Force:	Z: 0.230	Texture:	Z: 1.000		Nabla: 0.050	

Figure 10-4: Particle effect parameters for the campfire

4. Adjust the parameters as specified in the following list to make the animation follow our initial analysis of a real fire. If the scale of your scene is very different, you may have to make some adjustments in the proposed settings, but the ones given here should produce a good effect on the sample scene on the CD.

Sta Set to a negative value (like -20).

End Set to the desired animation length so that the fire will burn from the beginning of the animation and not suddenly go out.

Life Keep (the particle's lifetime) at 50.0 for now; once you've assigned the material you can set the flame's height more precisely by running a few test renderings.

Norm Keep at 0.000 or make it slightly negative (-0.008) to produce a fire with a somewhat bulbous base.

Force Set to a positive Z value of about 0.220 to produce the desired upward motion.

Damp Set to about 0.100 to make the flames move more slowly as they climb higher. Damp slows down the particles with a kind of friction (air resistance or the like).

Bspline Use to create a soft, flowing line of movement using a spline-based interpolation of the particle movements.

Rand Set to about 0.015 to produce somewhat random movements.

Tot Because we'll be working with large particles and textures, set the number of particles to between 130 and 150.

10.2.2 Add Material

Without a material, we can only test the animation in the 3D windows at this point. Let's add a material for the particles (see Figure 10-5).

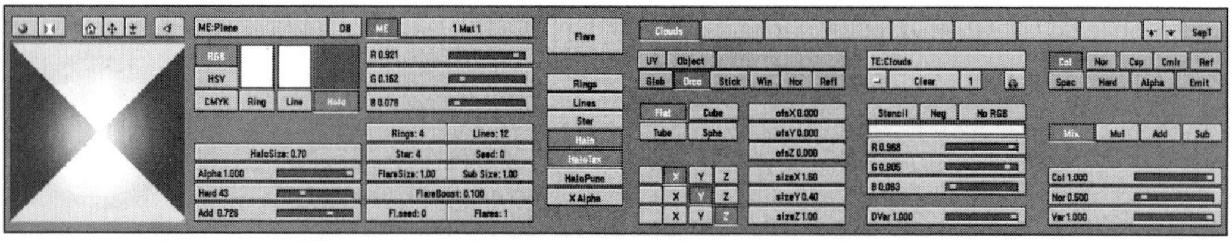

Figure 10-5: Settings for the fire's material

1. Select the particle emitter, change to the Material buttons (F5), and create a new material with ADD NEW in the Menu button. For clarity, change the material's name to fire.

2. Set the material's color to a glowing red and activate the Halo button, whereupon the halo material parameters will appear.

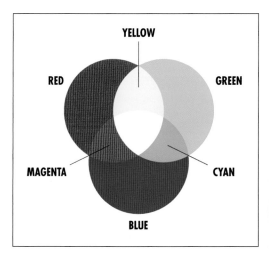

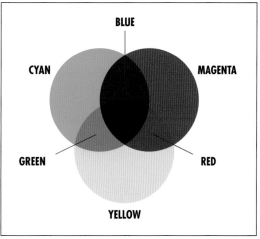

1. RGB uses the additive color model. Computer monitors and televisions use the RGB color model (Section 2.1).

2. CMYK uses the subtractive color model. The CMYK model is used primarily for printing (Section 2.1).

3. Here's a furball modeled with DupliVerts (Section 5.16). Objects like this furball, with many vertices and faces, may take a while to render.

4. The finished scene from the image texture tutorial (Section 6.4). The materials that make up the boards and legs use images as their textures (the computer monitor is not discussed in the tutorial but is in the scene on the CD).

5. Various halos created with the halo materials (Section 6.6). Note the different effects of the Rings, Lines, and Star parameters (the upper left halo has all three parameters disabled, the middle halo has only Star enabled, and the bottom right has all three enabled).

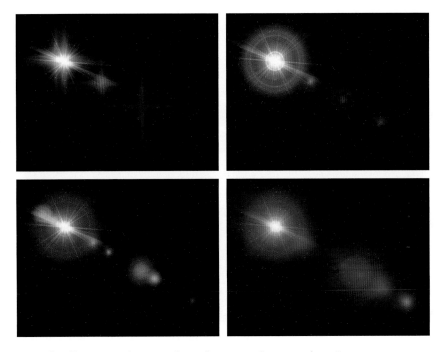

6. Use lens flares to simulate secondary reflections on the camera lens. Camera operators try to avoid them, but lens flares often make computer graphics scenes more believable (Section 6.7).

7. The transparent object on the left is rendered with reflection mapping, and the ones on the right with environment mapping (Section 6.8). Environment mapping lets you simulate reflections from other objects in a scene (notice the reflection of the floor in the right sphere).

8. Frames from the material and texture animation. The sphere is made to disappear by animating its material's alpha value (Section 8.2.5).

9. A few frames of the lattice animation of a cow going through the eye of a needle. Lattice animations are good for animating deformations in an object (Section 8.4).

10. This robot painter animation uses an IKA to animate the robot arm and a particle animation to simulate the paint. Image textures are used for the wall and floor (Section 9.1.7).

11. Some frames from the bottle animation in Section 9.2. IKAs are used to create a skeleton for the bottle, complete with feet, legs, hip, spine, and head.

12. This campfire was created with a particle system; the round glow with halos (Section 10.2).

13. A school of fish animated with a particle system; DupliVerts multiply the fish on the particle positions, and a lattice steers the school through the animation (Section 10.6).

14. A 3D function rendered in Blender with the aid of a Python script. A particle system is used to create the stream of sparks erupting from the center (Section 12.7).

15. A simple radiosity scene. Note the red reflection on the wall made by the pyramid—in a radiosity rendering objects emit light, and color their surroundings (Section 13.3).

16. A scene rendered with the radiosity method. Textures were added after the radiosity method was applied (Section 13.3).

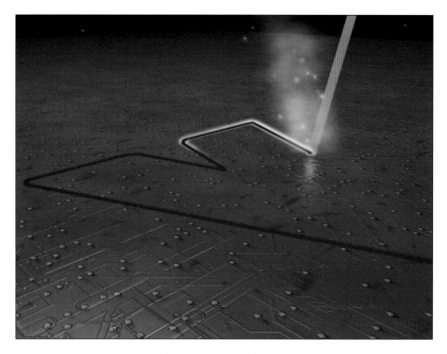

17. A frame from the laser tutorial (Chapter 14). The laser's afterglow is created by a path animation and particle system with an animated material.

18. A frame from the torpedo tutorial (Chapter 15). Even though shadows are not strong under water, the shadow here clearly adds to the scene.

A test rendering at this point should show something of the particles for the first time, which should form a kind of circular glow and go out near the top. If you render a short animation, you should be able to see if the flames move at the right speed.

3. Set the HaloSize to 0.50 to increase the flames' coherence.

4. Set Hard to about 43 and Add to 0.7 to improve the flame effect, though the flame now appears as a large, single flame—more like that of a candle.

5. With the emitter selected, change to the Texture buttons (F6) and create a new texture. Choose Clouds for the texture type.

6. Set NoiseSize to 0.900 to make each flame visible; NoiseDepth to 3 to create a finely structured flame; and raise the contrast (Contr) of the texture to about 1.500.

7. Return to the Material buttons (F5) and activate the HaloTex option.

8. Since the halo now has a violet color, a test rendering at this point should produce a red-violet flame. You can fix this by setting the texture's RGB controls (on the left in the Material buttons) to a bright yellow. A test rendering with F12 will produce a red and yellow veined flame.

9. To lengthen the flames, set the texture size controls SizeX and SizeY to 1.6 and 0.4, respectively.

10.2.3 Making the Flames Fade

We still have to address the last item on our list—making the flames fade out. To do this,

1. Set the frame slider to Frame 1, mouse over the fire's Material buttons, and press I to add a keyframe for a material animation; then choose HaSize.

2. Toggle a 3D window to an IPO window, and select the material IPO (the sphere icon); a green line should appear in the IPO window.

3. Drag the frame slider to Frame 100, change the HaloSize value in the Material buttons to 0.0, and insert a keyframe for the halo's size by pressing I and choosing HaSize. The green line in the IPO window should turn into a rounded Bezier curve representing the course of the halo's change in size.

NOTE   *In material animations for particle systems, Frames 1 through 100 always relate to the entire lifetime of the particles, regardless of how long the lifetime actually is.*

The IPO curves shown in Figure 10-6 decrease the halo's size over its lifetime until it reaches zero (the end of the particles' life). You can adjust these curves like normal Bezier curves (for example, to achieve a steep falling off at the end of the curve).

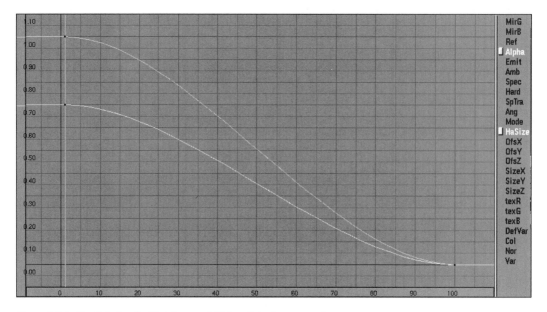

Figure 10-6: The IPOs for the HaloSize and Alpha of the fire material

Go ahead and insert two keys for the halo's alpha value (its "coverage") as you did for the halo's size. (If you're still on Frame 100, it's okay to stay there.)

1. Set the alpha value to 0 in the Material buttons.

2. Press I, and choose Alpha from the pop-up menu. A blue line should appear in the IPO window.

3. Now press SHIFT-← to go to Frame 1, set the alpha value to 1.0, and create another key by pressing I.

To refine your animation, try varying the brightness of the lights in the fire to make the fire flicker. Another especially good effect is to slightly animate the positions of three or four spotlights to project changing shadows on the ground. See Color Plate 12 for a frame from the finished animation.

10.3 Smoke

In principle, smoke is nothing more than rising gas. To produce a smokestack with a particle system that simulates smoke, bear in mind that smoke exits a chimney very fast (so set Norm high), then cools and quickly slows down (Damp). (The X and Y components of Force let you simulate wind.)

When working with smoke, use a texture (created with the paint brush or air brush in a graphics program like the GIMP or Photoshop) with an alpha channel (transparency information) instead of a lot of particles. Also, depending on the kind of smoke or steam you want to depict, Blender's procedural clouds texture produces good effects.

Load the scene chimney01.blend from the CD or model your own smoke-stack. You'll find a brick texture, including the appropriate bump map, in the texture directory on the CD. Once you have your basic scene, create a plane in the smokestack's opening for the particle emitter. Leave EditMode and add a new particle effect in the Animation buttons (F7).

Figure 10-7 shows a few suggestions for smoke particle parameters, but experiment a bit with the settings to create smoke that looks best for your animation. Various types of smoke look and act differently, so consider the real properties of the smoke you're simulating: cigarette smoke is light and transparent, while the smoke coming from a burning car is thick and black. And consider what your customer wants to see—I once had to modify the exhaust from a visualized industrial site so much that only some small white puffs came out of the chimney!

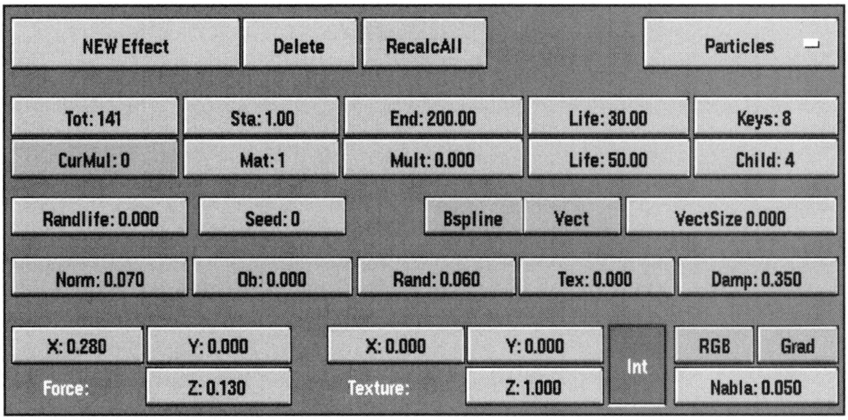

NEW Effect	Delete	RecalcAll		Particles
Tot: 141	Sta: 1.00	End: 200.00	Life: 30.00	Keys: 8
CurMul: 0	Mat: 1	Mult: 0.000	Life: 50.00	Child: 4
Randlife: 0.000	Seed: 0	Bspline	Vect	VectSize 0.000
Norm: 0.070	Ob: 0.000	Rand: 0.060	Tex: 0.000	Damp: 0.350
X: 0.280	Y: 0.000	X: 0.000	Y: 0.000	Int	RGB	Grad
Force:	Z: 0.130	Texture:	Z: 1.000		Nabla: 0.050

Figure 10-7: Parameters for the smoke particles

The smoke particles' material will play an important role in making your smoke look more realistic. Remember to limit the number of particles by setting a large HaloSize of about 0.50. You might animate the halo's size from zero at the beginning of the particles' life to the final value within a few frames to simulate the smoke expanding at the chimney's opening, and animate the alpha value over the particles' life to make the smoke slowly disappear. Figure 10-8 shows a frame from the animation.

Figure 10-8: A frame from the chimney animation

10.4   Happy Holiday: Fireworks

The characteristic feature of fireworks is that they spread out, requiring an increase in the number of particles used to depict them. First you see the rocket's trail of fire, and then it explodes into a starburst, which may then divide further or change color as it burns. The CurMul (current multiplication) particle parameter produces precisely this effect by letting a particle multiply itself into up to 600 new particles at the end of its life. These new particles can then multiply at the end of their lives, making three generations of particles possible, each of which can have a different material attached to it (see Section 6.5).

10.4.1   Setting the Scene

To begin our experiment, use the scene `particle/fireworks00.blend` on the CD or create one with stars and a black sky, so that the fireworks will show up well against the background. A city silhouette, made from simple base objects, refines the scene even further. For the city's texture, use an image map with randomly distributed yellow rectangles for the windows.

In a top view (PAD 7), create a plane for the particle emitter and name it `launching_pad`. The launching pad should, of course, lie near ground level. Rotate the emitter in the front view about 10 degrees so that the rockets launch at an angle.

10.4.2 Set the Parameters

With the emitter still active, change to the Animation buttons (F7) and add a new particle effect. Advance 50 frames in the animation so that the preview shows some particles, and then set the particle system's parameters as shown in Figure 10-9, in the order introduced below. The following list spells out the purpose of each parameter.

NEW Effect	Delete	RecalcAll		Particles
Tot: 328	Sta: 1.00	End: 100.00	Life: 30.00	Keys: 8
CurMul: 0	Mat: 1	Mult: 1.000	Life: 20.05	Child: 28
Randlife: 0.500	Seed: 0	Bspline	Vect	VectSize 0.000
Norm: 0.500	Ob: 0.000	Rand: 0.100	Tex: 0.000	Damp: 0.000

				Int	
X: 0.000	Y: 0.000	X: 0.000	Y: 0.000		RGB / Grad
Force:	Z: −0.300	Texture:	Z: 1.000		Nabla: 0.050

Figure 10-9: The parameters for fireworks particles

Tot Sets the total number of particles, including the products of the original particle's division.

Norm Determines the strength of the particles' acceleration from the emitter. Since the particles should climb high into the sky, use a high value.

Life Use the Life button in the second row to determine how high the particles will climb before they multiply (that is, before the rocket explodes).

Force Z Defines the strength of the gravitation that pulls the particles back to earth.

Mult Determines the percentage of particles that will multiply themselves at the end of their lives. A value of 1.0 makes every rocket explode; 0.5 would make 50 percent of them duds.

Child Determines the number of children each parent divides into.

Life Use the Life button in the third row (the same line with the green CurMul button) to indicate how long the new generation of particles exists.

Rand Gives the particles different flight paths. When you set this to 0.1 or higher, you should see a fireworks effect in an animation preview.

10.4.3 Add a Material

Without a material the particles will not be rendered, so let's add one now.

Select the particle emitter and change to the Material buttons (F5), where you'll create a new material via the Menu button. Activate the Halo button to create a halo material.

The following is an overview of the material parameters (see Figure 10-10).

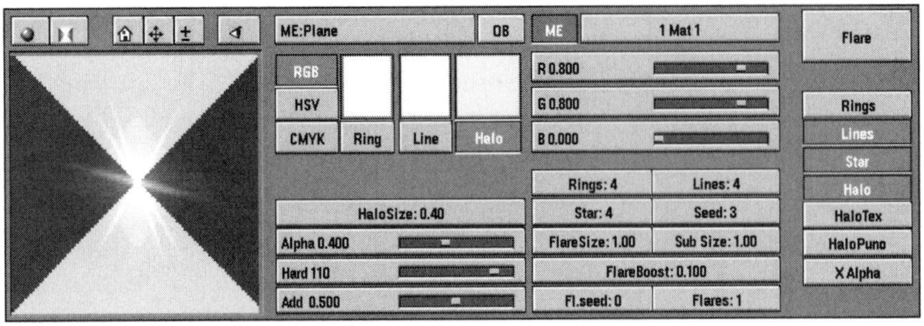

Figure 10-10: Parameters for the fireworks material

RGB	Defines the halo color; colors for rings and lines are defined separately.
HaloSize	Scales the size of your halo to fit your scene. In the example scene, 0.4 works well.
Alpha	Defines the halo's transparency.
Hard	Makes the halos fade toward their edges; in fact, they dissolve into the environment.
Add	Makes halos additive so that when they overlap they intensify and produce a bright "glow"; lower values weaken this effect. Try 0.0 for smoke or 0.8 for plasma.
Lines	Use this setting to give halos rays protruding from their centers. You can also use this setting to make the halos look more like sparks.
Star	Makes halos look like stars.

10.4.4 Keep the Action Going

In many fireworks displays, rockets are continually fired and their starbursts change colors or explode again. You can easily create color changes with a material animation (as described in Section 10.2), and you can produce the additional explosions with CurMul.

To get the additional explosions, select the particle emitter and change to the Animation buttons (F7). Change the CurMul value to 1 so that the settings in the buttons to the right will be applied to the second multiplication of particles (Blender begins counting with 0 here). Adjust the other parameters as follows:

Mat	Set to 2 since the new generation of particles will have a different material.
Mult	Set this to 0.5 so that every other particle will produce a new generation of particles.
Life	Determines the life span of the new generation of particles; I set it to 10.

Child	Set to 4 in the example scene, so that four new particles will come from each old one.
Tot	Set to 500 to limit the total number of particles in the scene at any time. Thus, the disappearance of particles produces more rockets, but the rate at which new particles are produced is governed by this total.

10.4.5 Creating Multiple Materials

If you now preview or render the animation, you'll see only the particles multiply—the material remains as defined at the beginning. To fix this, we'll create multiple materials for the particle system, using the procedure described in Section 6.5. (See that section if the following explanation is unclear.)

Creating multiple materials

1. Select the emitter and change to the Edit buttons (F9).

2. Create a new material index by choosing New in the material indices. The display 2 Mat: 2 now appears in the button under the material name ("fireworks" in this example).

Material index

3. Change to the Material buttons (F5). The material name field should now be highlighted blue and have a 2 next to it. The blue indicates that the material is being used multiple times, and the number indicates the number of times it is used. Click the 2 and answer the dialog positively. You have now created a copy of the material, which is automatically named fireworks.001.

   You can now change the color (to violet, for example). A rendering should show that the second generation of particles uses the second material.

10.5 Moving Emitters

If you're animating a rocket airplane and want to create a vapor trail for your creation (Figure 10-11), you'll need to use a *moving emitter* (an emitter that has been animated to rotate or move through a scene). The Ob parameter determines how strongly a moving emitter influences the particles (particles receive the velocity and rotation of their parent objects).

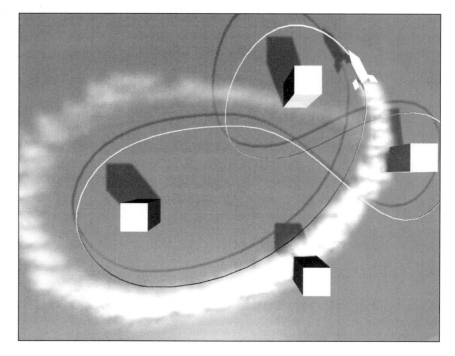

Figure 10-11: Creating a vapor trail to make the rocket's path clearer

To observe Ob's effect, create a plane in a top view and make it rotate with a keyframe animation. Now if you turn the plane into a particle emitter, thus creating a moving emitter, Ob will determine how strongly the rotation hurls the particles away. Give Norm a small value and the two parameters produce a lawn sprinkler.

10.5.1 Creating a Vapor Trail

Let's experiment by using a moving emitter to create a rocket's vapor trail. To begin, load the scene we used in Section 8.3.3 (`particle_rocket00.blend`) to animate a rocket along a path.

1. Construct a plane on the rocket's end to serve as the particle emitter.

2. The plane you've created will probably be much too large and positioned incorrectly. Press TAB to leave EditMode and adjust the plane's size and position so that it is at the end of the rocket.

3. Hold SHIFT and select the plane and rocket, then make the rocket the parent of the emitter with CTRL-P. Confirm that the emitter now follows the rocket by playing the animation in a 3D window with ALT-A.

4. Select the emitter plane and use the Animation buttons (F7) to assign a particle effect to it. A trail of particles should immediately appear on the rocket's flight path.

The Norm, Ob, and Damp parameters are the most important parameters for the vapor trail. Norm determines how fast the particles are ejected out of the emitter; if you raise its value and begin to see strange effects, the emitter plane is probably facing in the wrong direction and is hurling the particles in the direction of the rocket. Real vapor trails quickly lose velocity, so set Damp high to create this effect.

In the animation we just created, the effect Ob has on the particles is opposed to the particle movements created by Norm; the effect manifests itself especially on the curves where the particles are hurled outward (the Ob setting makes the particles follow the emitter while the Norm setting hurls them out of the emitter). This effect would also be good for the dirt a car throws up when driving in the sand.

If the particle motion does not appear correct, raising the Keys value will let you calculate the particles' movement more precisely.

10.6 Mass Movement: A School of Fish

Animating a big swarm of uniform objects like the school of fish shown in Color Plate 13 can require a lot of manual work if you need to model each object precisely. Fortunately, swarms are often in the background and are only there to liven up the scene, so precise modeling usually isn't necessary.

Blender's particle systems let you create a swarm effect, and lattices can be used to influence the particles so that the swarms can curve, split, and merge. But your swarms will have limitations: you can't avoid overlapping individual objects nor can you animate an individual object—all objects are copies of the main object.

Load the scene fish_school00.blend from the CD. I created the fish by tracing an image loaded into the background of the scene with Bezier curves and then extruding it with Ext1. This simple way of creating objects works well when the camera doesn't show the object too closely and when the fish is not seen head on. The fish image also serves as the color texture for the fish. Fog and some blue lamps simulate an underwater atmosphere. Now let's create our school of fish.

1. Create a plane in the side view, and, without leaving EditMode, divide it twice with Subdivide (in the Edit buttons, F9).

2. Staying in EditMode, use the Hash function to make sure the sequence of vertices is calculated randomly. Since the particles are created on the vertices, Hash ensures that they don't all line up.

3. Leave EditMode for the emitter and create a particle effect in the Animation buttons (F7). Set the parameters as shown in Figure 10-12, paying special attention to the following parameters:

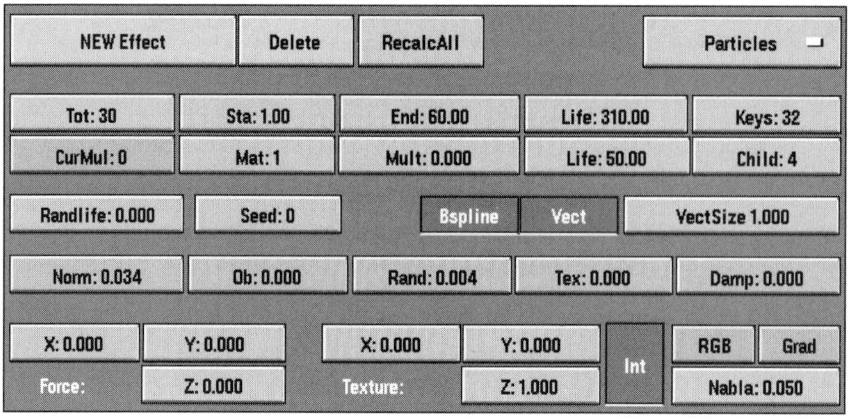

Figure 10-12: The swarm particle parameters

Tot Sets the number of fish (30 in our example). If you use a lot of particles, you run the risk of overlapping particle objects.

End Determines when the particle emission ends. The school of fish will be more or less thick depending on how long the particles are emitted.

Life Use higher values here to make sure the fish won't just disappear when the particle life span ends.

Keys Set this to the maximum value of 32 to produce very fluid movements.

Vect Use this to ensure that particle rotations are transferred to the fish so that the fish are aligned in the direction of movement.

Norm Set this to a low value so that the fish do not move too fast.

Rand Set this to a low value so the movements are not too orderly.

4. Now place the emitter (the plane created in Step 1) at the far end of the lattice so that the particle swarm slowly moves through the frame.

5. To assign the particle system to the fish, select the fish and then the particle emitter and press CTRL-P to make the emitter the parent object.

6. Select the emitter alone and switch to the Animation buttons (F7).

7. Select the DupliVerts button in the left of the window, and an image of the fish should promptly appear at every particle position. The fish may now be swimming on their sides. To correct this, rotate the emitter or clear the rotation of the original fish by pressing ALT-R.

8. Push the original fish out of the camera's field of vision—it does not move with the school, and you don't want it just sitting there.

10.6.1 *Steering the School with a Lattice*

To steer the school of fish, we'll use a lattice object, since otherwise only the Force parameter can divert the school a bit.

1. In the front view, create a lattice and insert (in the Edit buttons, F9) additional segments in the U direction by repeatedly clicking the U button until the lattice is the desired length.

2. Scale the lattice until it encloses the school of fish like a tube, and place the left end over the particle emitter.

3. Now select the emitter and then the lattice and make the lattice the parent object by pressing CTRL-P.

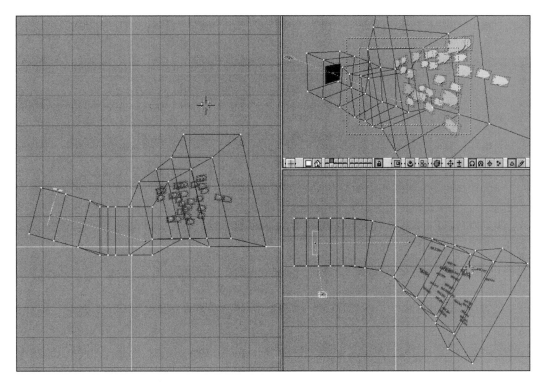

Figure 10-13: The lattice for steering the school of fish

You should now be able to steer the school by deforming the lattice. Enlarging parts of the lattice in EditMode will widen the school when it crosses this spot; decreasing the lattice size has the opposite effect. You can make the school curve by rotating individual lattice segments.

11

THE FINAL CUT:
POSTPRODUCTION

Once you've modeled and animated your scenes (and spent dozens of hours in the process), you're ready to put everything together to make your final product. The process of putting scenes together (*editing*, that is, combining takes from different camera angles or several animations) and polishing the resulting sequence is called *postproduction*. Postproduction also includes adding titles, inserting fades and dissolves from scene to scene, adding other special effects like fades to color, and combining live action video with computer animation (for example, adding titles to a movie of your vacation or visualizing how a building you're designing will fit into the landscape). Postproduction is an extremely important phase in filmmaking: it's where the raw material (footage, animations, 3D graphics) gets massaged into a tight, unified whole.

This tutorial covers the most important ways to use Blender's postproduction tool, the *Sequence Editor*, to apply postproduction effects. (Unfortunately, Blender does not yet let you edit sound or music in the Sequence Editor; if it did, you'd be able to use the program to make a completely computer-generated film.)

NOTE *Working with video images requires a lot of memory and a fast computer, and playing these images in real time is possible only with special hardware or in a low resolution (such as AVI). On some SGI computers, the finished SGI movies can be output via Cosmo hardware in video quality.*

11.1 The Sequence Editor

To begin, call up the Sequence Editor by turning a window into a Sequence window. (Because the Sequence Editor takes up so much space, create a new screen for working with sequences and save it in your default scene, .B.blend.)

Figure 11-1 shows a typical screen for working with the Sequence Editor. Note that the Sequence Editor is larger than all but the often-used Buttons window (in the lower part of the screen). We limit the 3D windows to an IPO window, a camera view, and an orthogonal view. The second Sequence window at the upper right has been toggled with the Image window icon to show the sequence's images.

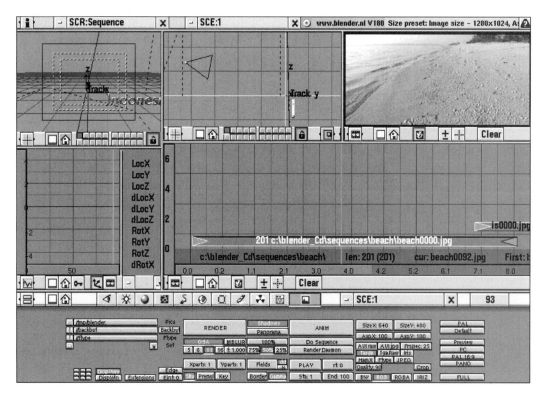

Figure 11-1: The Sequence Editor screen

The sequences directory on the CD contains some sequences from a travel and documentary film about Indonesia, courtesy of Imago Viva (http://www. imago-viva.de/). (You may use these sequences for noncommercial projects.) The images are in individually numbered frames, and most of the resolutions have been lowered to 320x240 pixels to limit the amount of data and processing time. (The scenes in the reef/ directory are in PAL resolution and will be used in the Chapter 15 torpedo tutorial.)

Let's create a small vacation movie using the available sequences, give it a title, and add fade-ins and fade-outs.

11.2 Placing the First Scene

1. If you've made your own default scene, reset Blender by pressing CTRL-X and create a new screen with the SCR option in the Menu button, dividing it like the screen in Figure 11-1. This screen will be the basis for your work with sequences. Or use the scene in postproduction/Indonesia00.blend.

2. Switch to the Sequence screen with the SCR option in the Menu button.

3. Move the mouse cursor over the big Sequence window and press SHIFT-A • Images to tell Blender you want to insert an image sequence. The File window appears.

4. Choose the sequences/beach/ directory in the File window. The images beach0000.jpg through beach0200.jpg should be listed.

5. Press A to select all the images. If a .Bpip file appears on the list, deselect it with a right-click; this image overview file will put a black frame at the beginning of the scene.

NOTE *In new Blender versions these dot files can be blanked by activating the ghost icon in the File window.*

6. Press ENTER to transfer the selected images to the sequencer. The view should change back to the Sequence window and the scene (the series of beach images) should now be attached to the mouse pointer and can be moved to the beginning of the sequence (Frame 1).

7. Translate the scene in the lower strip until the triangle at the beginning of the scene shows a 1, and then left-click. You have now placed the first scene.

NOTE *When the scene moves over the green line in the Sequence window (indicating the frame slider's current position) and the image icon is activated, the corresponding image of the sequence is displayed.*

The number at the bottom of the Sequence window shows the animation's length in seconds. The first scene goes from zero to eight seconds; this time axis depends on the Frs/Sec (frames per second) setting in the Display buttons. The standard setting is 25, which means, in the case of our example scene with 200 frames, our animation is 8 seconds long (200 frames per second divided by 25 frames). The vertical axis of the Sequence window is numbered with channels or strips.

11.2.1 Previewing the Scene

A left-click in the Sequence window places the green line, and lets you view the scene's individual images. You can set the scene's resolution in the Display buttons (F10), and the scene will then be displayed in the preview window at the chosen resolution. If the resolution is low enough, you should be able to play the animation in the preview window with ALT-A to see how the sequence looks. (If you have a lot of RAM, Blender will store the images in memory and display the animation faster if you play it again.) And, as in all windows, you can translate or zoom in or out on the contents of the Sequence window.

11.3   Dissolves: Adding the Second Scene

We'll now load a second scene and define a dissolve between the two scenes.

1. Insert another scene with SHIFT-A • Images and choose the scene in the sequences/rice folder.

2. Translate this new scene on the second strip until it slightly overlaps the first scene and fix its position with a left-click. (The exact value of the overlap is not important just yet.)

11.3.1   Cuts

Play the sequence with ALT-A in the preview window. You should see that Blender basically makes a hard cut between overlapping scenes or scenes that immediately follow each other. Hard cuts are the most commonly used transitions between scenes. (The next time you watch a film or TV show, note how often hard cuts are used.)

11.3.2   Soft Dissolves

Depending on a scene and the film's dynamics, soft dissolves may be used between scenes, or hard cuts may be "blunted" with a two- or three-frame dissolve. Use GammaCross to define a soft dissolve.

1. Select the scene in Strip 1 and then, holding SHIFT, select the scene in Strip 2.

2. Press SHIFT-A and choose GammaCross to insert a dissolve; place it on the third strip with a left-click. The dissolve is only as long as the overlap of both scenes and can only be translated vertically (see Figure 11-2).

3. With the left mouse button, place the green line at different spots on the red GammaCross effect. Depending on the position, you'll see a more or less intense dissolve effect between the scenes.

4. Zoom in on the Sequence window by pressing the PAD + key (or CTRL-left-click and move the mouse to the right) until you can read all of the text on the red effect strip. (If the effect ends up outside the frame, translate the view by holding the middle mouse button.)

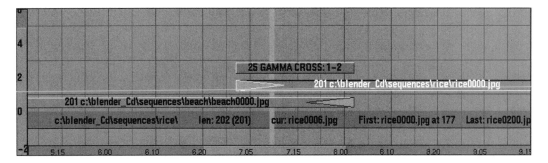

Figure 11-2: Using GammaCross to create a dissolve between two scenes

GammaCross

The text in the GammaCross effect provides some important information on the type of dissolve. At the left is the effect's length, in frames, and its name. The numbers following the colon indicate which strips the effect corresponds to. (You should see "1-2" in our example, which means that we are dissolving from Strip 1 to Strip 2.) The dissolve should come to 25 frames, or one second in PAL.

Right-click the scene in Strip 2 to select it and switch to translation mode by pressing G. If you translate the scene horizontally, you should see the effect's length automatically adjust to the scenes' overlap, and then be redisplayed. If you translate the scene vertically, the information after the colon should be adjusted. Set the overlap so that the effect's length is 25 frames.

11.3.3 Other Sequence Editing Possibilities

Besides translation, there are a whole bunch of editing possibilities for sequences, the most important of which are called up with the C key. If you press C when a scene is selected and confirm the dialog, you can replace the scene with new images. If you press C when over an effect (like the GammaCross we defined), a menu similar to the one for SHIFT-A appears with these options:

Change effect
Switch a-b
Switch b-c
Plugin
Recalculate
Cross
GammaCross
Add
Sub
Mul
AlphaOver
AlphaUnder
AlphaOverdrop

Sequence effects

Switch a-b — Changes the effect's strip sequence. In our example above, the dissolve would be reversed.

Switch b-c — Changes Strips 2 and 3 for effects that have three strips.

Plugin — Loads a sequence plug-in that enlarges the effect palette (see Section B.5).

Recalculate — Recalculates the effect.

Cross — Creates a fluid transition between two scenes.

GammaCross — Creates a dissolve between two scenes that takes the scenes' brightness into account to produce soft transitions.

Add — Adds two scenes according to their brightness.

Sub — Subtracts two scenes according to their brightness.

Mul — Multiplies two scenes according to their brightness.

AlphaOver — Places scene A over scene B, taking their transparency information (Alpha channel) into account.

AlphaUnder	Places scene A under scene B, taking their transparency information into account.
AlphaOverdrop	Like AlphaOver except that a shadow is also added.

11.4 Integrating a 3D Title

Unlike conventional title generators, Blender puts all of its animation and effect features at your disposal for title creation, letting you make incredibly original titles. (Be sure when creating titles, though, that in each case your title is legible and harmonizes with your film's content.)

Let's create 3D text for our title and run it along the bottom edge of the screen.

1. Switch from SCR:Sequence to SCR:3D with the Menu button to move the Sequence window out of your way. To better judge the placement of the title in the camera view, add a still frame from the beach animation to the view.

2. Mouse over the camera view and press SHIFT-F7, then select a background image for the camera view from the Buttons window that appears.

3. Activate BackGroundPic (see Figure 11-3) and click Load; the File window should appear so that you can choose an image from the beach sequence.

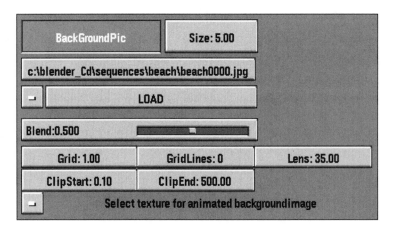

Figure 11-3: Defining a background picture for the camera view

4. Switch back to the camera view (SHIFT-F5) and the still frame should be blended into the background.

> **NOTE** *You can easily activate or deactivate the background picture with the image icon in the camera view's button header.*

5. Create a text with Space • Add • Text and edit it into your title (see Section 5.17).

6. Place the title in the camera view on the lower edge of the screen (see Figure 11-4) and scale it to the desired size. (Keep in mind that the outer broken line in the camera view is the frame's outer border. If the animation is intended for video, place the text within the inner broken line so that it will be completely visible on a television set.)

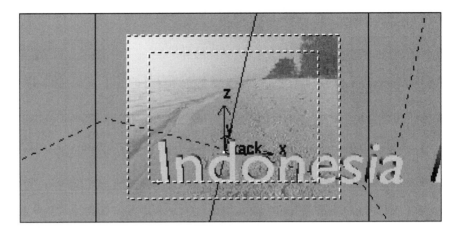

Figure 11-4: The title in the camera view

7. Remove any floor from the scene that would otherwise be rendered, and delete any defined worlds in the World buttons (F8); the fog settings would be especially bothersome here.

8. Switch to the Animation buttons (F7) and set the animation length to 100 frames by adjusting End.

9. Drag the frame slider to Frame 1 and move the text to the right, out of the camera view. Add a location key with I • Loc.

10. Advance to Frame 100, move the text out of the frame to the left, and add a second location keyframe. You can now judge the success of the animation by pressing ALT-A; the text should move through the frame along its bottom edge. Left-clicking lets you place the green line in the Sequence window so you can check the animation frame by frame.

11. Once you've created the animation, switch to the Sequence screen by clicking the SCR: button. Select the first scene (the beach, Strip 1) with the right mouse button and press PAD . (the period key on the numerical keypad) to have the scene take up the entire Sequence window.

12. With the mouse pointer in the Sequence window, press SHIFT-A and choose Scene from the menu. A selection of scenes to insert appears, which shows only one scene in this case. Left-click the 1 or press ENTER to confirm the selection, use the mouse to place the scene around Frame 50 in the second strip (the frame number is displayed in the left of the new film strip), and then left-click to set the scene (see Figure 11-5).

Figure 11-5: A single rendered frame from the title animation

NOTE *If the scene extends over the green line, Blender immediately renders the relevant images, which, depending on your computer's speed, may cause a delay. For this reason, it's a good idea to set the frame slider to Frame 1 with SHIFT-← or disable the sequence image preview by pressing the Image icon. If you inadvertently misplaced the scene, select it with the right mouse button and translate it with G.*

13. Select the beach film segment in Strip 1 and then, holding SHIFT, select the scene you just added.

14. Add the AlphaOver effect by pressing SHIFT-A and place it in Strip 3 with a left mouse click.

To render an animation of the sequence, activate the blue Do Sequence button in the Display buttons (F10) and adjust the Sta and End values to correspond to the entire sequence length. Use the resolution settings to define an appropriate resolution; if set higher (or lower) than the sequence's images, Blender will scale it accordingly. (It's especially important to enable oversampling with OSA so that this scaling does not generate any ugly, coarse pixels or aliasing.)

You can now supply the title with a material or try to have it appear from afar. To do the latter, define a world with a completely black background color and have the title appear out of the black fog, resulting in a soft fade-in.

11.4.1 Spiffing Up the Scene with Shadows and Other 3D Objects

You can have the title cast shadows on a beach by using a plane that catches shadows but is otherwise not rendered. The scene Indonesia08.blend on the CD is such a scene. Chapter 15 uses similar effects to combine computer graphics with live action. Try your hand at putting a deck chair on the beach (see Figure 11-6)!

Figure 11-6: Combination of a title and the integration of 3D objects in a real-life scene

Adding a deck chair highlights a general problem: The beach scene was recorded without a tripod and therefore shakes a bit, but an added computer graphic of a deck chair stays completely still—the eye immediately realizes that it doesn't belong in the scene. It's even harder to deceive the eye if you're trying to integrate 3D objects into a scene with camera movements. One method for overcoming this problem is to manually set the 3D objects at fixed points in the video image, which, depending on how exact you want it, has to be redone in each frame. This requires a *lot* of work—the only reasonable way to get around this problem is to use a good tripod when capturing your images. In particular, rotations along the camera's longitudinal axis are almost impossible to correct by hand.

11.5 Effects and Sequence Plug-ins

The Sequence editor offers a number of additional effects, some of which result from combining existing effects. In addition, there are many sequence plug-ins for realizing different special effects.

As of Blender 1.68, Blender's plug-in interface has been free, so some programmers will surely develop new plug-ins. (Since the necessary C compiler is free on the free Unix-like platforms, I expect a lot to happen in this area.) Section B.5 introduces some of the plug-ins already available.

One important effect is fading in or out of scenes, either to or from black or a color (as shown in Figure 11-7). While there is as yet no such direct effect available, it's easy to create one using a normal dissolve and an individual image that is imported to the desired fade length.

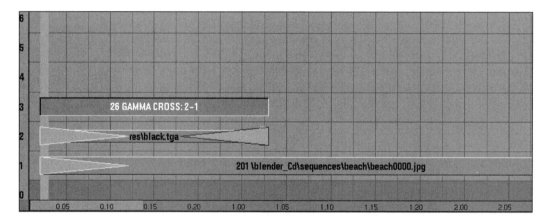

Figure 11-7: A sequence fading in an animation from black

Let's use the beach scene to practice fading in from black:

1. Position the mouse cursor over the Sequence window, press SHIFT-A, and select Images from the menu.

2. In the File window, select black.tga from the texture directory on the CD. Place the scene at the beginning of the beach scene.

> **NOTE** *Individual imported images are always 50 frames long in the Sequence Editor by default. A new scene thus goes from Frame 1 to Frame 50.*

3. Right-click the triangle at the right of the imported scene to select the triangle, then press G and translate the scene's end to the left until the scene is 25 frames long.

4. Select the black frame scene with a right-click and then, holding SHIFT, select the beach scene. Press SHIFT-A and select GammaCross, then place the effect that appears in Strip 3. The dissolve should now go from Strip 2 (the black frame) to Strip 1 (the beach scene).

5. Follow the same procedure to create a fade-out at the end of the entire sequence, but reverse the order of the strips. Again, the effect strip shows the length of the effect, its name, and the strips being used.

You can also use differently colored frames to make fade-ins, fade-outs, and dissolves between scenes. Dissolves to white between scenes have become especially popular lately.

12

PYTHON TUTORIALS

In this chapter I'll describe some applications of Python—a portable, interpretive, object-oriented scripting language developed by Guido van Rossum (who still leads its development). This is by no means an exhaustive tutorial on programming with Python, and it assumes that you have some programming experience.

NOTE *For more information on Python, visit the official site at http://www.python.org/, where you'll find many Python tutorials and complete documentation.*

Python has been Blender's embedded programming language since version 1.68, and, along with all the standard libraries, is free for all platforms and available as source code. Both Blender and Python are object-oriented, so the two fit very well together—and Python's integration with Blender keeps improving, keeping pace with Blender's own incredibly fast progress. (See http://www.blender.nl/blender/index.php for current developments.)

I hope this chapter's sample Python scripts will give you a sense of how Python works with Blender, and that they will be of use to you in your own creations. Scripts are always useful in automating a function that repeatedly comes up or in creating a function that's not yet available in Blender.

12.1   What You Need to Begin

For Python to work correctly within Blender, you'll need a working Python installation. The Python package is certainly on the installation CDs of the free Unix clones and should be installed with the distribution's appropriate package manager.

Blender provides a small Python library for Windows users, but it has only the modules that are absolutely necessary. It lacks, for example, the module for generating random numbers, which is very important for scripts later in this chapter. If you're a Windows user, take a look at Appendix E, Section E.2.3, and follow the instructions for installing Python (which is on the book's CD) under Windows. The short documentation in Appendix D lists the Blender module's current Python functions. This overview was created with a Python script that called up the Blender module documentation texts and output them as HMTL pages. The Blender scene for creating such HTML documents is on the CD under Python/docstrings.blend.

12.2   Writing Scripts

When programming with Python from within Blender, start Blender from the command line—any output from your Python script (including errors) will be displayed in this window. If you're using Microsoft Windows, start Blender as normal and a DOS window will come up automatically.

Blender's simple text editor (the Text window—see Section 12.3) should be sufficient for writing smaller scripts. For more complex scripts, use a more flexible external editor. You can write scripts with the text editor of your choice, as long as it can save files as ASCII text. These scripts can then be loaded in Blender. Many editors provide special capabilities such as coloring key words or automatic indenting (the latter especially useful in the case of Python) to help you with your work on source programs.

NOTE   *It's very important to indent precisely when writing Python scripts because logical blocks in the Python language (parts of Python's syntax that belong together) are formed by indenting, not with parentheses or brackets as in many other languages. In practice, you should use TAB for indenting (many external editors will support the use of TAB).*

12.3   The Text Window

Blender's Text window (Figure 12-1) is a simple text editor with basic functions for entering text (for example, a script or a description of changes to a scene). The Icon Slider in the button header of the Text window lets you toggle between window types. The icon next to the Icon Slider switches to a view that fills the whole screen.

The Menu button lets you select from already available text files, and rename, add new (ADD NEW), load (OPEN NEW), and delete text files. To the right of the Menu button you can select the font for the text.

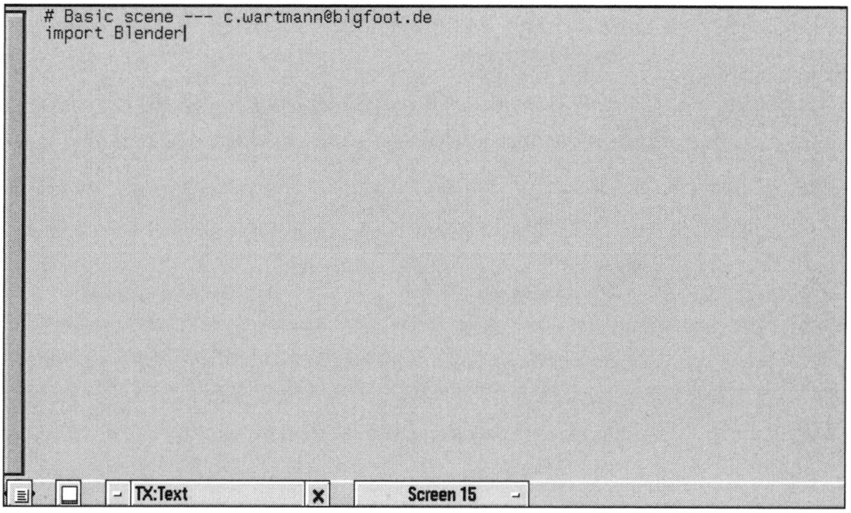

```
# Basic scene --- c.wartmann@bigfoot.de
import Blender|
```

```
[≡]  [▢]  [-]  TX:Text        [x]        Screen 15    [-]
```

Figure 12-1: Blender's text editor

Clicking and dragging with the left mouse button selects an area of text, which can then be cut or copied via the keyboard. Here are the important keyboard commands for the Text window:

ALT-C	Copies the selected text to the clipboard
ALT-X	Cuts the text and stores it on the clipboard
ALT-V	Pastes the text from the clipboard
ALT-S	Saves the text as a text file (calls up a File window)
ALT-O	Loads a text file (calls up a File window)
SHIFT-ALT-F	Calls up the Text window's file menu
ALT-J	Calls up a Number button in which you can enter a line number for the mouse cursor to jump to
ALT-P	Executes the text as a Python script
ALT-U	Undoes the last action in the Text window (unlimited undo)
ALT-R	Redoes the last undo
ALT-A	Selects the entire text

NOTE *When you're writing your script or looking for errors, it's especially bothersome to have to reload your script after each change. In future Blender versions, a new feature will allow you to load an external script at run time. This feature will also function with relative path-names so that the scripts can be put in the same directory as the Blender files. Currently, though, it's possible to integrate a Python script at the script's run time with this call:*

```
execfile("<path><file.py>")
```

The disadvantage to this type of call is that you have to give the absolute path name for the script because the information for the current directory is not available.

12.4   Your First Python Script: Keeping an Object Above a Floor

Let's get started with a script that will keep an object above a floor—that is, makes sure that it will not penetrate your scene's floor.

1. Change the Blender window to a Text window with SHIFT-F11 or select the Text window with the Icon Slider for the window type.

2. Click and hold the Menu button in the footer of the Text window and select ADD NEW to create new text.

3. Rename the text "OnGround" by clicking the TX:Text field and typing OnGround as a name for the text.

4. Enter the following script (without the line numbers, which are only for reference).

NOTE   *Lines 1 through 3 with the pound (#) signs are comment lines added to explain the script. Although these lines are not necessary to the code, it's a good idea to add them— they make it easier to understand the script and will serve as reminders later.*

```
1 # Keeps objects above the floor!
2 # Script from
3 # http://www.blender.nl/complete/scripting.html
4
5 import Blender
6
7 if (Blender.bylink):
8     obj = Blender.link
9     if (obj.LocZ <0.0): obj.LocZ = 0.0
```

Now let's test the script.

Once you have correctly entered the script, change to the Script buttons and follow these steps:

1. Create an object in a 3D window (a sphere or even an empty object).

2. Select the icon for linking scripts to objects (in the Script buttons). This will bring up two new Script buttons.

3. Click the New button on the left to attach a new script to the selected object.

4. In the empty button that appears, enter the name of the script you just edited. (Remember to use correct capitalization.)

5. Now select the object with the linked script and move it with G.

If the script is working properly, you should notice that it won't let you move the object below the floor since z=0.0. If the script doesn't work, look for error messages like the following in Blender's start-up window:

```
File "<string>", line 8
    obj = Blender.link
        *
SyntaxError: invalid syntax
SystemError: bad argument to internal function
```

Compare your script again with the one in the book. There's a good chance the error is near whatever line number is mentioned at the beginning of the message—which is line 8 in this case. The error described here resulted from not indenting the eighth line.

12.4.1 How It Works

Here's how this script works.

- Line 5 contains one of the most important Python (and Blender) statements—the import statement—which integrates a module into Python that, like a library, makes specific information and routines available. Line 5 imports the Blender module, which defines the interface between Python and Blender.

- Line 7 begins an *if block*, or a query as to whether a certain condition has been fulfilled. The Blender module imported earlier is used here for the first time. The Blender.bylink variable is true when the script is linked to an object. With this if construction, the script is executed only when it's linked to an object. Since the rest of the lines are all indented, this condition holds for the rest of the script.

- Line 8 assigns the value link from the Blender module to the variable obj. Blender.link references the object assigned to the script.

- After the obj variable tells the script which object to work with, the if statement in Line 9 tests if the object's z-position (obj.LocZ) is smaller than zero (<0.0). If it is, the statement after the colon will be executed and the object position will be set to zero (obj.LocZ = 0.0).

NOTE *Try adding* print obj *to the script after Line 9 (indented like Line 9). If you now call the script in the start-up window, it will output the object's name followed by its coordinates. Comment the line out again by putting a pound sign (#) before the line.*

Even this tiny script can come in handy, as it lets you prevent an object from leaving a certain area. With a somewhat more refined script, you could make a ball bounce off the floor or prevent a character's foot from penetrating the ground in an animation.

12.5 A Second Script Example: Turbulence

The following sample script (on the CD under python/turbulence.blend) simulates the vibrations or turbulence of an aborted airplane landing, and can also be used to simulate the vibrations of a shock wave. It works by increasing the turbulence as the object with the linked script gets closer to a defined object.

When assigned to an object, the script calculates the turbulence when the object approaches <object_name>.turb, thus the turbulence depends on the scaling of <object_name>.turb.

This script improves over a normal keyframe animation because the parameters can be changed quickly and the effect can be quickly assigned to different objects.

```
1  # Turbulence.py, 08/99, mailto:C.Wartmann@bigfoot.de
2
3  import Blender
4  import whrandom
5  import math
6
7  link=Blender.link
8  turb=Blender.Object.Get(link.name+".turb")
9
10 t=Blender.Get(Blender.Const.CURTIME)
11 if t==1:
12    try:                    #try to set ta[name]
13      ta[link.name]=0.0
14    except :                # we have to init ta
15      ta={}
16      ta[link.name]=0.0
17
18
19 dt = t-ta[link.name] # change in time
20 ta[link.name]=t # store old time
21
22 if (Blender.bylink):
23   if dt<>0: # execute only if time has changed
24     dx=link.LocX-turb.LocX # difference Obj/Turb
25     dy=link.LocY-turb.LocY
26     dz=link.LocZ-turb.LocZ
27     r=math.sqrt(dx**2 + dy**2 + dz**2)
28     link.dLocX=whrandom.random()*turb.SizeX/r #+ random
29     link.dLocY=whrandom.random()*turb.SizeY/r
30     link.dLocZ=whrandom.random()*turb.SizeZ/r
```

12.5.1 How It Works

The beginning of this script imports modules, the first of which is the `Blender` module. The `whrandom` module provides the random number generator, and the `math` module supplies the square root function.

- Line 7 loads the variable `link` with a reference to the linked object and Line 8 looks for an object with the base name of the linked object and `.turb` on the end of its name. The construction `link.name` refers to "the 'name' property of the object 'link.'" (An example of Python's object-orientation.)

- Line 10 returns the animation's current time—in simple terms, the position of the frame slider. (If you use field rendering or motion blur, you may get a nonwhole number here.)

- Lines 11 through 16 initialize the variable `ta` in the first frame of the animation. If `ta` does not yet exist, an exception is triggered (`except:`) that initializes `ta`. Because `ta` is a global variable, a second script would overwrite this variable and produce invalid results. Thus, the `ta` value is referenced with the name of the object: `ta[link.name]` and this variable is unique for the object that the script is linked to since Blender cannot have two objects with the same name.

- Lines 19 and 20 calculate the time since the script was last run and store this value in `dt`. The old time value `t` is stored in `ta[link.name]` for use the next time the script is run.

- Lines 22 and 23 ensure that the script is executed only when it's linked to an object (`Blender.bylink`) and time has elapsed (`dt` does not equal zero). This ensures that the script executes the rendering only once, when playing or rendering an animation, which is especially important when making timing calculations.

> **NOTE** *If a scene script (in the right-hand side of Script window) is supplied, these measures are not necessary since a scene script is called only once per frame. However, in this case we would need to know which object the script is linked to.*

- At Line 24 and following, the script finally performs its task. The difference in the objects' coordinates is calculated and Line 27 uses this difference to calculate the distance between the objects.

- Lines 28 through 30 then displace the object a small random distance using the object's relative position (`dLoc`), rather than its absolute coordinates.

The intensity of the turbulence depends on a randomization factor (`random.random()`), the size of the turbulence object (`turb.Size`), and, of course, the distance (`r`) from the turbulence object.

12.6 Creating New Objects with Python: A 3D Function Plotter

Blender can use Python scripts to create new objects and manipulate existing ones. The next script is a small 3D function plotter. It creates a divided plane (a kind of grid) on the xy plane and uses a function of (x,y) to determine its height (z coordinate).

You'll find this file on the CD (python/function.py).

To begin, load the file, put the mouse cursor in the Text window, and call up the function with ALT-P to make it draw. Use Set Smooth in the Edit buttons (F9) to smooth the result. You may have to translate or scale the object to get a view of it in its entirety, giving you something that looks like Figure 12-2.

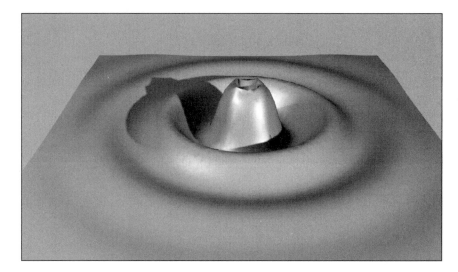

Figure 12-2: Blender as a 3D function plotter

```
1   # Function_plotter.py, Oktober 1999
2   # C.Wartmann@bigfoot.de
3
4   import Blender
5
6   from Blender import NMesh,Object
7   from Blender.NMesh import Col
8   from math import sin,cos,sqrt,exp
9
10  xw=0.5
11  yw=0.5
12  xmax=36 #x resolution
13  ymax=36 #y resolution
14
```

```
15 me2= NMesh.GetRaw()
16
17 # create the vertices
18 for y in range(0,ymax):
19      for x in range(0,xmax):
20              r=sqrt((x-xmax/2)**2+(y-ymax/2)**2)
21              z=sin(r*xw)*cos(r*yw)*exp(-r/5)*10
22              v=NMesh.Vert(x,y,z)
23              me2.verts.append(v)
24
25 # connect vertices to form faces
26 for y in range(0,ymax-1):
27      for x in range(0,xmax-1):
28              a=x+y*ymax
29              f= NMesh.Face()
30              f.v.append(me2.verts[a])
31              f.v.append(me2.verts[a+ymax])
32              f.v.append(me2.verts[a+ymax+1])
33              f.v.append(me2.verts[a+1])
34              me2.faces.append(f)
35
36 NMesh.PutRaw(me2,"Function",1)
37 Blender.Redraw()
```

12.6.1 How It Works

This script has several different mathematical functions that you can try in addition to the one shown. Here's how it works:

- Line 15 creates a new but empty polygon object with `Nmesh.GetRaw()`.

- The script creates an area by going through the x and y coordinates in two nested loops. The area is thus constructed line by line. A mathematical function then calculates the z coordinates for the corresponding x and y values.

- Line 22 then converts the individual coordinate triples into a set of vertices [`v=NMesh.Vert(x,y,z)`] and adds them to the new mesh [`me2.verts.append(v)`].

- An additional loop now connects four vertices into a face: `NMesh.Face()` (Line 29) creates a new face, `f.v.append` assigns the vertices to the face (Lines 30–33), and `me2.faces.append` then assigns the face to the object (Line 34).

- Finally, the mesh object is passed to Blender (`Nmesh.PutRaw`, Line 36) and `Blender.Redraw()` gives rise to a new icon in the Blender interface (Line 37); clicking it draws the object.

12.7 Blender-Python GUIs

Blender lets you supply Python scripts with a graphical interface while maintaining Blender's look and feel. In fact, the script GUIs fit into Blender so well that it's almost impossible to recognize right away whether you're dealing with a built-in Blender function or a script.

Currently, the Python GUI uses Blender's Text window and does not yet support all operations (for example, zooming or translating buttons). On the other hand, Blender does not inhibit this GUI; work in the windows (for example, the 3D windows) proceeds as normal.

12.7.1 Hello_GUI.blend

No tutorial would be complete without the obligatory "HelloWorld.xyz." But here we'll give a hearty greeting to the much-ballyhooed GUI instead of the whole world.

```
1  # Hello_GUI.py
2  # C.Wartmann@gmx.net
3
4  from Blender.Draw import *
5
6  def gui():
7          Button("Thanks Ton & Daniel", 1, 40, 100, 150, 19)
8
9  def event(evt, val):
10 #       print "event : ",evt,val
11         if (evt == ESCKEY and not val): Exit()
12
13 def bevent(evt):
14 #       print "bevent : ",evt
15         if (evt == 1): Exit()
16
17 Register(gui, event, bevent)
```

The listing for Hello_GUI.py doesn't look that complicated, does it? If you enter this script or load Hello_GUI.blend and run it with ALT-P, a button appears in the Text window that you can click to quit the GUI. Try working in Blender for a bit with the button displayed in the Text window. Everything works as normal, down to the Text window with its button!

12.7.2 How It Works

First, the script imports files. Here we're importing everything (*) from Blender.Draw, a module responsible for drawing the interface (Line 4). Then it defines three functions:

- gui() is responsible for drawing the interface (Line 6), which at the moment is just one button, defined with Button() (Line 7). (I'll explain the parameters a bit later.)

- event() handles keyboard input and mouse movements (Line 9). However, right now only the ESC key, which quits the GUI with Exit(), is recognized (Line 11).

- Finally, bevent() queries the button (Line 13), and, if it is clicked, the GUI is closed with Exit() (Line 15).

Why are these commands all packed in functions? In principle, one loop that waits for the action would be enough. However, having just one loop (called *polling*) would probably cause Blender (and other systems) to slow to a crawl. To serve us users, though, Blender has to process all input anyway. Therefore, we simply give it more work to do in Line 17 with Register(gui, event, bevent). This call registers the gui function, which is executed when the GUI is supposed to be redrawn, and also registers event() and bevent(), which are supposed to react to events. This produces an event-based GUI; that is, functions are called only when something is really happening, and the rest of the time the CPU's resources can be used for other tasks.

The gui() function, which displays the graphic interface, has no parameters, but the event() function takes two parameters: the event number and its associated value. If you want, you can insert a print evt,val in the function to have it output the events. If you then move the mouse over the Text window with the GUI, events 4 and 5, which represent the mouse coordinates in val, will be triggered. But since such numbers are hard to remember, two constants for the mouse coordinates, MOUSEX and MOUSEY, are defined in Blender.Draw. A similar constant is used for the ESC key (ESCKEY), which is much easier to remember than 65307.

In order of appearance, here are the parameters for Button():

1. The text displayed in the button

2. The event number generated by clicking the button, from which the script knows which GUI element triggered the event

3. The x and y coordinates for the button (the button's height and width)

   Appendix D has a list of the Blender.Draw module's functions.

12.7.3 OpenGL

You probably noticed that the button in the first script was drawn directly over the Text window. But if you examine the Blender.Draw module, you won't find any functions that could change that. Did someone forget something? The short answer is no. Instead of trying to reinvent the wheel, Blender takes advantage of the fact that its interface is displayed with OpenGL commands. Take a look at the listing for Hello_GUI2.py on the next page.

```
1   # Hello_GUI2.py
2   # C.Wartmann@gmx.net
3
4   from Blender.Draw import *
5   from Blender.BGL import *
6
7   def gui():
8   glClearColor(0.5, 0.5, 0.5, 0.0)
9   glClear(GL_COLOR_BUFFER_BIT)
10
11  glRasterPos2i(40, 130)
12  Text("Hello GUI!")
13  Button("Thanks Ton & Daniel!", 1, 40, 100, 150, 19)
14
15  def event(evt, val):
16              if (evt == ESCKEY and not val): Exit()
17
18  def bevent(evt):
19              if (evt == 1): Exit()
20
21  Register(gui, event, bevent)
```

Here something has happened to the gui() function! If you run this script, the Text window will be cleared and text will be drawn on the button. If you're an OpenGL expert, you probably recognize the command. Integrating OpenGL with Blender's Python makes it possible to create GUIs with interactive 3D elements and much more!

The functions come from the Blender.BGL module. What's important for us are the commands that place the OpenGL cursor [glRasterPos2i()] (so that the text appears where it should), and the commands that clear the Text window (Lines 8 through 10).

Using the functions from the two preceding sections, you can now program a function plotter with a graphical interface. The GUI is shown in Figure 12-3.

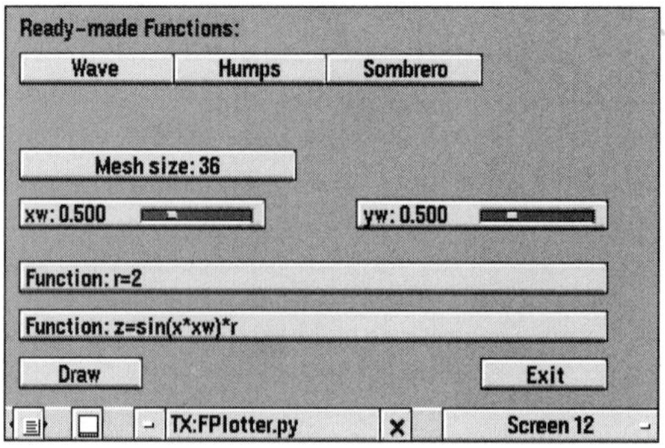

Figure 12-3: A GUI in Blender programmed with Python

```
1  # FPlotter.py
2  # Blender Function Plotter, Blender >=1.72
3  # C.Wartmann@gmx.net
4
5  import Blender
6
7  from Blender.Draw import *
8  from Blender.BGL import *
9
10 from Blender import NMesh,Object
11 from Blender.NMesh import Col
12 from math import sin,cos,sqrt,exp
13
14 from whrandom import random
15
16 ########## Predefined Functions ###############
17 def sombrero():
18      global zstring, rstring, xmax, ymax, xw ,yw
19      zstring = Create("sin(r*xw)*cos(r*yw)*exp(-r/5)*10")
20      rstring = Create("sqrt((x-xmax/2)**2+(y-ymax/2)**2)")
21      xw=Create(0.5)
22      yw=Create(0.5)
23      xmax = Create(36)
24      ymax = Create(36)
25      Register(gui, event, bevent)
26
27 def humps():
28      global zstring, rstring, xmax, ymax, xw ,yw
29      zstring = Create("sin(x*xw)*cos(y*yw)*r")
30      rstring = Create("1")
31      xw=Create(0.5)
32      yw=Create(0.5)
33      xmax = Create(36)
34      ymax = Create(36)
35      Register(gui, event, bevent)
36
37 def waves():
38      global zstring, rstring, xmax, ymax, xw ,yw
39      zstring = Create("sin(x*xw)*r")
40      rstring = Create("2")
41      xw=Create(0.5)
42      yw=Create(0.5)
43      xmax = Create(36)
44      ymax = Create(36)
45      Register(gui, event, bevent)
46
```

```
47
48  ########### Draw the functions #################
49  def draw(zfunk,rfunk,xw,yw,xmax,ymax):
50      me2= NMesh.GetRaw()
51      print zfunk,rfunk,xw,yw,xmax,ymax
52      # create the vertices
53      for y in range(0,ymax):
54          for x in range(0,xmax):
55              r=eval(rfunk)
56              z=eval(zfunk)
57              v=NMesh.Vert(x,y,z)
58              me2.verts.append(v)
59
60      #link the vertices to the planes
61      for y in range(0,ymax-1):
62          for x in range(0,xmax-1):
63              a=x+y*ymax
64              f=NMesh.Face()
65              f.v.append(me2.verts[a])
66              f.v.append(me2.verts[a+ymax])
67              f.v.append(me2.verts[a+ymax+1])
68              f.v.append(me2.verts[a+1])
69              me2.faces.append(f)
70
71      NMesh.PutRaw(me2,"Plot",1)
72      Blender.Redraw()
73
74  ############# draw the interface ############
75  def gui():
76      global zstring, rstring, xmax, ymax, xw ,yw
77
78      glClearColor(0.5,0.5,0.5, 0.0)
79      glClear(GL_COLOR_BUFFER_BIT)
80
81      Button("Exit", 1, 310, 10, 80, 19)
82      Button("Draw", 3, 10, 10, 80, 19)
83      rstring= String("Function: r=",
84          2, 10, 70, 380, 19, rstring.val, 70)
85      zstring= String("Function: z=",
86          4, 10, 40, 380, 19, zstring.val, 70)
87
88      xw = Slider("xw: ", 7, 10, 110, 160,
89          18, yw.val, 0.0, 2.0)
90      yw = Slider("yw: ", 8, 230, 110, 160,
91          18, yw.val, 0.0, 2.0)
```

```
92    xmax = Number("Mesh size:", 5, 10,
93         140, 180, 19, xmax.val, 5, 100)
94
95    glRasterPos2i(10, 230)
96    Text("Ready-made functions:")
97    Button("Waves", 9, 10, 200, 100, 19)
98    Button("Humps",10, 110, 200, 100, 19)
99    Button("Sombrero",11, 210, 200, 100, 19)
100
101 def event(evt, val):
102    if (evt== QKEY and not val): Exit()
103
104 def bevent(evt):
105    if (evt == 1): Exit()
106    elif (evt == 3):
107        draw(zstring.val,rstring.val,
108             xw.val,yw.val,xmax.val,xmax.val)
109    elif (evt == 9): waves()
110    elif (evt == 10): humps()
111    elif (evt == 11): sombrero()
112
113
114 ############ Here we go!#########################
115 waves()
```

12.7.4 How It Works

This script is definitely more complicated than what we've seen so far. In principle, though, its construction is the same.

- Three functions are defined (Lines 74 through 103) and then registered with Register(). The functions in gui() for displaying the buttons and controls should be easy to figure out using the preceding explanations and the description of the Blender.Draw module in Appendix D.

- The program then calls the waves() function, one of the three predefined Python functions that sets the values appropriately for a mathematical function (and the corresponding plot), and then Register() initializes the GUI. If you call the script with ALT-P, the GUI will appear as seen in Figure 12-3 on page 208. If you click the Draw button, Blender calculates a bit and then draws the wave function in the 3D window. Go ahead and try out your own functions or try changing the predefined parameters.

- Mesh size (as shown in Figure 12-3) determines how many points are generated per quadrant. The xw and yw controls display suggested values that can be used freely in the entered function. The text entry z= defines the main function that calculates the height value for the corresponding grid (raster) point. The r= is a helper function that I used to calculate the distance from the mesh's center in the sombrero picture. If this function is not used, you should set r=1.

Other important variables are xmax and ymax, which range from 0 to the value of the mesh size during the calculations. Color Plate 14 shows a mesh made with the function plotter. The stream of sparks erupting from the center was made with a particle system.

The actual function plotter works as described in Section 12.5.

13

THE BIG REWARD:
RENDERING

Rendering your image or animation is your reward at the end of your work with a 3D design and animation program. Your choice of image or animation format will depend on your output medium. If you will be printing your work you should produce high-resolution files with as little compression as possible. If outputting to PC video, you should produce files with lower resolution, which may incorporate file compression to reduce the amount of data you need to transmit. If you are outputting to videotape or even film, you will need to take special considerations into account since these media have hidden traps that can ruin a long and arduous rendering.

In my years of involvement in computer graphics and video, I have learned from my many mistakes. In this chapter I give you recommendations about using each rendering technique so that you can avoid the many pitfalls that await the unwary.

13.1 Saving Individual Images

Blender's Display buttons (F10) are its rendering control center (see Figure 13-1). Its most important settings are the buttons SizeX and SizeY, which set the image's width and height. Using the buttons 100%, 75%, 50%, and 25% you can quickly change to a lower resolution for test renderings.

Figure 13-1: The Display buttons in Blender

To save individual images after rendering, press F3. A File window will appear where you can enter the file name and directory path. The settings in the Display buttons will determine the file format.

At the right side of the Display buttons you'll find some defaults for image formats, including the PAL television format, the norm in many European countries (though France uses SECAM and the United States uses NTSC, which is also used in the United Kingdom). If you choose PAL, the settings for the pixel aspect ratio parameters AspX and AspY change automatically since PAL pixels are not square—that is, the pixel aspect ratio is not 1:1. PAL pixels differ from the target image format (the ratio of PAL to typical computer monitors is 4:3, and PAL to PAL+ is 16:9). As a result, a circle—a figure that looks round on a computer monitor (with a pixel aspect ratio of 1:1)—will show up as an oval on a television screen if you don't adjust the pixel aspect ratio.

Directly under the settings for image size and pixel aspect ratio are the buttons for setting the data format of the image to be saved. F3 saves a rendered image in the format that you select in the Display buttons:

Targa   A flexible graphics format that reduces image information loss using RLE compression. Choosing RGBA saves the alpha channel (transparency information), which is important if you will use the image independently of Blender or convert it to GIF or PNG format. Targa's compression format is not suited for colorbands or organic color transitions—and using Targa to save work with these characteristics can result in very large files.

TgaRaw   Like Targa but uncompressed. If your video editing software has problems with TGA (Targa) files, use TgaRaw.

Iris   Native SGI file format with RLE compression and an alpha channel option. Choosing IRIZ lets you save in a special Iris format that also contains the depth information of the rendered image (Z-buffer); useful for compositing.

HamX   An older graphics format that comes from the Amiga computer. Because this format produces small images that load quickly, it is good for when you want to play back a rendered animation with PLAY. However the image quality is not good enough for other purposes.

Ftype   Activating this button makes Blender save images in the format of the file name entered in the Ftype input field (left in the Display buttons), which is ideal for script-driven rendering.

JPEG	This file format is commonly used for photographs and rendered images; its lossy compression produces small image sizes. You can set the compression with Quality between 10% and 100%, though 100% does not mean that the compression is 100% lossless! (JPEG compression is adjusted to human perception, so you hardly even notice when JPEG images on standard video or computer monitors are highly compressed.) Many computer-based video editing systems use JPEG to store video images on a hard drive, and are often able to write in JPEG format without additional compression. (This is especially important because each JPEG compression introduces new errors that compound.)

Here are the various color settings:

BW	Transforms the rendered image to 8-bit grayscale. When saving the image, Blender attempts to retain its depth according to the capacities of the image format.
RGB	Saves color data.
RGBA	Adds transparency information (as long as the file format supports it).
IRIZ	Saves the depth information in Iris format.

In general I recommend the JPEG format if the images are either to be transmitted via the Internet or do not require further editing. To achieve maximal quality and flexibility for later editing, use the TGA format with alpha channel.

13.1.1 Saving Images for the Web

When integrating images into HTML documents for publishing on the Web, you have your choice of three image formats that all graphical browsers support: JPEG, GIF, and PNG. When saving to JPEG, set the quality as low as possible to reduce download times and file size.

GIF is a bitmap format with a palette of up to 256 colors. The pixel data is compressed using the LZW algorithm, which many free programs no longer support due to licensing difficulties. Because of its 256-color limitation, GIF is not suited for reproducing photorealistic images. Still, it has two properties that make it interesting:

Transparency	Defines a color that allows the background to shine through, allowing you to produce images that are not limited to rectangular boundaries.
Animation	This GIF file format allows you to save images on top of each other, which can then be played back in succession to produce an animation like a classic cartoon. Spinning logos and blinking buttons on the Web are typically GIF animations.

To produce either transparent or animated GIFs, use a program that can both accept at least one of Blender's image formats and save as GIF. Targa format is a good choice since TGA compression is lossless and includes transparency data, which is needed to create transparent GIFs.

A couple of programs worth considering are Photoshop and the GIMP. Photoshop is a big and expensive but also professional image-manipulation program available for Macintosh and Windows platforms. The GIMP (http://www.gimp.org) is a free program, with source code, that offers nearly the same functionality as Photoshop; it is available for UNIX, Unix-like platforms (Linux, FreeBSD), and Windows.

Besides Photoshop and the GIMP, a wide range of smaller programs for all platforms are often optimized for a certain task, such as creating animated GIFs. (There is also an almost unimaginable array of freeware and shareware tools.) Appendix B introduces some programs that serve these purposes.

NOTE *PNG format is likely to replace GIF since it has similar properties and is, in some respects, even better. Unfortunately, most Web browsers do not yet completely support PNG.*

13.2 Animations

When saving an animation for further editing as individual images, the comments from Section 13.1, "Saving Individual Images," generally apply. Click ANIM in the Display buttons (see Figure 13-1) and Blender will render the animation from start to final image as set in Sta and End. Files are saved in the selected file format, and you can enter the directory and the base file name into the field Pics on the left of the Display buttons, or click on the square gray button adjacent to the field to receive a choice of files.

Once you've entered the path and base file name (such as /tmp/image.), Blender adds an extension corresponding to the current image number (to include a "dot" between the base name and the extension, include it in the base file name at the outset). For example, if you use the path /tmp/image., Blender would save an animation with 100 images as /tmp/image.0001, /tmp/image.0002, /tmp/image.0003, . . . /tmp/image.0100. If you enter a new directory name that doesn't exist yet, Blender creates it (if you are using a multiuser system you must first, of course, have the requisite permissions).

To mark a file's type, Windows programs use a dot with a three-letter extension, like .jpg or .tga; add these automatically by pressing Extensions. (In this case, be sure to avoid including a dot in the base file name, which could confuse some Windows-based applications.)

When rendering in television resolution for a video editing system, activate the Fields button to enable support for the interlacing of fields (a process television and video systems use). Once this button is activated, Blender renders two fields for each image (frame); a trick that increases the image frequency. The fields are broadcast in succession, and the inertia of the picture tube allows the fields to blend together. (Some video editing systems may require you to activate the Odd button, which reverses the order of the fields.) Since computer monitors are faster than television sets (the light layer of the picture tube doesn't remain lit as long), playing an interlaced animation on them shows frayed edges.

13.2.1 Video Formats

Blender supports the following animation formats:

AVI Raw   AVI (audio video interlaced) files are simply a container for several audio and video formats, woven together, and subject to various compression methods. When using AVI Raw, Blender saves uncompressed images as large, uncompressed standard AVI files that every program accepting AVIs should be able to read.

AVI jpg   An AVI file in which the images are saved as compressed JPEGs. The Quality setting defines the compression level. Due to compression, these files are relatively small; they are likely to be readable by newer programs that accept AVIs.

SGI-Movie   Saves an SGI-Movie. This function applies only when using Blender on SGI Unix machines because it requires special SGI function libraries.

The input button Frs/sec sets the frame replay rate per second (f/s) for playback of an animation. Typical values are 15 f/s for AVIs played directly on the computer, 25 f/s for PAL video, 30 f/s for NTSC (U.S.) video, and 24 f/s for motion picture film.

13.2.2 Motion Blur

When you try to capture a quick movement on film, the object continues to move during the exposure time, resulting in motion blur. Like lens flares, motion blur is essentially a technological flaw.

By reducing the exposure time, one can reduce and almost eliminate this effect by capturing images at particular moments in the course of a movement. (Sports photography commonly employs this technique.) However, when you play back a recording taken with short exposure time, you get a movement that shakes significantly. Thus, though stop-motion may be desirable for sports photography (who wants to see a blurred view of a ball from the sidelines in a still shot?), it is best avoided in normal film and video production.

A virtual camera in a 3D program acts as if it has an unfathomably small exposure time, which means that even the quickest movement is always in focus. Our brains notice immediately that this goes against what we're used to seeing in films. Using motion blur, therefore, can add a realistic effect to 3D animations by suggesting movements that are out of focus (see Figure 13-2).

To render motion blur, Blender renders an image several times over a small time interval and dissolves the renderings together to compose the final image. Although this type of rendering requires a lot of processing time, it pays off in key scenes in video production situations that show quick movement.

To activate motion blur, press MBLUR in the Display buttons. The settings for OSA of 5, 8, 11, 16 (as shown in Figure 13-1) control the number of in-between images to be rendered. The blur factor Bf defines the camera's exposure time, with higher values resulting in more obvious motion blur. For example, the scene in Figure 13-2 uses 11 for OSA and 0.5 for Bf. An OSA setting of 5 is usually sufficient for video.

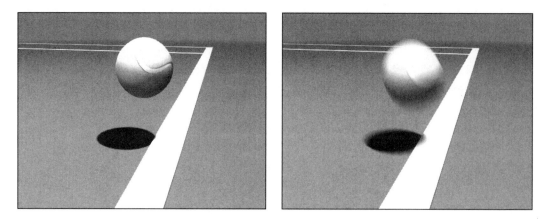

Figure 13-2: A scene rendered with and without motion blur

13.3 Lighting Simulation: Radiosity Rendering

In the real world, every object that is not absolutely black emits light, and colors surrounding objects with its own color. You can simulate this diffuse emission of light with a few strategically placed light-colored light sources. However, Blender contains a radiosity renderer that can give you a more exact picture of reality.

Not a Number considers the radiosity renderer a modeling tool, and it is not completely integrated into Blender; you will recognize its origins as an external tool. Its biggest disadvantage is that it works only with polygon objects, treating all of them as one large object; that means that you will lose all of your textures when you use it, and must replace them by hand once the radiosity rendering is complete. And you cannot have animated objects in a radiosity implementation. Despite these negatives, camera animations can be used in the final implementation.

Let's create a simple scene to render with the radiosity method.

1. Create a simple space that contains a few objects. Place a couple of surfaces on the ceiling to represent overhead lighting. (You only need lights to render a view during modeling.)

2. Create a self-lit material by placing a material on the lighting elements (in a color of your choice) with an Emit value of 1.0. (Surfaces with an Emit value larger than 0.0 are light-emitting.) Both the Emit value and surface size (surface x Emit value) determine the amount of light emitted. (You can simulate various light colors with varied material colors.)

3. Once you have finished and saved your scene, select all of the objects that belong in the radiosity implementation, then change to the Radiosity buttons (see Figure 13-3).

The individual steps for carrying out a radiosity implementation are in the Radiosity buttons, organized in columns from left to right. The second button row indicates how the objects are shown in the radiosity implementation.

Phase: COLLECT MESHES							
	PaMax: 500	PaMin: 200	Hemires: 300	GO		Element Filter	Add new Meshes
Collect Meshes	ElMax: 100	ElMin: 20	MaxEl: 10000	SubSh P: 1	SubSh E: 2	RemoveDoubles	Lim: 0	
	ShowLim		Max Subdiv Shoot: 0			FaceFilter	Replace Meshes
			Subdiv Shoot Patch	Convergence: 0.100			
Limit Subdivide	Wire	Solid	Gour	Subdiv Shoot Element	Max Iterations: 0	Mult: 30.00	Gamma: 2.000	Free Radio Data

Figure 13-3: The radiosity renderer

Collect Meshes	Collects the selected polygon objects and prepares them for radiosity rendering. Once activated, other buttons turn beige, indicating that a rendering is possible, and a status indicator for the scene appears in the Radiosity buttons. Emit: shows the number of light surfaces acting as light emitters; if this number is less than zero, everything remains dark.
Wire	Displays a wireframe, allowing you to control the subdivision of the surfaces (which Blender had performed earlier).
Solid	Shows filled colored surfaces.
Gour	Shows the rendering with smoothed polygon objects and allows the most control over it.

The remaining four settings in the first four button rows allow for exact control over the radiosity process. Leave these settings unchanged.

Now let's render the scene:

1. Activate Gour.

2. Begin the radiosity rendering by clicking GO. You can view the progress in the 3D window. If you need to interrupt it, press ESC (your work up to that point will be saved).

3. If the scene shows an unattractive distribution of light intensities on certain surfaces, use Element Filter to filter the light. (You will see the difference in the 3D window.)

4. If you are satisfied with the results of your rendering, integrate the radiosity rendering with the scene with Add new Meshes. The result is a large mesh with all elements, which is placed on the layer containing the original objects. Press M to place it onto a different layer.

5. To render the image, change to the main layer and press F12; you should see an image like Color Plate 15.

Note the red reflection on the wall made by the red pyramid on the left in Color Plate 15. To see this effect on your monitor, open the image in figures/radiosity_box on the CD. The CD also contains a number of both preliminary and finished scenes in the radiosity directory. The finished scenes have "_solved" added to the file name.

Because the information regarding the strength of the light emitted from each surface is stored in the object's vertices, saving a scene saves the radiosity implementation too. You need only load the scene to perform the radiosity function; there is no need for a new rendering.

13.3.1 Post-Radiosity Work

Because the radiosity implementation produces a large, composite object, you must again divide the mesh into individual objects to perform post-radiosity material and texture work.

1. Select the mesh and press TAB to enter EditMode.

2. Move the cursor over a vertex of the object you want to split off and press L to select all vertices belonging to the object.

3. Press P to separate the object from the original mesh. Once objects have been separated, you can apply normal textures. Be sure to activate VertexCol in the Material buttons (F5) so that the results of the radiosity rendering will influence the material color.

NOTE *You will often find it helpful to first split off a wall or other objects with large surfaces, to prevent the vertices of one selection from hindering those of another. The file* radiosity_box01_solved.blend *contains a split and rendered mesh from this example.*

You can also introduce new light sources into finished scenes, as shown in Color Plate 16 (conference_room04_solved.blend on the CD). In this example, normal spotlights are used for light coming through the window and for the desk lamp, but the radiosity renderer creates the rest of the lighting, including the glow of the computer monitor. A rendered animation of this scene is on the CD-ROM in the animations directory.

Radiosity rendering is a complex method; a full treatment is beyond the scope of this book.

14

LASER TUTORIAL

Lasers—weapons of the future, medical instruments of today—don't we all just love 'em? This chapter is an homage to lasers, especially those of the science fiction variety. In this tutorial, we'll use volumetric lighting and particle and material animations to animate a laser, complete with smoke, sparks, and burning glow, cutting away a piece of metal. (See Color Plate 17 for what the final product looks like.) If you're feeling more ambitious, try using the basics of this tutorial to create a space battle.

14.1 The Laser Beam

First let's create the laser beam:

1. Create a lamp over a surface and make it a spotlight by turning on the Spot button in the Lamp buttons (F4).

2. Set SpotSi to the lowest value (1.0) to get a small beam.

Unlike a real laser, this light beam widens with increasing distance, so don't let the distance between the lamp and end point become too large. If you need a very long laser beam for a particular scene, use a transparent, self-illuminating cylinder, but make sure that no other objects pass through it.

Activate the Halo option in the Lamp buttons to make the beam visible in the rendered image. When using this option, pay attention to the Halo step parameter, which determines how precisely shadows are rendered within halos. A value of 1 gives the highest level of quality, but 8 is adequate for most scenes. Increase the light intensity until a beam is visible and the laser's point of light on the surface is sufficiently intense. Figure 14-1 shows the other lamp parameters.

Quad	Lamp	Spot	Sun	Hemi	Dist: 10.00
Sphere					
Shadows	SpotSi 1.00			Energy 4.000	
Halo	SpotBl 0.800			R 1.000	
Layer	Quad1 0.000			G 0.000	
Negative	Quad2 1.000			B 0.000	
OnlyShadow	HaloInt 1.000				
Square					

BufSi 512	768	ClipSta: 0.50	Samples: 3	Bias: 1.000
1024	1536	ClipEnd: 11.00	Halo step: 8	Soft: 1.00

Figure 14-1: Parameters for the laser beam's Lamp buttons

To make it easier to aim the laser, do the following:

1. Choose ADD • Empty to create an empty that will function as the laser's target.

2. Select the laser beam and then the empty by holding SHIFT and right-clicking, then press CTRL-T to make the empty the laser's target.

If, after following these steps, the laser beam is off target, select Object • Clear Rotation (or ALT-R with the lamp selected); now, when you move the target empty, the laser beam should follow.

A test rendering (F12) should show a red laser beam that creates a bright point of light.

14.1.1 Making the Surface Reflect

In the real world, such a powerful laser beam would reflect brightly on the surface. We'll simulate this effect by placing a light source just above the surface. (This technique doesn't require a true reflection.)

1. Right-click to select the laser's target and place the 3D cursor directly on the target via the SNAP menu or by pressing SHIFT-S-4 to select the fourth menu option.

2. Create a light source with Add • Lamp in a side or front view.

3. Middle-click and press G (for translation mode) to move the lamp slightly above the surface.

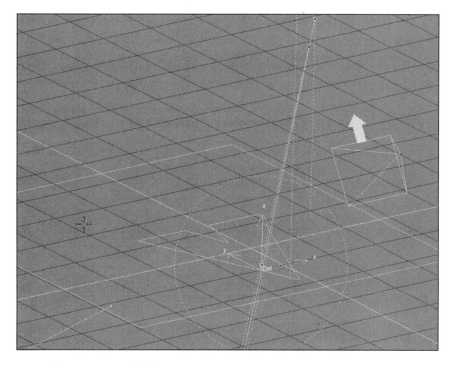

Figure 14-2: Overview of the laser scene

4. Select the lamp and then the target (hold SHIFT and right-click), then press CTRL-P to make the target a parent of the lamp; the lamp will now follow the target.

5. In the Lamp buttons (F4), set the color in the RGB control to bright red.

Try a test rendering with F12 to see if you like the effect. You may need to make the lamp brighter with Energy or raise it higher over the surface.

14.1.2 *Adjusting the Light Source*

By default (see Figure 14-2), once you've created a new light source, the lamp shines into infinity and its intensity decreases linearly in relation to the distance from the light source, both of which are unrealistic attributes. To correct this and make the laser more realistic, select Sphere as your light source and then adjust Dist to reduce the light's range, represented by the circular dotted line surrounding it. Next, make the light's intensity decrease more realistically by using Quad to make the relationship quadratic.

14.2 The World

Laser beams complement outer space scenes perfectly, so let's create one for our laser—a sci-fi surface under a starry sky.

Change to the World buttons (F8) and set the parameters as shown in Figure 14-3 to produce a uniformly black background with stars (Blend and Real are deselected and the horizon color is set to black). You may need to adjust the star size with Size depending on the rendering size. (You'll find more on additional parameters in Section 7.5.4.)

	Blend	Real	Paper		Mist		
					Qua	Lin	Sqr
					Sta: 0.00		
	ZeR 0.000				Di: 0.00		
	ZeG 0.000				Hi: 0.00		
	ZeB 0.000		Expos 1.000		Stars		
					StarDist: 15.00		
	HoR 0.000		AmbR 0.000		MinDist: 0.00		
	HoG 0.000		AmbG 0.000		Size: 2.000		
	HoB 0.000		AmbB 0.000		Colnoise: 0.000		

Figure 14-3: Parameters for the starry background

14.3 Surface Material

Since we are creating a science fiction scene, we need an appropriate material for the plane the laser is striking.

1. Right-click the plane to select it.

2. Change to the Material buttons (F5), and create a new material for the plane (assuming one is not already defined).

3. Change to the Texture buttons (F6) and add the texture scifi01color2.jpg (in tutorials/textures/) as an image texture to the material.

4. Insert the textures scifi01bump2.jpg and scifi05bump2.jpg into the second and third texture channels as bump maps, then deactivate Col and activate Nor (in the Material buttons) for these bump maps.

Figure 14-4 shows the textures for this scene. To make the bump maps look good, define a light source for the scene that shines at an angle onto the surface (use CTRL-T—see Section 7.4.1).

Since the texture is mapped over the entire surface, the structures in the textures will be much too large. However, these textures are designed to be *tiled* (set next to each other iteratively). To tile them, use the Xrepeat and Yrepeat parameters in the Texture buttons. These options have the disadvantage that you must set the parameters for each texture (the Size parameter in the Material buttons would have the same disadvantage).

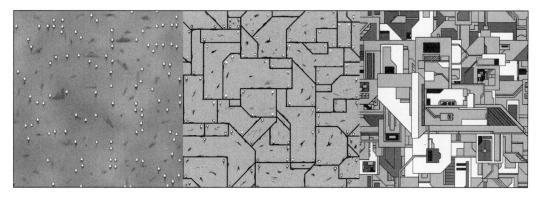

Figure 14-4: Textures for the surface material

Now change the entire texture area for the object:

1. Select the plane and press T. The resulting menu lets you move the texture area with Grabber or alter its size with Size.

2. Choose Size to reduce the size of the texture area. Using the mouse, reduce the size of the area (represented by the dotted line) by about 50 percent.

   If you perform a test rendering, the texture will repeat itself.

14.4   The Path

Now let's define the path to outline the piece the laser cuts out. If you want this piece to fall through later, use a single, closed path.

I chose the letter "V" from a PostScript character set, which I then converted into a curve section with ALT-C. You can see the "V" most of the way traced out in Color Plate 17. To use a letter that consists of two closed-curve sections ("O" for example), first split the object into two parts.

14.4.1   Creating the Path

1. Once you've converted the text into a curve, press TAB to enter EditMode and place the mouse cursor over a vertex of the path section that you want to break off.

2. Press L to select (link) all vertices that belong to the desired segment.

3. Press P to separate the segment from the main object.

4. Select the target and then the path and press CTRL-P to make the path the parent of the laser target (the empty).

5. Select the path and activate CurvePath in the Animation buttons (F7). Depending on the starting points of the target and the path, you may need to select the target and press ALT-O to place it directly onto the path.

Depending on the path, the laser beam may not follow the letter exactly (in our example, the left side of the V is left out). To fix this, select the path object, change to EditMode, select all vertices with A, and press H.

If you play the animation with ALT-A, notice that the laser beam cuts off when it makes abrupt direction changes. Fix this by increasing the value of DefResolU for the path to around 20 or 30 and applying it with Set.

NOTE *The default setting for a path is always 100 frames, but you can change the animation's length at any time with PathLen. The animation takes on the value immediately.*

14.4.2 Manipulating the Laser

To make the laser look like it's coming from a large, heavy cannon, we accelerate it at the start of the animation and decelerate it at the end. This makes the animation appear more natural.

In contrast to path objects, speed IPOs are not created automatically for curve paths, so we'll have to create a speed IPO to be able to manipulate the laser's acceleration.

1. Select the path and change a window to an IPO window.

2. Select the curved arrow in the IPO window to edit the IPOs for the path. The only channel available in this case is Speed.

3. Click twice in the IPO window while pressing CTRL to create the vertices for the IPO curve. Now an IPO curve should be displayed, showing the object's speed on the path. (As described in Section 8.2.1, the vertical axis indicates the object's position on the path and the horizontal axis indicates the animation time in frames.)

4. Select the IPO curve and press TAB to enter EditMode. Right-click to select a point on the curve and press N to call up the Number menu (Figure 14-5). Enter 1 for the x coordinate (the first frame) and 0 for the y coordinate (the start of the path).

5. For the curve's second control point, enter 200 for x and 1 for y. The laser beam should now cover the path within 200 frames, making an 8-second animation in TV or PAL video (a little less for NTSC).

6. In EditMode, move the IPO curve's handles horizontally so that the laser doesn't start so gently (test the animation by playing it in a 3D window with ALT-A).

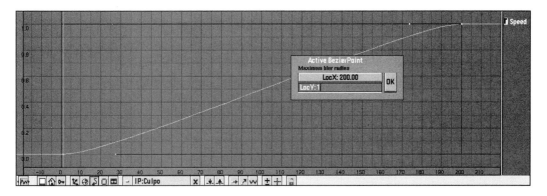

Figure 14-5: Speed IPO with Number menu

14.5 Making the Cut Glow

In reality, after a laser passes over metal, the metal continues to glow for a while. An animated texture, either drawn by hand or rendered separately in Blender, is one way to achieve this realistic effect. A particle system, though, lets you render the afterglow effect together with the rest of the animation.

14.5.1 Create the Particle System

1. Select the laser target and place the 3D cursor on it by pressing SHIFT-S-4.

2. Press PAD 7 to get a top view, then create a plane and scale it down until its diameter is a bit smaller than the laser beam's. This plane will be the particle emitter and will follow the laser beam.

3. Select the plane and then the target and press CTRL-P to make it a parent of the emitter.

4. To assign a new particle effect, select just the plane, switch to the Animation buttons (F7), and set the type in the Menu button to Particles.

5. Set the length of the particle generation to correspond to the animation length by setting End to 200 (if you used the animation length I suggested above).

6. Set the Randlife parameter to randomly vary the particles' life span and give the particle trail a frayed effect. Values around 0.5 are most effective.

14.5.2 Add a Material

If you play the animation in a 3D window with ALT-A, you'll see a particle trail, but you won't see one in a rendered image, because you have yet to apply a particle material.

1. Select the emitter, switch to the Material buttons (F5), and add a new material via ADD NEW in the Menu button.

2. Set the material type to Halo and Halosize to 0.07. The trail should now be visible in a rendered image.

3. Change the color as desired with the color controls in the Material buttons.

For an even better effect, animate the particle trail's material to change from light yellow to dark red and then slowly disappear. (As discussed in Section 10.2.3, a material animation for particle materials is always defined in the first 100 frames and applies to each particle's entire life.)

1. Move the frame slider to 1, select the emitter, and switch to the Material buttons (F5).

2. Use the color controls to set a light yellow color for the start of the material animation. With the mouse cursor in the material window, press I and select RGB from the pop-up menu to define a key for the color.

3. Set the frame slider to 100, change the material color to a dark red, press I, and choose RGB.

With the mouse cursor over the Material buttons, press ALT-A to preview the material animation. The trail's material color should change from yellow to red in the first 100 frames. You can edit the IPO curve for the material's keyframe animation (see Figure 14-6) in an IPO window.

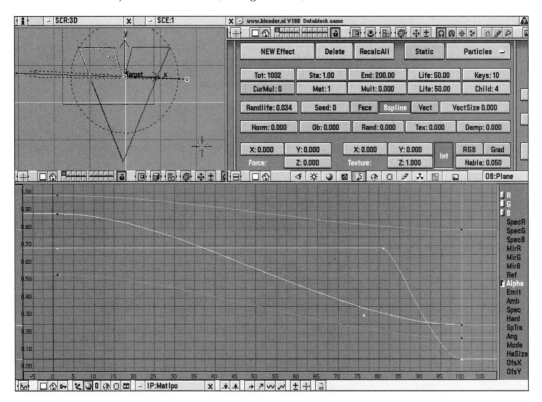

Figure 14-6: Particle parameters and material IPOs to make the laser cut glow

To make the trail gradually disappear, animate the alpha value just as you did with the color. Here you would use an IPO curve to set Alpha from 1.0 to 0.0 over Frames 80 through 100.

14.6 Leaving a Seam

If you want to leave a seam on the cutting path, use an additional particle system. A particle system as defined in the preceding exercises, with a long life and a skillfully constructed material animation, would usually suffice, but the IPO curves for the seam's material animation are difficult to create, and later adjustments to the animation would require almost the same amount of effort as creating the animation in the first place.

Let's the create the seam.

1. Create a plane directly on the target, and scale it significantly smaller than the first emitter. The seam should be quite small.

2. Press CTRL-P to make the laser target the parent of the emitter so that this second emitter also follows the laser beam.

3. Create a new particle system for the second emitter plane. Keep all default parameters except for End (adjust it to fit the animation length), and Life (which determines the particle system's life span). The life must be long enough to continue through the entire animation or the seam will disappear. My example uses a path length of 200 frames, which requires a setting of 200 for End. The entire animation lasts 250 frames, so I've set Life to 250.

I used the parameters shown in Figure 14-7 to define the scene's material; the halo is dark brown with a very small HaloSize to keep the seam narrow. Keep the Add parameter small so that the material does not glow (as is normally the case with halos).

Hard determines the material's transparency, and the standard value of 50 should produce a good effect. If you want a more visible seam you can reduce this value, but remember that decreasing Hard will increase the glowing effect.

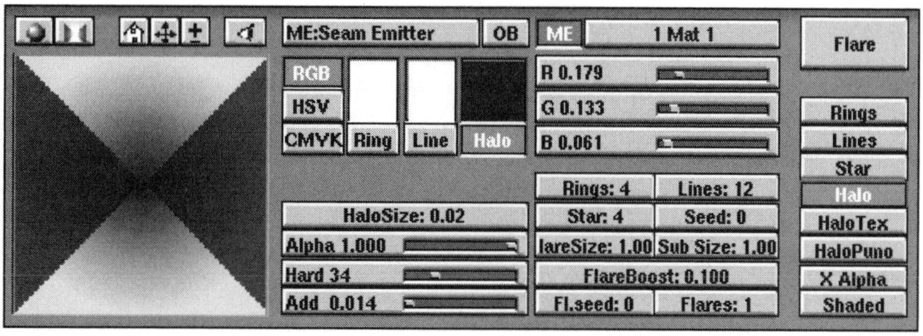

Figure 14-7: Material for the seam

14.7 Pyrotechnics: Sparks and Smoke

Now let's add some sparks and smoke to complete our animation, using the same steps we followed to add new particle emitters as described earlier. (You can use the material from Section 10.3 for the smoke by loading it with SHIFT-F1. For the sparks, apply a negative force in the z direction so that they fall to the ground.) The scene laser12.blend on the CD-ROM should give you some good ideas.

14.8 Turning Off the Laser

After 200 frames the laser should turn off. You can animate this effect by using the IPO curves for the energy of the laser lamp and the light point source that creates the red shine.

1. Create IPO curves of the lamps' full energy values for frames 1–199.

2. Make the energy value sink to 0.0 within one or two frames with a normal keyframe animation or by choosing the Energ channel in the IPO window for lamps (see Figure 14-8). To create keyframes, hold CTRL and left-click in the IPO window.

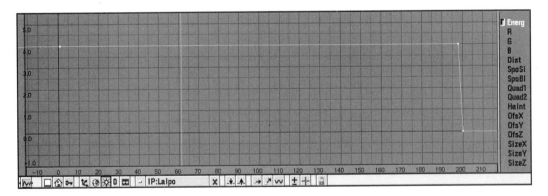

Figure 14-8: Energy IPO for the laser lamp

3. To make the change quick (the curves are still Bezier curves at this point, so the changes are slow and soft), right-click to select the curve, make sure the mouse is in the IPO window and press T, and select Linear from the pop-up menu. You can set the individual points in EditMode with N (the Number menu).

Because the brightness will be too strong, you will not be able to use the same IPO curve for the light point. To simplify the process, select the light point and then assign the laser beam's lamp IPO with the Menu button in the IPO window. The name field next to the Menu button will be highlighted blue, indicating multiple usage of the IPO. Clicking on the number 2 brings up a dialog box you can answer by choosing Single User or pressing RETURN. You can now edit this copy of the curve in EditMode, and adjust it to a lower energy value (for example, scale it in the y direction).

Take a look at Color Plate 17 again, and see how many of these effects you can spot in action on it.

15

ANIMATING A TORPEDO
THROUGH A SCHOOL OF FISH

The process of integrating effects, animations, or multiple scenes into one scene is called *compositing*. Compositing mistakes are very easy to spot, so it's important to integrate scenes as seamlessly as possible. To create a realistic impression, it's especially important that the scene to be integrated has harmonious lighting—unlike real-life scenes, computer-generated ones tend to be very precise and hard-edged, which makes small differences in lighting really stand out.

15.1 Compositing Methods

Depending on your goals, there are several ways to integrate computer graphics into video scenes.

15.1.1 Integrating Footage with an Editing System

One basic way is to render the scenes as usual with an alpha transparency and then to combine them with video footage on a video editing system. When you do that, the computer graphics would be the foreground, the real scenes (the video footage) the background, and semi-transparent objects would let the background show through appropriately.

Alternatively, you can use *colorkeying*, which puts the computer graphics in the background by replacing the colors blue or green (which of course must not show up elsewhere in the scene or they would disappear there too) with computer graphics. Colorkeying is commonly used by television news programs.

Several intermediate levels between these two methods let you create a complete virtual studio in which a moderator can wander around computer-generated objects.

15.1.2 Integrating Footage into a 3D Program

The second basic compositing method integrates the frames of a video or film into a 3D program. This direct integration gives you full control over compositing, and test renderings let you quickly judge individual frames.

You can use Blender's Sequence Editor to combine several scenes (see Chapter 11), just as you would use a computerized video editing system. You can also use animated image sequences or AVI films as textures and background images. While there are currently no sequence plug-ins that can perform colorkeying, combining alpha transparencies is quite easy. (As noted in Chapter 11, Blender's Sequence Editor does not yet support sound—but the system keeps growing. . . .)

15.2 Encounters of the Fourth Kind

In scuba circles a story makes the rounds of an encounter with a torpedo near a training ground. While viewing some underwater footage from Indonesia, I found an ideal scene for reconstructing this story in Blender. The scene takes place in the shallow water over a reef inhabited by scores of fish. For some reason, several fish suddenly dart into the reef—a perfect spot to make our computer-generated torpedo (see Color Plate 18) enter the scene as if it scared the poor fish into hiding.

You'll find the images from this underwater scene on the CD in JPEG format and PAL resolution. (Because they compress files, thus reducing their quality, JPEGs are not ideal for compositing, but space is limited on the CD.) The 900 images in this directory are PAL fields and take up about 70MB. Since the PAL television system uses frames consisting of two fields and displays 50 fields per second, the entire scene is 18 seconds long. If you want the animation to conform to the NTSC standard, then you need to adjust the Frs/Sec setting in the Display buttons to 30.

15.3 Background

To begin, load the scene torpedo/torpedo00.blend from the CD. This scene contains the finished torpedo on a kind of stage made out of two planes. The lower plane will pick up the torpedo's shadow and fade into the background scene, and the plane in the back will display the video images.

I modeled the torpedo "into" the scene by using a background image from the video sequence to adjust its size and position. (To insert a background image, press SHIFT-F7 and use BackGroundPic as described in Section 5.14.) Since the images are in PAL fields, I've used an image scaled vertically by a factor of two to set the correct aspect ratio.

I've defined a fog in the World buttons (F8) that extends just beyond the plane in the back. I've adjusted the fog's colors (turquoise changing to blue) to the background images to make the torpedo's entrance believable.

1. Select the back plane, create a new material in the Material buttons (F5), and name it "background".

2. Set the material's properties to Shadeless and No Mist so that it will not be included in the light rendering or be influenced by the fog (the background images already have enough natural "mist"). Press F12 for a test rendering, which should show this effect clearly: the torpedo should be rendered with shadows and fog while the background plane is not.

3. Set the texture coordinates in the Material buttons to Win so that the texture will be precisely adjusted to the size of the rendered image (window). (The size of the background plane is no longer a factor: it should fill the camera's entire field of vision.)

    Now let's call up the images by defining an animated texture.

1. With the background plane active, switch to the Texture buttons (F6), create a texture, name it "reef", and set its type to Image.

2. Click Load Image to select an image from the directory sequences/reef/. Choose any image—Blender will replace the name's four-digit number with the current frame number. (Figure 15-1 displays the Material parameters.)

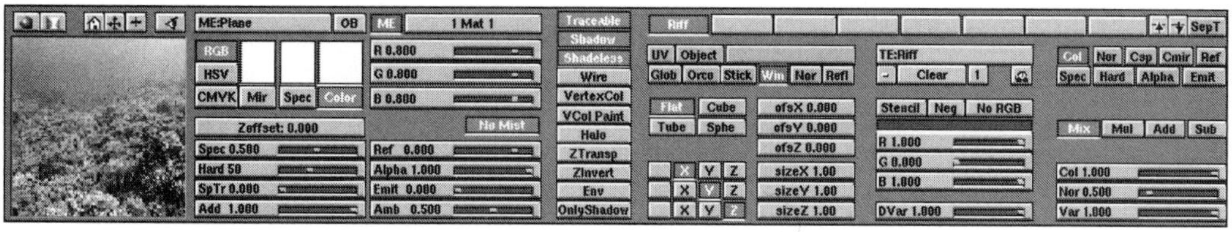

Figure 15-1: The background material with an animated texture

> **NOTE** *If it takes too long to preview the images, Blender is working on creating the directory's* .Bpip *file, which saves an overview of the directory's images. (Since the CD already contains a finished* .Bpip *file, the preview happens quickly.) If previewing still takes too long (the* .Bpip *file is almost 4MB for the underwater scene), try using the thin gray button near* Load Image *to call up the normal file window without thumbnails, or enter the file name directly with the keyboard. You can select an image once the first few thumbnails are displayed.*

3. Set the number of frames in the Texture buttons (F6) with Frames; if you're using the images on the CD, enter 905.

4. The Fie/Ima parameter tells Blender how many fields are in one image. Since the images are already fields, enter 1.

5. Set Offset to 400 so that the torpedo will be over the fish when they are hiding in the reef.

If you were now to render a frame of the animation, you'd see that it already looks pretty good. The lower plane still needs some work, however.

1. Create a material that receives only shadows but is otherwise transparent by right-clicking the lower plane to select it, changing to the Material buttons (F5), and creating a new material named "shadows". (The material's color is not important since the parameter Only Shadow makes sure only shadows are rendered.)

2. Make the material transparent by enabling Ztransp.

Now try rendering another frame. You should see that the torpedo is now well integrated into the background, but the underwater shadows are too strong. Correct this by setting the Alpha parameter to 0.5, which will produce shadows that aren't too obtrusive.

NOTE *In reality, there are hardly any well-defined shadows under water because the water's surface strongly scatters the sun's rays, even when there are few waves. Still, the impression created with shadows is much more believable than without shadows. This is a good example of how computer animation can use visual props to produce a believable (but not realistic) impression, which is ultimately what's important.*

15.4   Rendering for Video

Blender is commonly used to render animations for output to video; thus this capability has been well developed and integrated into several places in the program.

Today's primary television and video formats use fields, which are two half-resolution images interlaced line by line on the vertical axis and displayed one after the other. In general, the human eye is too slow to perceive the individual images so we see only one image. (Recording video uses the same method.) Thus, fast objects that move far within a short time (1/25 of a second in PAL, 1/30 of a second in NTSC) occupy different positions in the fields. So, if animations were rendered in the full PAL resolution and transferred to video, they would jerk slightly, since there would always be two identical images shown one after the other.

Therefore, the first step in preparing for the rendering is to activate Fields in the Display buttons (F10). Once activated, Blender will always create two fields that are 1/25 of a second apart (if you're using the PAL setting), to be combined into one frame at the end of the rendering. Figure 15-2 shows additional important buttons for rendering video.

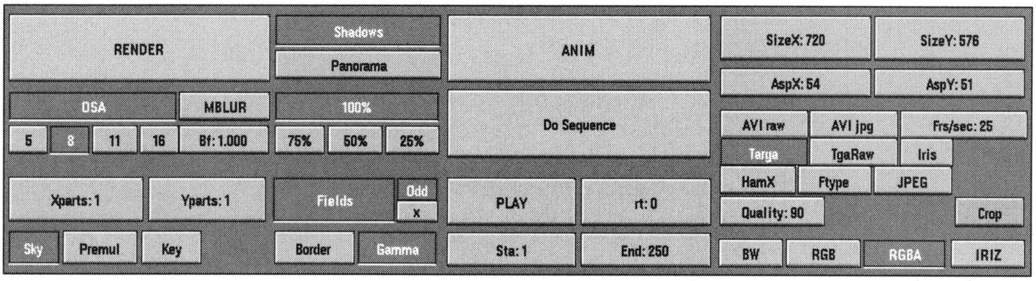

Figure 15-2: The relevant Display buttons for rendering video

You can clearly see the comblike structure on the tip of the torpedo in the individual rendered frames. You'll recognize this look if you've ever come across television images that have been recorded with a TV card.

15.4.1 Producing Good Video Output

Resolution and aspect ratio are two important factors affecting the quality of video output for your images.

The PAL standard has a resolution of 720x575 pixels and a pixel aspect ratio of 18:17. Thus, the pixels are not exact squares and can be regulated with AspX and AspY—though if you don't take the aspect ratio into account spheres will turn into eggs on television.

The resolution of your images need not correspond precisely to the PAL standard; many PC video editing cards use much smaller clips since normal televisions do not display the entire image area. For example, the editing system used to produce the background images for the torpedo uses a resolution of 688x560 pixels.

Consider too the order of fields in the finished rendered images. If you play a Blender animation on your editing system and it seems jumpy, your hardware is probably putting the fields in an order different from Blender's. Use the Odd button in the Display buttons to switch the order of the fields.

NOTE *Remember to save your animations in a format that your editing system can read.*

Whenever you use a video texture (as in this tutorial), remember these two additional points. First, activate the Fields option in the Texture buttons (F6) so that the fields will be handled correctly in the textures regardless of whether you render with fields or not. Second, pay attention to the number of fields in a texture image. In our case the texture images are already fields, so you have to enter a 1 in Fie/Ima (fields per image). If you use frames as an animated texture, then you must enter 2 here.

A

KEYBOARD COMMANDS

This appendix lists most of the Blender commands you will use on a regular basis. For a complete list, see the *Blender Manual* published by Not a Number.

Here are a few general tips to reviewing this appendix:

- A hyphen between two keys means press the two keys simultaneously.

- LMB, RMB, and MMB refer to the left, right, and middle mouse button, respectively.

- Most commands can only be executed in certain windows, as indicated.

- ESC always cancels a function.

A.1 Blender's Windows and Files

The function keys are primarily used for calling up Blender's various windows (including button groups) or for saving or rendering images or files. You can use these key combinations in any window, except where noted.

Table A-1: Keys for working with Blender windows and files

Key	Function
F1	Loads a file
F2	Saves a file
F3	Saves an image in the format set in the Display buttons
F4	Lamp buttons
F5	Material buttons
F6	Texture buttons
F7	Animation buttons
F8	World buttons
F9	Edit buttons
F10	Display buttons
F11	Moves the Render window to the front or back
F12	Renders current image
SHIFT-F1	Loads individual elements from a scene file
SHIFT-F2	Saves the current scene as a DXF file
SHIFT-F4	Data select window
SHIFT-F5	3D view window
SHIFT-F6	IPO window
SHIFT-F7	Button window
SHIFT-F8	Sequence window
SHIFT-F9	Oops window
SHIFT-F10	Images window
SHIFT-F11	Text edit window
SHIFT-F12	Image select window
A	Selects or deselects all files (only in File window)
CTRL-U	Saves current scene as the default scene (.B.blend)
CTRL-O	Opens a file
ALT-W	Saves a file in Videoscape format
CTRL-W	Quick save without calling up the File window
CTRL-X	Erases the current scene and starts over with the default scene
RMB	Selects a file (only in File window)
SHIFT-RMB	Multiple selection
Q	Quits Blender

A.2 Manipulating Views: The Number Pad

The keys on the number pad manipulate the view in the 3D window containing the mouse pointer. (In Windows, you may need to turn NUMLOCK on to activate this feature.) All numbers and symbols in the following list refer to the number pad keys.

Table A-2: The number pad keys

Key	Function
/	Local view
*	Rotate view to object
+	Zooms in on most windows
-	Zooms out of most windows
.	Centers and zooms in on the active object
0	Camera view
CTRL-0	Makes the active object the camera
ALT-0	Restores last camera to view
1	Front view
3	Side (right) view
7	Top view
2	Rotates view down
4	Rotates view to the left
6	Rotates view to the right
8	Rotates view up
SHIFT-2	Translates view down
SHIFT-4	Translates view to the left
SHIFT-6	Translates view to the right
SHIFT-8	Translates view up
5	Toggles between perspective and orthogonal view
9	Redraws
CTRL-MMB	Zooms in or out of view
SHIFT-MMB	Translates view

A.3 Working with Vertices, Faces, Objects, Curves, and Surfaces

The last three columns in this section's function tables indicate the window the mouse must be in, the required mode, and the type of data that must be selected (if any) for the given function to work. "None" in the Conditions column means that you don't have to have anything selected for the function to work.

A.3.1 Selecting

These are the commands for selecting objects and files.

Table A-3: Keys for selecting objects and files

Key	Function	Window	Mode	Conditions
A	Selects all	3D, File, IPO, Sequence, Image	Object, Edit	none
B	BorderSelect (selection box)	3D, IPO, Sequence	Object, Edit	none
B-B	CircleSelect	3D	Edit	none
L	Selects vertices linked to cursor	3D	Edit	none
CTRL-L	Selects vertices linked to selected vertex	3D	Edit	Mesh vertices
SHIFT-R	Selects row of NURBS in a surface	3D	Edit	Curve handles
RMB	Selects	3D, IPO, Sequence	Object, Edit	none
SHIFT-RMB	Multiple selection	3D, IPO, Sequence	Object, Edit	none

A.3.2 Creating and Manipulating Objects, Vertices, and Faces

These are the most important commands for working with objects.

Table A-4: Keys for working with objects

Key	Function	Window	Mode	Conditions
spacebar or **SHIFT-A**	Brings up the Toolbox (Blender's main menu). You can also call up the Toolbox icon by clicking the Toolbox icon.	3D, File, IPO, Sequence, Image	Object, Edit	none
CTRL-A	Applies location and rotation	3D	Object	Object
SHIFT-CTRL-A	Applies lattice deformation to an object's mesh	3D	Object	Object
ALT-C	Brings up the Convert menu (for example, to convert a font to a curve)	3D	Object	Object
CTRL-C	Brings up the Copy menu (copies information from active object to selected objects)	3D	Object	Object
ALT-D	Adds linked duplicate (copies selected objects)	3D	Object	Object

Table A-4 (continued): Keys for working with objects

Key	Function	Window	Mode	Conditions
CTRL-D	Displays alpha of image as a wire	3D	Object	Object
SHIFT-D	Adds duplicate object	3D, Sequence	Object	Object, Datablock, Sequence strip
E	Extrudes vertices	3D	Edit	Datablock
F	Connects selected vertices into an edge or face	3D	Edit	Mesh vertices, Curve handles
ALT-F	Beauty fill (forms equally sized faces)	3D	Edit	Datablock
CTRL-F	Sorts faces of active mesh object	3D	Object	Object
SHIFT-F	Fills selected closed polygons with triangular faces	3D	Edit	Mesh vertices
G	Grab (translate) mode	3D, IPO, Sequence	Object, Edit	Sequence strip, IPO keys, Datablock, Object
ALT-G	Clears location	3D	Object	Object
H	Hides selected vertices and faces	3D	Edit	Mesh vertices
ALT-H	Redisplays hidden vertices and faces	3D	Edit	none
SHIFT-H	Hides deselected vertices and faces	3D	Edit	Mesh vertices
CTRL-J	Joins selected objects to active object	3D	Object	Object
SHIFT-L	Brings up the Select links menu (selects objects linked to the same datablock as the active object)	3D	Object	Object
CTRL-L	Brings up the Make links menu (for copying links)	3D	Object	Object
N	Calls up Number menu (for example, to specify exact value of the x coordinate)	3D, Sequence	Object, Edit	If in EditMode, Mesh vertices must be selected
CTRL-N	Recalculates normals and sets them in the same direction outward	3D	Edit	Mesh vertices
SHIFT-CTRL-N	Recalculates normals and sets them in the same direction inward	3D	Edit	Mesh vertices

Table A-4 (continued): Keys for working with objects

Key	Function	Window	Mode	Conditions
ALT-O	Clears origin	3D, IPO	Object, Edit	Object
P	Separates vertices into objects	3D	Edit	Datablock
CTRL-P	Makes active object a parent	3D	Object	Object
CTRL-P	Makes selected vertices (you must have either 1 or 3 vertices selected) parent	3D	Edit	Object, Datablock
ALT-P	Clears parent (unlinks child objects)	3D	Object	Object
R	Rotate mode	3D	Object, Edit	Datablock, Object
ALT-R	Clears rotation	3D	Object	Object
S	Scaling mode	3D, IPO	Object, Edit	Datablock, Object
ALT-S	Clears size	3D, IPO	Object, Edit	Datablock, Object
CTRL-S	Shear (makes selected forms slant)	3D	Edit	Datablock
SHIFT-S	Calls up the Snap menu	3D, IPO	Object, Edit	Datablock, Object
T	Texture space mode (lets you change size and position of texture space)	3D	Object	Object
ALT-T	Clears track	3D	Object	Object
CTRL-T	Converts selected faces to triangles	3D	Edit	Mesh vertices
CTRL-T	Make track (gives selected objects rotation constraint toward active object)	3D	Object	Object
TAB	Starts or ends EditMode	3D	none	none
U	Reloads original data upon entering EditMode	3D	Edit	none
V	Vertex paint mode	3D	Object	none
ALT-V	Sets selected objects' dimensions to aspect of image texture	3D	Object	Object
W	Specials menu	3D	Edit	none
SHIFT-W	Warps selected vertices around cursor	3D	Edit	Datablock
X	Brings up the Erase menu	3D, IPO, Sequence	Object, Edit	Datablock, Object
Y	Splits selected part of a mesh	3D	Edit	Mesh vertices
Z	Toggles between wireframe and solid view	3D	Object, Edit	none

Table A-4 (continued): Keys for working with objects

Key	Function	Window	Mode	Conditions
SHIFT-Z	Toggles between wireframe and shaded view	3D	Object, Edit	none
CTRL-LMB	Adds vertex	3D, IPO	Edit	none

A.3.3 Curves and Surfaces

Table A-5: Keys for working with curves and surfaces

Key	Function	Window	Mode	Conditions
C	Sets selected curves or surfaces to cyclic	3D	Edit	Mesh vertices
E	Extrudes a curve; extrudes selected curves into surfaces	3D	Edit	Datablock
F	Connects two curves at selected end vertices	3D	Edit	Mesh vertices, Curve handles
H	Toggles between aligned and free handles	3D, IPO	Edit	IPO handles, Curve handles
SHIFT-H	Changes to an auto handle	3D, IPO	Edit	IPO handles, Curve handles
CTRL-H	Automatic handle calculation	3D	Edit	Curve handles
L	Selects vertex nearest the mouse and all vertices of curve or surface	3D	Edit	none
SHIFT-L	Deselects selected vertex and all vertices of curve or surface	3D	Edit	none
SHIFT-R	Selects row of NURBS in a surface	3D	Edit	Curve handles
T	Tilt mode	3D	Edit	Curve handles
ALT-T	Clears tilt	3D	Edit	Curve handles
V	Vector handle	3D, IPO	Edit	IPO handles, Curve handles

A.3.4 IKAs

Table A-6: Keys for working with IKAs

Key	Function	Window	Mode	Conditions
E	Extrudes the IKA (adds a limb)	3D	Object, Edit	Object
CTRL-K	Makes skeleton	3D	Object	Object
CTRL-P	Makes parent (3 options: vertex, limb, or skeleton)	3D	Object	Object

A.3.5 The 3D Cursor

Table A-7: Manipulating the 3D cursor

Key	Function	Window	Mode	Conditions
C	Centers window on 3D cursor	3D	none	none
SHIFT-C	Puts cursor on origin and window on home	3D	Object, Edit	none
SHIFT-S	Calls up the Snap menu	3D, IPO	Object, Edit	Datablock, Object
LMB	Sets 3D cursor	3D	none	none

A.4   Working with Layers

The numbers above the letters on the keyboard (*not* the number pad) activate the layers in the 3D windows. You can be in either EditMode or ObjectMode.

Table A-8: Keys for working with layers

Key	Function
0–9	Changes layers (for layers 1–10)
SHIFT-0–9	Changes layers (for layers 11–20)
M	Moves to layer (or layers) (view or change layer setting of all selected objects)

A.5   Working with Keys and Animations

Table A-9: Keys for working with animations

Key	Function
ALT-A	Plays the animation in the window the mouse is in
SHIFT-ALT-A	Plays the animation in all 3D windows
ESC	Stops animation
I	Calls up the Insert keyframe menu (in 3D or IPO windows, either ObjectMode or EditMode)
CTRL-J	Joins selected keys
K	Shows keys of selected objects (PgUp and PgDn switch between keys)
SHIFT-K	Shows and selects all keys
→	Advances one frame
SHIFT - →	Displays the last frame (set in the Display buttons)
←	Goes back one frame
SHIFT - ←	Goes to the first frame

Table A-9 (continued): Keys for working with animations

Key	Function
↑	Advances ten frames
↓	Goes back ten frames
C	Snaps current frame to selected key

B

TIPS, TRICKS, AND
USEFUL PROGRAMS

In this appendix I've compiled information and tips that have been useful to me in my work with Blender. My selections are, of course, subjective and do not represent the entire variety of possible solutions to problems you may encounter. I've also included URLs for additional information and programs you can download. If you encounter a dead link, go to http://www. nostarch.com/blender_updates.htm, where I've posted the current links.

B.1   Importing and Exporting 3D Data

Blender was developed as an in-house tool, so the exchange of 3D data was not an issue—and creating conversion engines would have required a huge expenditure. At first, VRML and the VRML predecessor Inventor were Blender's only interfaces to the outside world. (This was a common format in use on the SGI machines where Blender was developed and used.) Blender could also import and export ASCII files of 3D data using conventions introduced for Videoscape—the great-grandfather of all 3D animation programs—which was developed for the Amiga computer.

Once Blender became more widely available, the demand for better ways to import and export 3D data grew quickly. Since then, VRML import has been improved, VRML export has been added, functions have been added to the Videoscape format, and a DXF import and export facility has been added. The ability to process VRML and DXF, *the* two multi-platform 3D data formats, makes it possible for Blender to exchange files with almost any program. (Later in this appendix, I'll cover additional converters that can convert diverse 3D file formats into formats Blender can read.)

B.1.1 Videoscape

Although there is, as far as I know, no other program that still supports the Videoscape format, this easily parsed ASCII format is ideal for using Blender to visualize 3D data from your own programs, or for converting 3D Blender models into formats for different game engines. (The Videoscape format as enhanced by the Blender team is described in detail in the *Blender Handbook*.)

B.1.2 VRML

If you don't want to tie yourself down to an interface that's easy to understand but not really open, you should use VRML (virtual reality modeling language). VRML is a standardized interface for 3D data based on the SGI Inventor format. Because nearly every Web browser has VRML plug-ins, VRML is without a doubt the ideal medium for making 3D models available on the Internet.

An updated, interactive version of VRML (VRML97) makes it possible to build entire 3D worlds that can integrate multiple users. Unfortunately, Blender currently supports only VRML-1 as ASCII files.

B.1.3 DXF

The DXF format introduced by Autodesk (in AutoCAD or 3DStudio) has become the de facto standard for exchanging 3D data in the CAD field. Unfortunately, it's not really an established standard—it gets modified and expanded with each new AutoCAD version. In principle, DXF is also a format that uses ACSII characters for descriptions, but (unlike VRML) it cannot be read by a human being, much less edited. There are also binary formats for DXF, but Blender is not yet able to read them.

B.2 3D Tools

Before you can use Blender with the many 3D models available on the Internet you must convert them to a format Blender can read. There are a ton of programs for doing this, and I'll list just a few freeware or shareware programs here. (Linux and other Unix programs still lack these conversion utilities, so it's helpful to have access to a computer that runs Windows.) In general, however, CAD and 3D animation programs can also write VRML or DXF files, so a converter is not always necessary.

B.2.1 Crossroads 3D

The Windows 95/NT freeware program Crossroads by Keith Rule converts many 3D formats and writes the formats important for Blender—DXF and VRML-1. The program has a graphical interface that offers a preview of the object's geometry and a couple of features for editing models. Keith Rule is the author of *3D File Formats: A Programmer's Reference* (Addison Wesley Longman, 1996), which contains the source code for his converter.

In addition to Crossroads 3D, Rule also offers an older program called WCVT2POV, which not only converts into the POV Ray format but also supports most of the Crossroads formats. (A version of this program even runs under Windows 3.1.) One import format makes this program especially interesting for Blender users and puts it a notch above Crossroads: It can convert TrueType fonts into 3D objects.

The two programs are available on the author's home page at http://www.europa.com/~keithr/.

B.2.2   3DWin

The 3DWin homepage (http://www.stmuc.com/thbaier/) has a collection of various shareware converters by Thomas Baier. (If you use them regularly, you must pay a license fee, which is used for further development of the programs.)

3DWin itself sports a graphical interface with a four-sided view of the model. In addition to 3DWin, you'll also find various versions of the command-line converter 3Dto3D. Of special interest to Linux and Unix users is a source code version that can be compiled on common systems to then serve as a good converter for diverse file formats.

B.3   2D Tools

Even the pure 3D artist often has to post-process rendered images or prepare textures for use in Blender. Don't neglect this area, since 2D post-processing makes up a big part of films—even the ones with the latest special effects.

B.3.1   The GIMP

The GIMP (http://www.gimp.org) is a complete and very mature image editor. While developed under Linux, the GIMP has been ported to various Unix platforms and a Windows version is under development.

The GIMP's functionality is comparable to Photoshop, but unlike Photoshop, the GIMP is free—covered by the GNU Public License (GPL) by Richard M. Stallman—and available in source code.

B.3.2   Windows and Macintosh Programs

Image editors and tools for Windows and Macintosh are almost too numerous to be counted. The palette runs from high-end professional programs costing thousands of dollars to shareware and freeware.

If you get a 2D program for either Windows or Macintosh, make sure it supports creating textures on multiple levels and working with alpha masks (transparency information)—and, of course, that it has mastered the file formats supported by Blender.

B.4   Creating Animations

Blender writes AVI RAW (uncompressed) and AVI JPEG (JPEG compressed) as its animation formats. These formats are native to Windows platforms and thus often cause difficulties on other platforms. MPEG-1, which can be played back on most platforms, is a good alternative for producing animations.

(Appendix C has a description of how Blender itself can be used to play back all the formats it generates.)

B.4.1 Berkeley MPEG Tools

The Berkeley MPEG tools (http://bmrc.berkeley.edu/frame/research/mpeg/index.html) from the University of California at Berkeley (ucbmpeg) are a reference implementation of the MPEG-1 standard. The programs are in the public domain and include a player for MPEG-1 (mpeg_play), a program for creating MPEG-1s (mpeg_encode), and MPEG-1 video analyzers. (There are packages for the various Linux distributions as well.) MPEG-1 is an ideal format for putting animations on the Internet due to its high level of compression.

The program mpeg_encode offers many options for creating MPEG-1 files out of individual images. The process takes a lot of computing resources, but leads to very small files. The following is a simple example of a *control file* (a file that describes how and from which input files an MPEG will be created) that should work in most cases:

```
# Torpedo

# the following is necessary but need not be understood
PATTERN IBBPBBPBBPBBPBB
IQSCALE         8
PQSCALE         10
BQSCALE         25
PIXEL           HALF
RANGE           10
PSEARCH_ALG     LOGARITHMIC
BSEARCH_ALG     CROSS2
REFERENCE_FRAME DECODED
GOP_SIZE        30
SLICES_PER_FRAME        1

# important for the user as of here
# output name
OUTPUT Torpedo.mpg

# images in JPEG
# BASE_FILE_FORMAT      JPEG
# or in PPM
BASE_FILE_FORMAT        PPM

# use an external program as a filter here
# no filter
INPUT_CONVERT *
```

```
# TGA to PPM
INPUT_CONVERT tgatoppm *

# image directory
INPUT_DIR            .

# all the images from Torpedo.0001 to Torpedo.0400
INPUT
Torpedo.* [0001-0400]
END_INPUT
```

Now call mpeg_encode with the following:

```
cw@mero /tmp >mpeg_encode mpeg.param
[··· a lot of output ···]
```

After a while you will be able to watch the MPEG animation with any MPEG player.

B.4.2 avi2mpg: Producing MPEG-1 under Windows

Take advantage of avi2mpg (http://www.mnsi.net/~jschlic1/), a small, free, command-line–based program for producing MPEG-1 films under Windows. Originally released in 1997 as a freeware alternative to commercial encoders available at that time, it has been enhanced by various contributors since then to include numerous new features and enhancements. At this writing, a beta version of a GUI wrapper by Tom Holusa (to make it easier to use from Windows) is also available from the program's Web site.

B.4.3 MainActor

Mainconcept's MainActor (http://www.mainconcept.de) is one of the few programs available for both Linux and Windows. Like Blender, MainActor is distributed over the Internet and the registration key is good for Windows, Linux, and OS/2. MainActor's graphical interface lets you interconvert GIF animations, image sequences (numbered as in Blender), MPEG-1 and -2, QuickTime, and AVI files.

B.5 Plug-ins

The current version of Blender includes a plug-in interface that lets you quickly add new functions for textures and the Sequence Editor as you need them. Plug-ins are written in C and the C compiler must translate them into binary files necessary for each platform. (Before you download finished plug-ins, make sure that they match your operating system and hardware platform—if not, they will not run and may even crash Blender.)

You'll find documentation on Blender's Web site on how to create plug-ins; source programs of available plug-ins are also a good source of information.

NOTE *The URLs for the following plug-ins, other interesting Blender links, and information on this book are located at http://www.nostarch.com/blender/.*

B.5.1 Texture Plug-ins

The following are examples of the kind of texture plug-ins currently available. There have, of course, been many more plug-ins for some time now, and with the integration of the texture interface as of Blender 1.68, there are certainly more on the horizon.

Clouds2	An improved clouds texture. Author: Not a Number
Dots2	Texture plug-in for creating points, dots, and much more. Author: Bernd Breitenbach
Led	Texture plug-in for generating static or animated LED digits. Author: Bernd Breitenbach
musgrave	Texture plug-in for creating, with a little imagination, everything from dinosaur skin to metal surfaces; especially well-suited for bump maps. Author: Rob Haarsma
fixNoise	Generates smoke. However, unlike the built-in Noise texture, it is not animated. Author: "Excellent Whale," Joeri Kassenaar

B.5.2 Sequence Plug-ins

Sequence plug-ins are meant to expand the Sequence Editor's effects palette.

Alphamatte	Generates image masks from a sequence's alpha information, which can then be used for compositing in an external program. Author: Bart Veldhuizen
Chromakey	(also called Blue Screen) Chromakey removes a color you choose (typically blue but also green or red) from a composite image. For example, you could create a blue screen composite image with a subject that has been photographed in front of an evenly lit, bright, pure blue background, then use compositing to replace all the blue in the picture with another image, known as the background plate. Author: Stefan Gartner
Robocop	Simulates the view from a security camera or robot. Author: Joeri Kassenaar
Scatter	Adds distortion to a sequence to make it look like bad videotape. Author: Not a Number
WipeOut	Renders various wipes between scenes, with the help of masks. Author: Joeri Kassenaar
zblur	Renders depth of (un)focus into Blender animations. As a result of its aperture and exposure time, the depth of focus of a real camera has a defined range, outside of which objects appear more or less out of focus. A virtual camera does not have these properties—they must be simulated with a plug-in. Author: Martin Strubel

C

COMMAND LINE
ARGUMENTS

Blender has several arguments that can be issued from the command line at start-up. For example, it's possible to have Blender render an animation without calling up the graphical interface or, if you'll be away for a while, to have it render multiple animations, one after the other.

The -h parameter yields a short overview of the parameters.

```
cw@mero ~/work/texte/BlenderBuch >blender -h
Blender V 1.73
Usage: blender [options ...] [file]

Render options:
    -b <file>    Render <file> in background
    -S <name>    Set scene <name>
    -f <frame>   Render frame <frame> and save it
    -s <frame>   Set start to frame <frame>
                 (use with -a)
    -e <frame>    Set end to frame (use with -a)<frame>
    -a            Render animation

Animation options:
    -a <file(s)> Playback <file(s)>
    -m           Read from disk (Don't buffer)
```

```
Window options:
  -w               Force opening with borders
  -p <sx> <sy> <w> <h> Open with lower left
                   corner at <sx>, <sy>
                   and width and height <w>, <h>

Misc options:
  -f               Prevent forking in foreground mode
  -d               Turn debugging on
  -h               Print this help text
  -y               Disable OnLoad scene scripts,
                   use -Y to find out why its -y


cw@mero ~/work/texte/BlenderBuch >
```
....

The last argument to declare is the Blender file (<file>) to be loaded or rendered. These are the individual options:

Options for Rendering in the Background

-b <file>   Renders the Blender file in the background as set in the file.

-S <name>   Selects a scene from the file to render.

-f <image_number>   Renders and saves the image <image_number>.

-s <image_number>   Begins rendering with image <image_number>.

-e <image_number>   Ends rendering with image <image_number>.

-a   Renders the animation and saves the images.

The following call taken from a command line renders the entire animation as set in the Display buttons (F10):

....
```
cw@mero /tmp >blender -b test.blend -a
Saved: /tmp/blender.0001 Time: 00:01.28 (0.00)
Saved: /tmp/blender.0002 Time: 00:01.28 (-0.01)
Saved: /tmp/blender.0003 Time: 00:01.28 (0.05)
[...]
```
....

The above output indicates the rendered and saved image together with the processing time. The images are saved to the path set in the file (in the Display buttons).

The following call renders images 4 through 6 from the "logo" scene in the Blender file test.blend in the background and saves the images as specified in the file.

```
cw@mero /tmp >blender -B test.blend -S Logo -s
4 -e 6 -a
Saved: /tmp/blender.0004 Time: 00:01.19 (0.01)
Saved: /tmp/blender.0005 Time: 00:01.19 (0.01)
Saved: /tmp/blender.0006 Time: 00:01.19 (0.00)
Blender quit
```

Options for Displaying Animations

The following options turn Blender into a player of image sequences or AVIs created by Blender.

-a <file(s)>	Plays a rendered animation or image sequence. Plays all formats supported by Blender.
-m	Plays directly from the hard disk.

The following call plays all frames beginning with `blender.0001`. You can resize the playback window on a continuum. Press ESC to abort playback.

```
cw@mero /tmp >blender -a blender.0001
cw@mero /tmp >
```

Additional Options

-p sx sy w h	Opens the Blender window with a width of w and a height of h on the coordinates (sx, sy), measured from the bottom left of the screen.
-f	Prevents Blender from going into the background after the call, releasing the command line window. Helpful for batch rendering in shell scripts (Bash, *.bat, and so on).
-y	Prevents the execution of Python scripts when loading a file.

D

OVERVIEW OF
BLENDER MODULES

D.1   Blender's Main API Module

The Blender module contains all modules that are part of the Blender/Python API, as well as some general functions and variables.

D.1.1   Functions

Method: Blender.Get(request)

This is the general data access function; request is a string identifying the data that should be returned. Currently the Get function accepts the following requests:

curframe	Returns the current animation frame
curtime	Returns the current animation time
filename	Returns the name of the last file read or written
version	Returns the running Blender version number

The curtime request returns a floating point value, which incorporates motion blur and field calculations; curframe returns the integer value of the current frame.

Method: Blender.Redraw()

Forces an immediate redraw of all 3D windows in the current screen and can be used to force display of updated information (for example, when an IPO curve for an object has been changed).

D.1.2 Variables

Boolean: Blender.bylink

Tests to see whether the script was executed by a ScriptLink (see Section D.12, the ScriptLinks section).

Object: Blender.link

This variable exists only when scripts have been called by ScriptLinks and contains the object that the script was linked to (see the ScriptLinks section).

String: Blender.event

This variable exists only when scripts have been called by ScriptLinks and contains the name of the event that called the script (see the ScriptLinks section).

D.2 BGL: Blender's OpenGL Module

The BGL module allows scripts to draw sophisticated interfaces within Blender. It is essentially a flat wrapper around the entire OpenGL library, allowing the use of standard OpenGL tutorials and references to program Blender/Python interface scripts. Neither extensions nor platform-specific functions are supported.

All function names remain the same as with the C OpenGL implementation, although in some cases this makes less sense; for example, the function variants with f, i, and s are meaningless to Python. Functions that take pointer arguments are the only exception to this rule.

Since Python has no direct pointer access, the BGL module includes a special type (buffer) that essentially provides a wrapper around a pointer/malloc (memory allocator). Any OpenGL functions that take a pointer should be passed to a buffer object instead.

The BGL module is a flat wrapper that performs no extra error checking or handling. This means that it is possible to cause crashes if you try to pass a buffer object of incorrect size to an OpenGL function.

Because Blender uses one OpenGL context, and the entire interface is drawn with OpenGL, scripts must not inadvertently alter some critical state value. To effectively "sandbox" the scripts, Blender sets up the window to be drawn during drawing, and pushes all OpenGL stack attributes onto the attribute stack. When the draw function returns, the attributes are popped; BGL calls should be made *only* during the draw function.

D.2.1 Functions

Method: Buffer(type, dimensions, [template])

Creates a new buffer object to be passed to OpenGL functions expecting a pointer. The type argument, indicating the type of data the buffer is to store, should be GL_BYTE, GL_SHORT, GL_INT, or GL_FLOAT.

If a one-dimensional list is to be created, the dimensions argument should be a single integer; if a multi-dimensional list is desired it should be a list of dimensions. For example, passing in [100, 100] would create a two-dimensional square buffer (with a total of 100x100 = 10,000 elements). Passing in [16, 16, 26] would create a three-dimensional buffer, twice as deep as it is wide or high (with a total of 16x16x32 = 8192 elements).

The template argument can be used to pass a multi-dimensional list to be used to initialize the values in the buffer; the template should have the same dimensions as the buffer to be created. If no template is passed, all values are initialized to zero.

D.2.2 Object

The buffer object can be indexed, assigned, sliced, and so on, just like a Python multi-dimensional list (list of lists), except that its size cannot be changed. list returns the contents of the buffer as a multi-dimensional list.

D.3 Camera: Camera Object Access

The Camera access module.

D.3.1 Functions

Method: Get([name])

If name is specified, this function returns the camera object with the same name (or none if a match is not found). If name is not specified, the function returns a list of all the camera objects in the current scene.

D.3.2 Objects

name	Name of the camera referenced by this object
block_type	"Camera"
properties	List of extra data properties
ipo	Link to the IPO for the camera
Lens	Lens value for the camera
ClSta	Clip start value
ClEnd	Clip end value

The name, block_type, and properties fields are common to all BlockType objects. If the camera does not have an IPO, the Camera.ipo field returns none.

D.4　Draw: The Window Interface Module

The Draw module is broken into two parts, and provides the basic function that lets Blender/Python scripts build interfaces that work inside Blender. The first part handles the functions and variables needed to give a script control of a window, and the second part allows scripts to use the Blender internal user interface toolkit (buttons, sliders, menus, and so on).

Blender/Python interface scripts (GUI scripts for short) provide Blender with a set of callbacks to allow passage of events and drawing, after which the script takes control of the text window it was run from.

Before it can initiate the interface, the script must call the Draw.Register function to specify the script functions to be used to control the interface. Generally, a draw and event function are passed, though either one can be left out.

Once the script has been registered, the draw callback is executed (with no arguments) each time the window is redrawn. Drawing uses the functions in the Blender.BGL module to give scripts full control over the drawing process. Before drawing is initiated, Blender sets up the OpenGL window clipping and stores its own state on the attribute stack to prevent scripts from interfering with other parts of the Blender interface.

When the draw function is called, the window matrix is set to the window width and height, so the coordinate to pixel mapping is 1:1. Because Blender manages its windows internally, drawing should take place *only* inside the draw function; if an event must trigger drawing of some kind, the event function should send a redraw event (Draw.Redraw).

The script event function is called when the Blender window receives input events and the script window has input focus (the mouse is in the window). The function is called with two arguments: the event and an extra value modifier (see the Events section below for more information).

Scripts can unregister themselves and return control to the Text editor by calling the Draw.Exit function. If the script fails to provide a method to exit, the key combination CTRL-ALT-SHIFT-Q will force a script to exit.

D.4.1　Events

The Draw module contains all the event constants that can be passed to a registered Python event callback. Table D-1 lists the events that are currently passed, and the meaning of the extra value argument passed with the event.

Table D-1: List of events

Event names	Value/meaning
[x]KEY (AKEY, F2KEY, and so on)	The value is 0 or 1; 0 means a key-release, 1 a key-press.
PAD[x] (PAD1, PADENTER, and so on)	The value is 0 or 1; 0 means a key-release, 1 a key-press.
MOUSEX, MOUSEY	The values are the window x and y coordinates of the mouse position.
LEFTMOUSE, MIDDLEMOUSE, RIGHTMOUSE	The value is 0 or 1; 0 means a button-release, 1 a button-press.

The list of all events is quite long, and most are fairly obvious (AKEY, BKEY, CKEY, and so on) so they have been shortened to [x]KEY and PAD[x]. To find the exact name of an event, print the contents of the Draw module with

```
print dir(Blender.Draw)
```

(or guess).

D.4.2 Functions

Method: Draw()

Forces an immediate redraw of the active Python window; returns *after* the window has been redrawn.

Method: Exit()

Unregisters Python from controlling the windowing interface and returns the window control to the text editor.

Method: Redraw([after])

Adds a redraw event to the window event queue. If the after flag is not passed (or false), the window receives the redraw event as soon as program control returns to Blender (that is, once the running function completes.) If the after flag is true, the window receives the event after all other input events have been processed. This allows a window to continuously redraw while receiving user input, allowing the rest of the Blender program to receive input at the same time.

Redraw events are buffered internally, so the window is redrawn only once per queue-flush regardless of how many redraw events are on the queue.

Method: Register(draw, [event, button])

The Register function is the basis of the Python window interface. It is used to pass three callbacks, which handle window events. The first function, the draw function, is used to redraw the window when necessary and should take no arguments.

The second function, the event function, handles all input events. It takes two arguments: the event number and the value modifier. (See the Events section above for more information on the events that are passed.)

The third function, the button event function, handles events that are generated by the various button types.

Any of the functions can be passed as a none, and Blender will take a default action for events that are not handled by a callback. At least one function must be passed for the Register function to have any effect.

Method: Text(string)

Draws the string using the default bitmap font at the current GL raster position (use the glRasterPos functions to change the current raster position).

D.4.3 Button Functions

Method: Button(label, event, x, y, width, height, [tooltip])

Creates a new push button, drawn at the specified x and y coordinates with the specified width and height, and with the specified label drawn on top. If a tooltip is specified, it will be displayed when the user mouses over the button (if the system has Tooltips enabled).

When this new button is pressed it passes the event number specified by event to Python's button event callback, if one was specified to the Draw.Register function.

Method: Create(value)

Returns a new button object containing the specified value; the type of button (Int, Float, or String) is determined by the type of the value.

Method: Menu(options, event, x, y, width, height, default, [tooltip])

Creates a new push button, drawn at the specified x and y coordinates with the specified width and height. If a tooltip is specified, it will be displayed when the user mouses over the button (if they have Tooltips enabled).

The menu options are encoded in the options argument and are separated by the "|" (pipe) character. Each option consists of a name followed by a format code. Valid format codes are:

%t   The option should be used as the title for the menu

%xN   The option should set the integer N in the button value

The default argument determines the value that will initially be present in the button object, and the menu option that will initially be selected.

When the menu item is changed, the button value is set to the value specified in the selected menu option and the button passes the event number specified by event to Python's button event callback (assuming one was specified to the Draw.Register function).

For example, if the menu options argument is Color %t| Red %x1| Green %x2| Blue %x3, and the default is 2, then the menu will initially display "Green," and when the user selects it, it will display three items ("Red," "Green," and "Blue") and the title "Color." Selecting the "Red," "Green," or "Blue" options will change the button value to 1, 2, or 3 respectively, and the event will be passed to the button event callback.

Method: Number(label, event, x, y, width, height, initial, min, max, [tooltip])

Creates a new number button that will be drawn at the specified x and y coordinates with the specified width and height; the label will be drawn to the left of the input field. If a tooltip is specified, it will be displayed when the user mouses over the button (if Tooltips are enabled).

The number button's type is determined by the type of the initial argument: If an Int, the number button will hold integers; if a Float, it will hold floating point values. The value of the button return will range between min and max, with the initial argument determining which value is set by default.

When the button is pressed, it passes the event number specified by event to Python's button event callback, assuming one was specified to the Draw. Register function.

Method: Scrollbar(event, x, y, width, height, initial, min, max, [update, tooltip])

Creates a new scrollbar button that will be drawn at the specified x and y coordinates with the specified width and height; the label will be drawn to the left of the input field. If a tooltip is specified, it will be displayed when the user mouses over the button (if Tooltips are enabled).

The scrollbar type is determined by the type of the initial argument: If an Int, the number button will hold integers; if a Float, it will hold floating point values. The value of the button return will range between min and max, with the initial argument determining which value is set by default.

When the scrollbar is repositioned, it passes the event number specified by event to Python's button event callback, assuming one was specified to the Draw.Register function. If the update argument is not passed (or true) then the events will be passed for every motion of the scrollbar; if the update argument is false the events will be sent only after the user releases the scrollbar.

Method: Slider(label, event, x, y, width, height, initial, min, max, [update, tooltip])

Creates a new slider button that will be drawn at the specified x and y coordinates with the specified width and height; the label will be drawn to the left of the input field. If a tooltip is specified, it will be displayed when the user mouses over the button (if Tooltips are enabled).

The type of slider button is determined by the type of the initial argument; if an Int, the slider button will hold integers; if a Float, the slider button will hold floating point values. The value of the button return will range between min and max, with the initial argument determining which value is set by default.

When the slider is repositioned, it will pass the event number specified by event to Python's button event callback, assuming one was specified to the Draw.Register function. If the update argument is not passed (or true) then the events will be passed for every motion of the slider, otherwise (if the update argument is false) the events will be sent only after the user releases the slider.

Method: String(label, event, x, y, width, height, initial, length, [tooltip])

Creates a new string button that will be drawn at the specified x and y coordinates with the specified width and height; the label will be drawn to the left of the input field. If a tooltip is specified, it will be displayed when the user mouses over the button (if Tooltips are enabled).

The button will return a String value, reflecting the current state of the toggle. The initial argument determines which value is initially present in the button. The length field specifies the maximum length of the string that may be entered in the button.

After the string has been edited, it passes the event number specified by event to Python's button event callback, assuming one was specified to the Draw.Register function.

Method: Toggle(label, event, x, y, width, height, default, [tooltip])

Creates a new toggle button that will be drawn at the specified x and y coordinates with the specified width and height; the label will be drawn to the left of the input field. If a tooltip is specified, it will be displayed when the user mouses over the button (if Tooltips are enabled).

The value of the button return will be 0 or 1, reflecting the current state of the toggle. The default will determine which value is initially set.

When the button is pressed, it passes the event number specified by event to Python's button event callback, assuming one was specified to the Draw. Register function.

D.4.4   Objects

The val object has the current value of the button. Depending on the method used to create the button, the val field will have several different types, including Int, Float, and String.

D.5   Lamp: Lamp Object Access

The Lamp access module.

D.5.1   Functions

Method: Get([name])

If name is specified, this function returns the Lamp object with the same name (or none if a match is not found). If name is not specified, the function returns a list of all the Lamp objects in the current scene.

D.5.2   Objects

name	Name of the lamp this object references
block_type	"Lamp"
properties	List of extra data properties
ipo	Link to the IPO for the lamp
R	Red light component
G	Green light component
B	Blue light component
Energ	Lamp energy value
Dist	Lamp distance value
SpoSi	Lamp spot size

SpoBl	Lamp spot blend
HaInt	Lamp halo intensity
Quad1	Lamp quad1 value
Quad2	Lamp quad2 value

The name, block_type, and properties fields are common to all BlockType objects. If the Lamp does not have an IPO, the Lamp.ipo field returns none.

D.6 Material: Material Object Access

The Material access module.

D.6.1 Functions

Method: Get([name])

If name is specified, this function returns the Material object with the same name (or none if a match is not found). If name is not specified, the function returns a list of all the Material objects in the current scene.

D.6.2 Objects

name	Name of the material this object references
block_type	"Material"
properties	List of extra data properties
ipo	Link to the IPO for the material
R	Red material color component
G	Green material color component
B	Blue material color component
SpecR	Red material specular component
SpecG	Green material specular component
SpecB	Blue material specular component
MirR	Red material mirror component
MirG	Green material mirror component
MirB	Blue material mirror component
Ref	Material reflectivity
Alpha	Material transparency
Emit	Material emittance value
Amb	Material ambient value
Spec	Material specular value
SpTra	Material specular transparency
HaSize	Material halo size
Mode	Material mode settings
Hard	Material hardness

The `name`, `block_type`, and `properties` fields are common to all BlockType objects. If the `Material` does not have an IPO, the `Material.ipo` field returns `none`.

D.7 NMesh: Mesh Access

The vertex editing functionality is planned for low- and high-level access. Low-level access is intended for programmers who are familiar with mesh editing and the data structures involved (and links between them), and who intend to write intensive modules to work with Blender. High-level access is for people who do not want to take the time to handle the basic data structures themselves, or who need only a quick effect. Low-level editing is completely independent of Blender, while high-level editing uses and builds on Blender's features.

The `NMesh` module represents the first step toward providing vertex-level access from Python.

D.7.1 Functions

Method: NMesh.GetRaw([name])

If `name` is specified, Blender will try to return an `NMesh` derived from the Blender mesh with the same name; if a mesh with that name does not exist, `GetRaw` returns `none`. If `name` is not specified, a new empty `NMesh` object will be returned.

When the `NMesh` is created, Blender sets the `NMesh` name, `has_col`, and `has_uvco` based on the mesh read.

Method: NMesh.PutRaw(nmesh, [name, renormal])

If `name` is not given (or `none`), `PutRaw` creates a new Blender object and mesh, sets the mesh data to match the `nmesh` field, and returns the created object.

If the `name` is given, `PutRaw` attempts to replace the Blender mesh with that name with the `nmesh` value, and will return `none` (regardless of success or failure). If a mesh with the name is in Blender but has no users, the effects are as if the name was not given (an object will be created and returned).

The `renormal` flag determines whether vertex normals are recalculated. They should not be recalculated only if they have been specifically modified to achieve a particular effect.

The `nmesh.has_uvco` and `nmesh.has_col` flags determine whether the mesh should be created with UV coordinates or vertex colors, or both.

Method: NMesh.Vert([x, y, z])

Returns a new `NMVert` object, created from the given `x`, `y`, and `z` coordinates. If any coordinates are not passed they default to 0.0.

Method: NMesh.Face()

Returns a new `NMFace` object.

Method: NMesh.Col([r,g,b,a])

Returns a new NMCol object created from the given r, g, b, and a color components. If any components are not passed they default to 255.

D.7.2 Objects

NMesh

name	Name of the mesh this object was derived from
verts	List of NMVert objects
faces	List of NMFace objects
mats	List of material names
has_col	Flag for whether mesh has mesh colors
has_uvco	Flag for whether mesh has UV coordinates

The name field of the NMesh object allows scripts to determine what mesh the object originally came from when it is otherwise unknown, for example when the mesh has been obtained from an object's data field.

To keep mesh sizes low, mesh colors and UV coordinates are stored only when needed; if a mesh has colors or UV coordinates when it is accessed by the GetRaw function, the has_col and has_uvco flags will be set accordingly. Similarly, before a mesh is returned to Blender with the PutRaw functions, the has_col and has_uvco flags must be set properly.

The mats field contains a list of materials that are attached to the mesh indices (which differs from the list of materials attached to objects). The PutRaw function remakes the material list, so the mats field can be used to switch the materials linked by the mesh.

The verts field should contain a list of all vertices in the mesh. If a vertex is listed in a face but not in the verts list, it will not be present in the face.

NMFace

v	List of NMVert objects
col	List of NMCol objects
mat	Material index number for face
smooth	Flag indicating whether face is smooth

The v field lists NMVert objects. If a face is to be part of an NMesh, each object should be in the NMesh.verts list. The vertices determine the face in clockwise ordering. Faces should have two, three, or four vertices stored in a mesh; two vertices form an edge, while three or four form a face (a triangle or quad).

The col field lists NMCols, always with a length of 4. NMCol matches the NMVert in the v list with the same index. Extra objects in the list (for example, if a face has fewer than four vertices) are ignored.

The mat field contains the material index for the face; if the face is part of an NMesh its value is used with the NMesh.mats list to determine the face's material.

NMVert

index	Vertex index
co	Coordinate vector
uvco	UV coordinate vector
no	Normal vector

If the vertex is from an NMesh that has been read with the GetRaw function, the index field will contain the index of the vertex within the array. This field is ignored by the PutRaw function, and exists only to simplify some calculations relating to face-to-vertex resolution.

The co, uvco, and no fields return a VectorType object, which is used to interact efficiently with Blender data structures. A VectorType object can generally be used like a list of floating point values, but its length cannot be changed.

The uvco field contains the vertex UV coordinates for the mesh, which are used by the Sticky mapping option. This field is a three-member vector, but the last (z) member is unused.

The no field can be used to alter the vertex normals of a mesh to change the way some calculations (like rendering) are performed. A flag must be passed to the PutRaw function to prevent the normals from being recalculated if they have been modified for this purpose (though the vertex normals will still be recalculated if the user enters EditMode or performs other operations on the mesh, regardless of the flag passed to the PutRaw function).

NMCol

r	Red color component
g	Green color component
b	Blue color component
a	Alpha color component

D.8 Object: Object Object Access

The Object access module.

D.8.1 Functions

Method: Get([name])

If name is specified, this function returns the Object object with the same name (or none if a match is not found). If name is not specified, the function returns a list of all the Object objects in the current scene.

Method: GetSelected()

Returns a list of all selected objects in the current scene. The active object is the first one in the list.

Method: Update(name)

Updates the object with the specified name during user-transformation. This is an experimental function for combating lag, mainly with regard to calculating IKA properly.

D.8.2 Objects

name	Name of the Blender object this object references
block_type	"Object"
properties	List of extra data properties
parent	Link to this object's parent
track	Link to the object this object is tracking
ipo	Link to the IPO for the object
data	Link to the data for the object
math	The object matrix
loc	The location coordinate vector
dloc	The delta location coordinate vector
rot	The rotation vector (angles are in radians)
drot	The delta rotation vector (angles are in radians)
size	The size vector
dsize	The delta size vector
LocX	X location coordinate
LocY	Y location coordinate
LocZ	Z location coordinate
dLocX	X delta location coordinate
dLocY	Y delta location coordinate
dLocZ	Z delta location coordinate
RotX	X rotation angle (in radians)
RotY	Y rotation angle (in radians)
RotZ	Z rotation angle (in radians)
dRotX	X delta rotation angle (in radians)
dRotY	Y delta rotation angle (in radians)
dRotZ	Z delta rotation angle (in radians)
SizeX	X size
SizeY	Y size
SizeZ	Z size
dSizeX	X delta size
dSizeY	Y delta size
dSizeZ	Z delta size
EffX	X effector coordinate
EffY	Y effector coordinate
EffZ	Z effector coordinate
Layer	Object layer (as a bitmap)

The name, block_type, and properties fields are common to all BlockType objects.

The loc, dloc, rot, drot, size, and dsize fields all return a vector object, which is used to interact efficiently with Blender data structures. It can generally be used like a list of floating point values, but its length cannot be changed.

If the object does not have content in the parent, track, ipo, or data fields, or the content is not accessible to Python, the fields return none.

D.9 World: World Object Access

The World access module.

D.9.1 Functions

Method: Get([name])

If name is specified, this function returns the World object with the same name (or none if a match is not found); if name is not specified, the function returns a list of all the World objects in the current scene.

Method: GetActive()

Returns the active world (or none if there isn't one).

D.9.2 Objects

name	Name of the world this object references
block_type	"World"
properties	List of extra data properties
ipo	Link to the IPO for the world
HorR	The red horizon color component
HorG	The green horizon color component
HorB	The blue horizon color component
ZenR	The red zenith color component
ZenG	The green zenith color component
ZenB	The blue zenith color component
Expos	The world exposure value
MisSta	The mist start value
MisDi	The mist distance value
MisHi	The mist height value
StarDi	The star distance value
StarSi	The star size value

The name, block_type, and properties fields are common to all BlockType objects. If the world does not have an IPO, the World.ipo field returns none.

D.10   Types: Blender Declared Types

This module holds the type objects for all the Blender declared objects, which can be compared with the types returned by the type (object) function.

D.10.1   Variables

BezTripleType	**NMColType**
BlockType	**NMFaceType**
BufferType	**NMVertType**
ButtonType	**NMeshType**
IpoCurveType	**VectorType**
MatrixType	

D.11   IPO: IPO Object Access

The IPO access module.

D.11.1   Functions

Method: Get([name])

If name is specified, this function returns the IPO object with the same name (or none if a match is not found); if name is not specified, the function returns a list of all the IPO objects in the current scene.

Method: BezTriple()

Returns a new BezTriple object.

Method: Eval(curve, [time])

Returns the value of the curve at the given time. If the time is not passed, the current time is used.

Method: Recalc(ipo)

Recalculates the values of the curves in the given ipo, and updates all objects in the scene that reference the ipo with the new values.

D.11.2   Objects

IPO

name	Name of the IPO this object references
block_type	"IPO"
properties	List of extra data properties
curves	List of IPOCurve objects making up this IPO block

The name, block_type, and properties fields are common to all BlockType objects.

IPOCurve

name	Name of this IPO curve
type	The type of interpolation for this curve
extend	The type of extension for this curve
points	List of BezTriples comprising this curve

To quickly and easily edit IPO curves, Blender needs a way to recalculate curve-specific data without recalculating the data in every script operation. To handle this, the points field returns a list of the BezTriples that make up the curve, which can be edited without any intervention by Blender. To update the curve, the list must be reassigned to the points field. (Note that single points cannot simply be edited, however, and editing IpoCurve.points[0] in place will not update the curve.)

The type field returns one of the following values:

Constant	Curve remains constant between points
Linear	Curve uses linear interpolation of points
Bezier	Curve uses Bezier interpolation of points

The extend field returns one of the following values:

Constant	Curve remains constant after endpoints
Extrapolate	Curve is extrapolated after endpoints
Cyclic	Curve repeats cyclically
CyclicX	Curve repeats cyclically, and is extrapolated

BezTriple

h1	The first (leftmost) handle coordinate vector
pt	The point coordinate vector
h2	The second (rightmost) handle coordinate vector
f1	Flag for h1 selection (true=selected)
f2	Flag for pt selection (true=selected)
f3	Flag for h2 selection (true=selected)
h1t	The first (leftmost) handle type
h2t	The second (rightmost) handle type

The h1, pt, and h2 fields all return a vector object, which is used to interact efficiently with Blender data structures. A vector object can generally be used like a list of floating point values, but its length cannot be changed.

The h1t and h2t fields determine the handle types that return and can be set to these values:

Free	Handle is free (unconstrained)
Auto	Handle is automatically calculated
Vect	Handle points toward adjoining point on curve
Align	Handle is aligned with the other handle

D.12   ScriptLinks: Linking Scripts to Blender

Python scripts can be attached to datablocks and assigned to events that trigger them in the Script buttons window. When the Script buttons have been selected, the header buttons change to display the datablocks that can be given ScriptLinks.

ScriptLinks can be added for the following datablocks:

Objects	Available when an object is active
Cameras	Available when the active object is a camera
Lamps	Available when the active object is a lamp
Materials	Available when the active object has a material
Worlds	Available when the current scene contains a world

If you can add a ScriptLink, an icon appears on the header. Selecting one of the icons brings up the ScriptLink buttons group on the left of the Script buttons window.

Datablocks can have an arbitrary number of ScriptLinks attached to them—additional links can be added and deleted with the New and Del buttons, similar to material indexes. Scripts are executed in order, beginning with the script linked at index 1.

When you have at least one ScriptLink, the event type and link buttons are displayed. The link button should be filled in with the name of the Text object to be executed. The event type controls when the script will be executed. Currently there is only one event: FrameChanged. This event is executed every time the user changes frames, including during rendering and animation playback. This script is also executed continuously when objects are edited.

Event-triggered scripts receive additional input through Blender module objects:

Blender.bylink	Set to true to indicate that the script has been called through a ScriptLink (as opposed to the user pressing ALT-P in the Text window)
Blender.link	Set to contain the datablock referenced by the script (material, lamp, object, and so on)
Blender.event	Set to the name of the event that triggered the ScriptLink, allowing one script to be used to process different event types

D.12.1 Scene ScriptLinks

The ScriptLink buttons for scenes are located in the right of the Script buttons window. Events available for scene ScriptLinks are:

FrameChanged   Executed every time the user changes frames, as well as during rendering and animation playback

OnLoad   Executed whenever a scene is loaded (when a file is initially loaded, or when the user switches to the current scene)

E

INSTALLING BLENDER

Blender is currently distributed only over the Internet. You can download it from http://www.blender.nl/download/index.php or directly via FTP: ftp://ftp.blender.nl/pub/. Be sure to download the correct package for your operating system and processor.

The CD accompanying the book contains all Blender versions current when this book was published or last updated. Since the pace of Blender's development is so rapid, however, consider downloading the most current version. (The installation files usually fit on a single 3.5-inch diskette.)

Normally, installing Blender on any platform and operating system is simply a matter of unpacking Blender and any plug-ins and copying them to a directory, from which you can then start the program. When you start Blender for the first time, it copies its standard font and a default scene either to the user's home directory or, in the case of Windows, to the Windows directory.

Unlike many other 3D programs, Blender is very frugal about hardware requirements—it even functions on machines that are quite old. Still, your machine and hard disk must be fast enough to render, manipulate, and display 3D graphics and images. 3D graphics demand a lot from the graphics system, and a powerful graphics card is highly recommended for complex modeling.

The system configurations listed here, which are based both on the author's experience and Not a Number's recommendations, will give you reasonable performance for a reasonable price. A three-button mouse is highly recommended for all systems, though you can use a two-button mouse in Windows 9x and Windows NT as well as under X windows by replacing the third button with a key combination. However, this will be a frustrating adaptation since Blender makes extensive use of all three buttons.

E.1 Installing under Linux

E.1.1 Recommended System Requirements

- Intel Pentium PC (at least 90 MHz), Alpha PC, or PowerPC 32MB RAM

- Graphics card with a 16-bit color depth (required) that allows resolutions of at least 800x600 pixels

- Slackware, RedHat, Debian, SuSE

- Mesa 3.*x*; you can support your hardware with graphics cards (other than Voodoo game cards) and a customized Mesa/GLX/X server

- Three-button mouse strongly recommended

E.1.2 Unpacking the Files

The installation file for Unix-like systems is compressed with the usual tar and GNUZip programs to keep the files small for the Internet data transfer. To unpack the files, copy or drag the file to the target directory, change to the directory with the cd command, and enter the following command:

```
tar zxvf blender1.80a_Linux_xxx.tar.gz
```

This creates a `blender1.80a_Linux_xxx` directory. The version number and the xxx, which stands for the library version number, the processor type, and the type of link, will differ depending on your distribution.

NOTE *Versions with* stat *in their name have the necessary libraries set in the program code. These versions are bigger, but if there are system conflicts with the shared libraries they allow you to fix them quickly. In general, though, you should get a dynamic version (*dyn*) since it's smaller and faster to load.*

A glance in your distribution's manual or a question posted to a Linux user group should help to clarify any problems. Some Linux distributions already contain distribution-specific packages, but they seldom have a current Blender package. Depending on the windows or desktop manager you're using (Gnome or KDE), you can also unpack and install Blender with the integrated file manager and start it with a mouse click.

Start Blender in the installation directory with the call `./blender`. If you log in as the root, you can establish a link in a binary directory that points to Blender's installation directory by entering the following at the shell prompt:

```
ln -sf _pwd_/blender /usr/local/bin/
```

(Be sure to use back ticks around the pwd command.) This sets a link to /usr/local/bin and you should now be able to start Blender immediately from any directory with the simple blender call.

When Blender is started for the first time, it creates the following files in the user's home directory ($HOME):

.B.blend   The user-dependent start file (a completely normal Blender file) with personal settings.

.Bfs   A text file with paths to the files that serve as abbreviations to specific directories.

.Bfont   Blender's standard PostScript font.

E.1.3 Configuring X Windows Systems

On some Linux distributions the ALT key, which is extremely important for Blender, may not work correctly (though I have not had this problem with either RedHat or Debian). If you encounter the problem, try changing the following in the ~/.Xmodmap file (the tilde stands for the home directory) with the text editor of your choice: Replace the line

```
keycode 64 = Meta_L
```

with

```
keycode 64 = Alt_L
```

E.1.4 Configuring Mesa

Blender's 3D window and interface are drawn with Sun's 3D graphics OpenGL library. On free Unix systems, Mesa (also free) takes over this function from OpenGL.

Experiment with Mesa's settings to make Blender draw the 3D window with optimal speed (though rendering speed depends only on the CPU and memory). Use a dynamically linked Blender version—you want to be sure you're using the system's own libraries, because the libraries embedded in the program code are apt to be out of date.

Mesa's documentation has a whole bunch of pointers for increasing its performance. The most important for Blender are:

- Disable the dithering with the environment variable MESA_NO_DITHER. A simple setting is enough to disable dithering.

- Tell Mesa directly what kind of display you're using with the environment variable ESA_RGB_VISUAL.

- Stop the 3D window from flickering when it is drawn by setting the environment variable MESA_BACK_BUFFER; this setting can actually double the drawing speed.

Environment variables are set differently depending on the shell. For the standard bash shell and variants, set the environment variable, in either your personal or the systemwide shell default settings, with

```
export MESA_RGB_VISUAL="TrueColor 24"
```

To test Blender's drawing speed, start Blender in a terminal window under X11. After loading a (not too simple) scene, call the timer menu with CTRL-ALT-T in a 3D window. Select Draw to test the drawing speed and the result will be output in the terminal window. Next, test the speed for the shaded view (Z or CTRL-Z) too.

On my system, this parameter yields the following output from Blender:

```
cw@mero >export MESA_BACK_BUFFER="Ximage"
cw@mero >./blender -p 250 200 900 700 blacksmith/blacksmith.blend
cw@mero >start timer
draw 209
start timer
draw 676
Blender quit

cw@mero >export MESA_BACK_BUFFER="Pixmap"
cw@mero >./blender -p 250 200 900 700 blacksmith/blacksmith.blend
cw@mero >start timer
draw 384
start timer
draw 1311
Blender quit
```

The "Blacksmith" scene is also Blender's "Blenchmark" (coined by Cesar Blecua as a combination of the words Blender and benchmark). You'll find a number of system configurations that have been tested with the Blenchmark at http://www.blender.nl/blender/blench.php.

E.2 Installing under Windows

E.2.1 Unpacking the Files

Double-click the .exe file in Explorer to expand the self-extracting Windows archive and you'll have the option to install Blender in c:\Blender\. To install Blender elsewhere, adjust the path accordingly or call up WinZip directly.

NOTE *If you are installing under Windows NT, the install program may complain that your operating system does not use long file names—which is, of course, not the case; ignore this message.*

E.2.2 Recommended System Requirements

*   Intel or Intel-compatible PC with Windows 95 or higher or Windows NT or higher

*   32MB RAM

*   Graphics card with a 16-bit color depth (required) that allows resolutions of at least 800x600 pixels

*   OpenGL library

If you get the cannot find glu32.dll or cannot find opengl32.dll error upon starting Blender, your Windows 95 installation is too old; download and install the OpenGL update from ftp://ftp.microsoft.com/softlib/mslfiles/opengl95.exe.

While a three-button mouse is strongly recommended, you can set 2-Mouse in Blender's Info window to configure the ALT-left-click as the middle mouse button if your mouse has only two buttons.

When Blender is started for the first time with a double-click on its icon, it installs the following three files in the Windows directory:

.B.blend A Blender scene file that's automatically loaded at start-up and functions as the default setting.

.Bfs A text file with preset paths to directories and drives.

.Bfont Blender's vector character set.

E.2.3 Windows Plug-ins

Many of the tools necessary for programming Blender plug-ins under Windows are only available commercially. Still, make or project files for common compilers are available with which you can compile Windows plug-ins. Some users have compiled many of the available plug-ins for Windows and made them available to all users.

For further information and discussion on this topic, visit the Windows section of the Blender news server (http://www.blender.nl/discussion/search.php?f=2 and search for "Windows plug-ins.").

E.2.4 Python under Windows

The file pyth151.exe on the CD in the python/Windows directory contains the installation program for Python 1.5.1. After you start it, the program asks the usual questions, in particular which directory to install Python in.

After installing Python, delete the file python15.dll from the Blender directory. This file has most of the necessary Python libraries and modules—but you don't want to leave it around. Blender will turn to it first, and that will hinder use of your complete Python installation.

E.3 Installing under FreeBSD

E.3.1 Recommended System Requirements

- Intel Pentium PC with at least a 90 MHz clock rate

- 32MB RAM

- Graphics card with a 16-bit color depth (required) that allows resolutions of at least 800x600 pixels

- FreeBSD version 2.2.6-RELEASE (newer versions should also work)

- Mesa 3.x; you can support your hardware with graphics cards (other than Voodoo game cards) and a customized Mesa/GLX/X server

- Three-button mouse strongly recommended

E.3.2 Unpacking the Files

The installation file for Unix-like systems is compressed with the usual tar and GNUZip programs to keep the files small for the Internet data transfer. To unpack the files, copy or move the file to the target directory, change to the directory with the cd command and enter the following command:

```
tar zxvf blender1.80a_BSD_i386_2.2-xxx.tar.gz
```

This creates a blender1.80a_BSD_i386_2.2-xxx directory. The version number and the xxx, which stands for the type of link, will differ depending on the version loaded.

When Blender is started for the first time, it creates the following files in the user's home directory ($HOME):

.B.blend   The user-dependent start file (a normal Blender file) with personal settings.

.Bfs   A text file with paths to the files that serve as abbreviations to specific directories.

.Bfont   Blender's standard PostScript font.

For installing and configuring Mesa under FreeBSD, see the Linux section above.

E.4 Installing under SGI IRIX

To install Blender on SGI IRIX, change to the directory with the installation file and unpack it with the following commands:

```
gunzip blender1.80a_SGI_.xxx.tar.gz
tar xvf blender1.80a_SGI_.xxx.tar
```

This creates a `blender1.80a_SGI_xxx` directory. The version number and the xxx, which stand for the IrixGL or OpenGL version, will differ. In general, the OpenGL versions display interactive graphics faster on newer SGI systems like Indigo2 Impact, O2, and Octane. Use the IrixGL version for Indy and Indifo systems.

You can now start Blender from the installation directory with the call `./blender` or by clicking the icon on the desktop.

When Blender is started for the first time, it creates the following files in the user's home directory ($HOME):

.B.blend	The user-dependent start file (a completely normal Blender file) with personal settings.
.Bfs	A text file with paths to the files that serve as abbreviations to specific directories.
.Bfont	Blender's standard PostScript font.

E.5   Installing under Sun Solaris

To install Blender under Solaris, change to the directory with the installation file and unpack it with the following commands:

```
uncompress blender1.80a_Sun_.xxx.tar.Z
tar xvf blender1.80a_Sun_.xxx.tar
```

This creates a `blender1.80a_Sun_xxx` directory. The version number and the xxx, which stand for the IrisGL or OpenGL version, will differ.

You can now start Blender from the installation directory with the call `./blender` or by clicking the icon on the desktop.

When Blender is started for the first time, it creates the following files in the user's home directory ($HOME):

.B.blend	The user-dependent start file (a completely normal Blender file) with personal settings.
.Bfs	A text file with paths to the files that serve as abbreviations to specific directories.
.Bfont	Blender's standard PostScript font.

F

GLOSSARY

(anti-) aliasing   Distorted visual effects caused by resolutions or sampling frequencies that are too low. Aliasing can appear on superimposed structures (for example, a texture pattern and monitor raster) or on the edges of rendered objects. Anti-aliasing attempts to limit these effects. A feature employed by Blender for anti-aliasing is *oversampling*.

alpha channel   The alpha channel contains an image's transparency information; thus it can be used to combine rendered scenes. In principle, the alpha channel is a grayscale image in which black areas of the image are completely transparent, white areas completely opaque, and the intermediate levels in corresponding gray tones.

ambient light   Ambient light is environmental light; it comes from diffuse reflected light and brightens shadows or colors surroundings if the reflection is from colored objects. Ambient light is not rendered in the common rendering procedures; it can only be simulated by globally increasing the brightness level or skillfully placing additional light sources. The *radiosity method* is a rendering method that takes ambient light into account.

ASCII (American Standard Code for Information Interchange)   ASCII defines how letters of the alphabet are saved as digital information. The ASCII system defines only 127 symbols, so there are often problems with special national symbols when files are exchanged between different computer systems.

AVI (Audio Video Interleave)   A container format introduced by Microsoft for sound and moving images. The sound and video information is nested together to achieve synchronized sound and image. AVI files can contain sound and video streams at different levels of compression.

beveling   A method for creating complicated object edges with cross-sections (from bevels and curves to ornamental structures), or for extruding a cross-section along a path to create objects like tracks or profiles.

Bezier curve   The approximation of a curve that passes through at least two control points.

blue screen   An often-used variant of the *chromakey*, with blue as its key color (also called bluebox).

Bounding box   The smallest rectangular box that encloses an object.

bump map   Also called a normap in Blender. A trick used when rendering bump maps makes structures appear on an object that aren't really modeled. White spots on a bump map create a raised impression, black spots a sunken impression, and levels of gray produce the corresponding intermediate steps (see *displacement map*).

chromakey   Key color. Replaces a color in a video frame with another scene (or computer graphic). Common key colors are blue and green; when used as chromakeys, key colors must not otherwise appear in the scene.

CMYK   A color model for combining primary pigments. C stands for cyan, M for magenta, Y for yellow, and K for black.

colorspace   A mathematical space defining a range of colors.

compositing   The combining of two or more scenes (real or computer generated). The *alpha channel* is often used with compositing.

datablock   The general name for any element in Blender.

displacement map   During rendering, a displacement map takes a grayscale texture and deforms the object's geometry based on the image's brightness. You can achieve a similar effect with Blender's Noise function. (See also *bump map*.)

empty   A null object.

field   Video images (PAL, NTSC, SECAM) are made by combining two interlaced fields that quickly follow each other. One field contains odd image lines, the other even image lines. The field method is a trick used to produce a flicker-free image with the smallest possible frame frequency, and has arisen out of a need to overcome technical limitations encountered when developing for television.

frame   The combination of two fields in video or one frame in film. If you extract a frame from a video, fast horizontal movements produce comblike structures in objects because fields differ temporally and the object has moved during this time (1/50 of a second in PAL).

HSV   A color space that describes color using the basic components hue, saturation, and brightness.

inbetween   Intermediate frame between two keyframes.

inverse kinematics (IKA)   Inverse kinematics lets you move an entire skeleton by animating just the skeleton's ends. (For example, moving a hand animates the entire arm.) The intermediate joints follow specified rules.

IPO   Blender's animation curve system.

JPEG (Joint Photographic Experts Group)   This expert group developed the JPEG method to compress photorealistic images or frames. JPEG compression reduces the amount of information in an image, resulting in small images; thus it is best for images that will not be reworked. (The data loss is barely visible to the eye except when the image is enlarged.)

keyframe   A point in an animation that marks a specific condition of the animation (position, rotation, color, and so on). At least two keyframes are required for a keyframe animation; the program then automatically interpolates between the frames.

mesh   A surface described by a collection of one or more polygons.

metaball   An object (usually a sphere) that attracts and clings to other metaballs based on how close they are to each other and how strongly their attractive fields are defined. Useful in animating organic objects.

MPEG (Moving Pictures Experts Group)   This expert group has developed several very good compression formats for saving video digitally.

MPEG-1 (MPEG Standard One)   Describes the compression and digital saving of video data. An additional standard is the MPEG-1 Layer 3 for audio compression (.mp3).

MPEG-II (MPEG Standard Two)   Describes the compression and digital saving of video data. In contrast to MPEG-1, MPEG-2 supports interlaced video data (see *field)* for television formats and offers different levels to meet different requirements (such as DVD or video).

NTSC (National Television Standards Committee)   Developed in the United States, NTSC is a television standard for transmitting color images. It works with an image frequency of 60 Hz per second for 525 lines and 60 fields per second (or 30 frames per second).

NURBS (Non Uniform Rational B-Spline)   A type of curve with weighted control points.

orthogonal view   An orthogonal view presents items in a scene from an angle while showing the full size of each object; distant objects are not represented as smaller. This produces a weak 3D impression, but is good for reading distances between points. As a result, technical drawings and CAD programs use orthogonal projection for the three views (top, side, front), allowing the viewer to make measurements directly from the drawing.

oversampling   A type of rendering that involves capturing more image data than is required and then using averaging algorithms to define the value of each pixel in the final image. Oversampling avoids *aliasing*.

PAL (Phase Alternating Line)   PAL is the prevailing television standard in Europe. PAL works with a frequency of 50 Hz, corresponding to 25 frames and 50 fields per second, with a line resolution of 625.

parenting   A process that generates object hierarchies. One object becomes a superordinate (parent) of the other and transmits certain properties (such as position or rotation) to the subordinate (child) object. If the parent object is animated, the child object follows it according to the hierarchy.

particle system   A modeling technique for irregular objects like smoke, grass, fog, and so on. A particle system is a collection of independent objects (often points) that have their own motion properties (usually determined at random).

pixel   An image element or point. The pixel is the smallest unit in rasterized images; it holds the color and sometimes also the transparency value (see *alpha channel*). Computer monitors use square pixels and television uses rectangular pixels, a fact that must be kept in mind so as to avoid distortion.

plane normal   Defines a plane's orientation in space. The plane normal is a vector that points outward, perpendicular to the plane. In principle, every plane has two normals, and it is especially important to choose the correct one (in almost all cases the one pointing away from the object) when rendering lighting.

plug-in   A software enhancement that extends a program's functionality without changing the main program.

postproduction   The reworking of recorded or rendered material. Postproduction includes sound and graphics editing and the addition of effects like fades, titles, and so on.

QuickTime   A format developed by Apple Computer for storing video and audio streams; now available for Windows and with an extensive set of functions. (See *virtual reality*.)

radiosity rendering A rendering method that takes into account the diffuse light reflected by objects to produce very realistic lighting. It requires long rendering times and generally does not let you animate the displayed objects. However, once a radiosity rendering has finished, you can perform a camera animation without re-rendering, which makes the radiosity method ideal for architectural visualizations where judging light ratios in buildings is important.

raytracing A rendering method that renders photorealistic images and does an especially good job of simulating reflections and refracted light. Ray-tracing demands a lot from your computer.

rendering The conversion of 3D data into an image or animation. You can use various procedures with rendering, such as raytracing, scan line rendering, and radiosity rendering.

RGB A color model whose primary colors are added to produce other colors. R stands for red, G for green, and B for blue.

RLE compression (Run Length Encoding) Compresses same-colored pixels to save space; for example, 100 red pixels would be saved as "red 100 times." RLE doesn't work with photos and similar images that have lots of detail. In contrast to JPEG, RLE compression is not lossy.

rotoscoping A procedure derived from cartooning that uses individual frames from a live-action recording as a pattern for the cartoon; 2D and 3D programs support numerous semi-automatic rotoscoping functions. Rotoscoping can also be used to manually stabilize images (see *tracking*).

scan line rendering A line-by-line scanning of a 3D scene in relation to its image resolution. This is a fast procedure that's especially good for anima-tion rendering. Reflections and refracted light can only be approximated.

SECAM (Système Électronique Couleur Avec Mémoire) A television standard developed in France. SECAM resembles PAL but uses a different color procedure.

specular point The diffuse reflection of light on a surface. The specular point's size and intensity lead us to draw certain conclusions about the sur-face's roughness. To create realistic materials in computer animation, therefore, set the specular point with care.

title safe An area that by definition should be visible on all television sets without cutting out any writing.

tracking The extraction of information from film or video sequences for the integration of 3D objects. Even with the use of a good tripod, live action scenes are never completely still, and you'll often need to use a scene where the camera pans across the objects, which is bound to introduce some vibration. You can use 2D tracking to still just the image (to do so manually, see *rotoscoping*). To integrate 3D objects, use 3D tracking, which (semi)automatically defines the position of distinctive pixels and makes them available to the 3D program.

virtual reality   Virtual reality attempts to make another reality believable to the brain. The more senses that are affected, the deeper the "immersion" in the virtual reality.

VRML (Virtual Reality Modeling Language)   A 3D model description format suited for the Internet.

wireframe   A rendering style in which only the edges of faces are drawn.

world   A datablock that lets you set horizon colors, ambient lighting, fog effects, and stars in a Blender scene.

Z-buffer   A Z-buffer saves the depth information for the pixels of a rendered image and then quickly compares it with the z coordinates of new elements. This gives Blender a fast way to determine whether an element lies in front of or behind another element in a scene, a process that would otherwise require a resource- and time-intensive rendering for every element.

G

WHAT'S ON THE CD?

/figures (60MB)

Includes select figures from the book as Targa and JPEG files.

/animations (97MB)

Includes rendered animations from the tutorials as well as additional animations, as either MPEG-I or AVI movies. The animations are in various resolutions, and some are compressed.

/DigitalDesignBox (6MB)

Includes a bunch of textures in monitor-quality resolution from the Digital Design Box, taken from the *Digital Design Library* by Helmut Kraus, dpunkt.verlag (Heidelberg, 1995). The Digital Design Box also has many other textures (fractal textures, photo types, the Digital Paper Collection, nature textures, technical textures) in print-quality resolution.

/python (5MB)

Includes Python installation files and tools for Windows 95 and higher and Windows NT. (Installation files for Unix-like systems should be in their distributions—or you can download them from http://www.python.org/.)

/sequences (97MB)

Includes image sequences for animating textures and compositing, courtesy of Imago Viva (http://www.imago-viva.de/). Free for private, noncommercial projects.

The sequences are in numbered, JPEG-compressed frames (320x240 pixels). The sequence in the reef/ directory is in numbered fields in PAL resolution.

/tutorials (56MB)

Includes the scenes from the tutorials arranged by chapter, as well as Blender files used in creating the figures. Numbered files correspond to the intermediate steps of the individual tutorials.

The textures/, fonts/, and objects/ directories contain the textures, fonts, and objects belonging to the scenes.

/blender (94MB)

Contains Blender's installation files for all currently supported platforms, downloaded from ftp://ftp.blender.nl/. There are also some Blender scenes from Not a Number that illustrate Blender's newer capabilities. This directory also contains the Blender FAQ as well as a short manual in HTML (in various languages). The Blender versions included are as follows:

1.80a for Windows, BeOS, FreeBSD, Linux PPC, Linux x86, SGI IRIX, Solaris

1.80 for Linux Alpha

1.72 for SGI IRIX

1.73 for Linux x86

INDEX

Blender. *See also* Sequence Editor
  advantages over similar
    programs, 4–5
  basics, 39–62
  birth of, 1
  vs. CAD programs, 49
  command line arguments,
    255–257
  "Complete Blender," 1
  customizing, 60–62
  downloading, 277
  embedded programming
    language. *See* Python
  features, 2–4
  hardware requirements, 277
  installing, 24, 277–283
  jargon, 5, 104
  logo, created with metaballs, *97*
  operating systems that use, 4–5
  quick start lesson, 23–37
  screen. *See* scenes
  two-handed design, 6, 24–25
  uses, 2, 135
  versions, 4
  weaknesses, 5
  Web sites, 6, 220, 254, 277
Blender.BGL, 208
Blender.bylink, 201
Blender controls, 52–54
Blender.Draw, 207
Blender interface, *26*
  features, 9, 24
  Python GUI, 206, *208*
Blender.link, 21
Blender Manual (Roosendaal), 2, 5
Blender modules, 201, 203, 207, 208
Blender radiosity renderer, 218, 220
Blender text editor, 198–*199*
Blend (texture type), 105–106
Blue Screen (plug-in), 254
body parts, creating and connecting,
  163–164
Boolean operations, 77–80
BorderSelect, 65, 67
bottle animation, CP11

constructing model skeleton for,
  161–*162*
creating and animating its
  skeleton, 162–166
Box Modeling, 75
.Bpip file, 187
Bspline (Edit button), 172
B-Spline (interpolation curve), 150
Build, 171
Bump, 101
bump maps
  Blender's name for, 104
  enhancing, 224, *225*
  and Noise, 140
BUT, 53
buttons, Blender, 52–54
Button window, 30
  header, *31*
  icons, *57*–58
BW, 215

C

cabinet projection, 17
CAD programs vs. Blender, 49
CalcAlpha, 110
camera, 25
camera parameters, 133
camera projection, 133
camera symbol size, 133
camera view (SHIFT-F5), 30, *31*,
  132–133
  3D titles in, 190, *191*
  shifting, 91, 92
campfire animation, 170–174; CP12
car button, 54, 100
Card, 81
Cardinal, 150
CD-ROM accompanying this book,
  5, 109
change effect menu, *189*
character animation, 161
characters. *See* special characters,
  creating
Child, 177, 179

Sphere (Lamp button), 123, 171, 223
Sphere (Material button), 103
spiked ball, 94–95
spinal column
    creating and connecting, *163*, 164
    moving, 165
Spin and Spin Dup, 71–72
Spot, 123, 125, 221
spotlight beam, *126*–127
SpotSi, 123, 221
SpTr, 114
Sqr, 131
Sta (Display button), 36, 192, 216
Sta (particle parameter), 131, 170,
    172
StarDist, 131
Star (halo parameter), 112, 178; CP5
starry background, parameters for,
    224
stars, rendering, 129, *131*–132
Stars (World button), 131
Star Trek transporter effect, 140
Static, 119
steam, creating, 167
Stencil, 105
Steps, 72
Stick, 102
Stiffness, 98
stones, creating a ring of, 171
Stucci, 105–106
Subdivide, 74, 141
Subdivide Smooth, 74–*75*
Sub (sequence effect), 189
Subsize, 114
Sub (texture parameter), 104
subtractive color model, 9; CP2
Sun, 123, 125
sunset (image), 130
Surface, 148
surface coordinate systems, 12, *13*
surfaces. *See also* textures
    commands for working with, 241,
        245
    creating, *13*

defining, 12
materials and textures for, 99–106
mathematically defined, 81
NURBS patch, 83
reflective, 222–223
smooth-looking, 14, 30–31
swarm effect, 181
Switch a-b and Switch b-c, 189
switches, types of Blender, 52–54

T

TAB key, 41
table, wood, CP4, CP15
    creating, *107*–109
table legs, CP4
    creating, 107, 108
Targa, 214
teapot, *118*
test rendering (F12), 223
text, applying Warp to, 74
text editors, 198–*199*
text objects, 95–97
    creating, 128
TextOnCurve, 97
Texture buttons (F6), *33*, 57
    Colorband settings, *106*
    EnvMap settings, 119–*120*
    texture types, 105–106
texture channels, 102
texture coordinates
    converting from 2D to 3D, 103
    inputs, *102*
    outputs, *103*–104
texture datablock and color sliders,
    105
texture mapping, 102
texture output buttons, *104*
texture plug-ins, 254
textures
    animating, 140, *235*; CP8
    creating, 33, *76*
    defined, 32
    disabling, 77
    effect on halos, 112

V

values
    of buttons, 33
values *(continued)*
    HSV color model, 9
    Number Menu for entering, 50–*51*
vanishing point, 18
van Rossum, Guido, 197
vapor trails, creating, 179, *180*–181
Var, 104, 119, 140
Vect, 182
Vector handle, *82*–83, 138
vertex, 64
    adding between two vertices, 141
VertexCol, 220
vertex keys, 148–151. *See also*
      weighted vertex keys
    defined, *149*
    and EditMode, 149, 150, 151
vertices
    with Bezier curves, *82*–83
    commands for working with, 241,
      242–245
    defined, 49
    deleting and creating, 66
    editing, 52
    in EditMode, 64–*66*
    toggling between free and
      aligned handles, 83
video
    camera view, 133
    editing, 185
    integrating computer graphics
      into, 233
    lighting in, 120–122
    rendering for, 236–237
video formats, 217
Videoscape format, 249, 250
View buttons (SHIFT-F7), 50, 57
Viewmove, 44, 61
views, manipulating, 241
volumetric light, *126*
VRML format, 249, 250

W

wall, penetrated by an object,
    127–129
Warp, 74
water, bodies of, 77
water fountains, creating, 167
wavy line button, 146
WCVT2POV, 250–251
Weight, 84
weighted vertex keys, 146, 151–*154*
Width, 89
Win, 102, 235
wind, simulating, 174
window borders, *54*–55
windows, 54–58. *See also* 3D windows
    active, 25
    command line argument options,
      255, 257
    commands for working in, 240
    splitting, 54–*55*
    types of, 55–57
Window type icon, *26*
WipeOut (plug-in), 254
Wire, 219
wireframe graphic, 13, *14*
    reusing, 61
Wiresize, 97
Wood, 105–106
world, science fiction, 223–225
World buttons (F8), 57, *129*–132
    fog parameters, *131*
    star parameters, *131*
world textures, 129–130

X

X button, 54
xmax (variable), 212
X offset, 96
Xrepeat, 224
X Window System, 58
XY Constraint, 159

Y

Z

THE LINUX PROBLEM SOLVER

Hands-on Solutions for Systems Administrators

by BRIAN WARD

This book is a must-have for solving technical problems related to printing, networking, back-up, crash recovery, and compiling or upgrading a kernel. The CD-ROM supports the book with configuration files and numerous programs not included in many Linux distributions.

2000, 290 PP. W/CD-ROM, $34.95 ($53.95 CDN)
ISBN 1-886411-35-2, ITEM #352

LINUX MUSIC & SOUND

by DAVE PHILLIPS

Linux Music & Sound looks at recording, storing, playing, and editing music and sound and the broad range of Linux music and sound applications. The CD-ROM includes over 100 MIDI applications, including digital audio and music notation software, games, and utilities.

2000, 408 PP. W/CD-ROM, $39.95 ($61.95 CDN)
ISBN 1-886411-34-4, ITEM #344

THE LINUX COOKBOOK

Best Practices for Using Linux

by MICHAEL STUTZ

The Linux Cookbook shows Linux users of all levels how to perform a variety of everyday computer tasks such as: editing and formating text; working with digital audio; and creating and manipulating graphics. The quick-reference, "cookbook"-style format, includes step-by-step Linux "recipes."

FEBRUARY 2001, 300 PP., $29.95 ($44.95 CDN)
ISBN 1-886411-48-4, ITEM #484

LINUX GAME PROGRAMMING

by LOKI SOFTWARE, INC.

Linux Game Programming discusses important multimedia toolkits (including a very thorough discussion of the Simple DirectMedia Layer) and teaches the basics of game programming. Understand the state of the Linux gaming world and learn to write and distribute games to the Linux community.

JUNE 2001, 300 PP., $39.95 ($59.95 CDN)
ISBN 1-886411-49-2, ITEM #492

THE BOOK OF JAVASCRIPT
A Practical Guide to Interactive Web Pages

by THAU!

Rather than offer cut-and-paste solutions, this tutorial/reference focuses on understanding JavaScript, and shows Web designers how to customize and implement JavaScript on their sites. The CD-ROM includes code for each example in the book, script libraries, and relevant software.

2000, 424 PP. W/CD-ROM, $29.95 ($46.50 CDN)
ISBN 1-886411-36-0, ITEM #360

Phone:

1 (800) 420-7240 OR
(415) 863-9900
MONDAY THROUGH FRIDAY,
9 A.M. TO 5 P.M. (PST)

Fax:

(415) 863-9950
24 HOURS A DAY,
7 DAYS A WEEK

E-mail:

SALES@NOSTARCH.COM

Web:

HTTP://WWW.NOSTARCH.COM

Mail:

NO STARCH PRESS
555 DE HARO STREET, SUITE 250
SAN FRANCISCO, CA 94107
USA

Distributed in the U.S. by Publishers Group West

Linux Journal's team of industry experts has put together a complete line of reference materials designed for Linux operating system users, programmers, and IT professionals. Visit your local bookstore or the Linux Journal Web site for other Linux Journal Press products. You may also request a free issue of the monthly magazine, Linux Journal, online at http://www.linuxjournal.com.

UPDATES

This book was carefully reviewed for technical accuracy, but it's inevitable that some things will change after the book goes to press. Visit the Web site for this book at **http://www.nostarch.com/blender_updates.htm** for updates, errata, and other information.

CD-ROM LICENSE AGREEMENT FOR *THE BLENDER BOOK*

Read this Agreement before opening this package. By opening this package, you agree to be bound by the terms and conditions of this Agreement.

This CD-ROM (the "CD") contains programs and associated documentation and other materials and is distributed with the book entitled *The Blender Book* to purchasers of the book for their own personal use only. Such programs, documentation and other materials and their compilation (collectively, the "Collection") are licensed to you subject to the terms and conditions of this Agreement by No Starch Press, having a place of business at 555 De Haro Street, Suite 250, San Francisco, CA 94107 ("Licensor"). In addition to being governed by the terms and conditions of this Agreement, your rights to use the programs and other materials included on the CD may also be governed by separate agreements distributed with those programs and materials (the "Other Agreements"). In the event of any inconsistency between this Agreement and any of the Other Agreements, those Agreements shall govern insofar as those programs and materials are concerned. By using the Collection, in whole or in part, you agree to be bound by the terms and conditions of this Agreement. Licensor owns the copyright to the Collection, except insofar as it contains materials that are proprietary to third-party suppliers. All rights to the Collection except those expressly granted to you in this Agreement are reserved to Licensor and such suppliers as their respective interests may appear.

1. Limited License. Licensor grants you a limited, nonexclusive, nontransferable license to use the Collection on a single dedicated computer (excluding network servers). This Agreement and your rights hereunder shall automatically terminate if you fail to comply with any provision of this Agreement or the Other Agreements. Upon such termination, you agree to destroy the CD and all copies of the CD, whether lawful or not, that are in your possession or under your control. Licensor and its suppliers retain all rights not expressly granted herein as their respective interests may appear.

2. Additional Restrictions. (A) You shall not (and shall not permit other persons or entities to) directly or indirectly, by electronic or other means, reproduce (except for archival purposes as permitted by law), publish, distribute, rent, lease, sell, sublicense, assign, or otherwise transfer the Collection or any part thereof or this Agreement. Any attempt to do so shall be void and of no effect. (B) You shall not (and shall not permit other persons or entities to) reverse-engineer, decompile, disassemble, merge, modify, create derivative works of, or translate the Collection or use the Collection or any part thereof for any commercial purpose. (C) You shall not (and shall not permit other persons or entities to) remove or obscure Licensor's or its suppliers' or licensors' copyright, trademark, or other proprietary notices or legends from any portion of the Collection or any related materials. (D) You agree and certify that the Collection will not be exported outside the United States except as authorized and as permitted by the laws and regulations of the United States. If the Collection has been rightfully obtained outside of the United States, you agree that you will not reexport the Collection, except as permitted by the laws and regulations of the United States and the laws and regulations of the jurisdiction in which you obtained the Collection.

3. Disclaimer of Warranty. (A) The Collection and the CD are provided "as is" without warranty of any kind, either express or implied, including, without limitation, any warranty of merchantability and fitness for a particular purpose. The entire risk as to the results and performance of the CD and the software and other materials that are part of the Collection is assumed by you, and Licensor and its suppliers and distributors shall have no responsibility for defects in the CD or the accuracy or application of or errors or omissions in the Collection, and do not warrant that the functions contained in the Collection will meet your requirements, or that the operation of the CD or the Collection will be uninterrupted or error-free, or that any defects in the CD or the Collection will be corrected. In no event shall Licensor or its suppliers or distributors be liable for any direct, indirect, special, incidental, or consequential damages arising out of the use of or inability to use the Collection or the CD, even if Licensor or its suppliers or distributors have been advised of the likelihood of such damages occurring. Licensor and its suppliers and distributors shall not be liable for any loss, damages, or costs arising out of, but not limited to, lost profits or revenue; loss of use of the Collection or the CD; loss of data or equipment; cost of recovering software, data, or materials in the Collection; cost of substitute software, data, or materials in the Collection; claims by third parties; or other similar costs. (B) In no event shall Licensor or its suppliers' or distributors' total liability to you for all damages, losses, and causes of action (whether in contract, tort or otherwise) exceed the amount paid by you for the Collection. (C) Some states do not allow exclusion or limitation of implied warranties or limitation of liability for incidental or consequential damages, so the above limitations or exclusions may not apply to you.

4. U.S. Government Restricted Rights. The Collection is licensed subject to RESTRICTED RIGHTS. Use, duplication, or disclosure by the U.S. Government or any person or entity acting on its behalf is subject to restrictions as set forth in subdivision (c)(1)(ii) of the Rights in Technical Data and Computer Software Clause at DFARS (48 CFR 252.227-7013) for DoD contracts, in paragraphs (c)(1) and (2) of the Commercial Computer Software Restricted Rights clause in the FAR (48 CFR 52.227 - 19) for civilian agencies, or, in the case of NASA, in clause 18-52.227-86(d) of the NASA Supplement to the FAR, or in other comparable agency clauses. The contractor/manufacturer is No Starch Press, 555 De Haro Street, Suite 250, San Francisco, CA 94107.

5. General Provisions. Nothing in this Agreement constitutes a waiver of Licensor's or its suppliers' or licensors' rights under U.S. copyright laws or any other federal, state, local, or foreign law. You are responsible for installation, management, and operation of the Collection. This Agreement shall be construed, interpreted, and governed under California law. Copyright © 2001 No Starch Press. All rights reserved. Reproduction in whole or in part without permission is prohibited.

Get a Free Issue!

Linux Journal has been bringing readers the information they need to stay ahead in the fast-paced world of Linux since 1994. Inside the covers you'll find great programming tricks, interviews with leading industry innovators, concise product reviews and thorough how-tos for both the novice and professional Linux user.

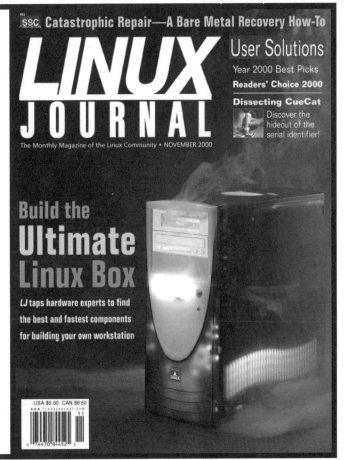